HTML5 Canvas and
CSS3 Graphics Primer

HTML5 CANVAS AND
CSS3 GRAPHICS PRIMER

Oswald Campesato

MERCURY LEARNING AND INFORMATION
Dulles, Virginia
Boston, Massachusetts
New Delhi

Publisher: David Pallai

Mercury Learning and Information
22841 Quicksilver Drive
Dulles, VA 20166
info@merclearning.com
www.merclearning.com
1-800-758-3756

This book is printed on acid-free paper.

Oswald Campesato. *HTML5 Canvas and CSS3 Graphics Primer*
ISBN: 9781936420346

Library of Congress Control Number: 2012940865

121314321

Our titles are available for adoption, license, or bulk purchase by institutions, corporations, etc. For additional information, please contact the Customer Service Dept. at 1-800-758-3756 (toll free).

I'd like to dedicate this book to my parents –
may this bring joy and happiness into their lives.

CONTENTS

PREFACE

The following list of points, in no particular order, is lengthy, but the complete list will clarify what you can expect to find in this book.

The first point is both strategic and tactical: the goal of this book is to show you some interesting functionality that is possible with HTML5 Canvas and CSS3, with an emphasis on the *what* and the *how* with respect to creating HTML pages that contain HTML5 Canvas and CSS3 graphics effects. The *why* and *when* are decisions best made by you. Consequently, although you should be mindful of best practices, this book will not provide a list of do's and don'ts, nor statements such as, "Just because you can doesn't mean you should," regarding the use of HTML5 Canvas or CSS3 features. As a professional, you already know these things, and you don't need such reminders. The intent is to share code samples and show what is possible with CSS3, HTML Canvas, and Scalable Vector Graphics (SVG). Some of the CSS3 code samples illustrate unusual effects and innovative techniques, and perhaps they will inspire you to enhance these code samples to create effects that reveal your own originality. In any case, after you finish this book, you will have a broader view of the capabilities of CSS3 and HTML5 Canvas, thereby enabling you to make more informed decisions regarding the functionality that is most appropriate for your Web site.

Second, this book is primarily for front-end Web developers, as well as for Web designers who want to learn the topics that are covered in this book. Most of the code samples in this book are not available on the Internet, which differentiates this book from other books that cover similar topics, so the question is this: Are you interested in learning about the techniques that are presented in the code samples in this book? Prerequisites consist of a basic understanding of HTML and JavaScript, but the code samples in this book do not use jQuery or any other JavaScript toolkit. You also need to know how to reference CSS stylesheets in an HTML page, and how to define basic CSS selectors. You need to have a basic familiarity of CSS, including how to use properties such as `position`, `top`, `left`, `font-size`, `width`, and so forth, because we will move quickly through code samples containing selectors with CSS3 transforms, animation, and 2D/3D effects. Of course, *basic understanding* is subjective; consequently, if you encounter unfamiliar CSS concepts, you can find free online tutorials that explain those concepts in greater detail.

Third, the CSS3-based code samples in this book are written for WebKit-based browsers (Chrome™ and Safari®), and the code samples have been tested on Chrome on a MacBook® computer. Keep in mind that sometimes code samples render differently on Chrome/MacBook than on Chrome/Windows Vista® operating system (apparently because of platform-specific device drivers), so it's always a good idea to test your code on different platforms or with different WebKit-based browsers (or both). In addition, some of the code samples in this chapter contain browser-specific prefixes, but the majority of the code samples in subsequent chapters only contain WebKit-specific prefixes. The rationale for this approach is two-fold: first, we want to focus on the key ideas and second, we also want to control the page count of the book. If you want to use the code samples in browsers that are not based on WebKit, you can manually add the code with browser-specific prefixes, or better yet, use a CSS framework (several are discussed in Chapter 2, "CSS3 2D/3D Animation and CSS Frameworks") that will generate the browser-specific code for you, which is definitely good news!

Fourth, this book does not discuss paragraph and document structure, the historical aspects of the evolution of CSS3, or how HTML5 `Canvas` became part of the HTML5 specification. Although context is relevant, this information is readily available by performing a quick Internet search, so it will not be repeated in this book. Instead of covering those topics, you will get more code samples for the topics in this book.

Fifth, this is not a book about game programming. Although you will learn pixel-level manipulation of JPG files in Chapter 5, "2D Shapes with Linear and Radial Gradients," and you will find rudimentary game mechanics in Chapter 9, "HTML5 `Canvas` and Animation Effects," you need to refer to a different book if you want to become a game programmer.

We don't want you to purchase this book unless you believe that its content is relevant to you, and that you are comfortable with the writing style of the author. Skim through the images (which are in black and white in the printed book to reduce costs) in order to get a sense of the material in this book. As you can see, this is a highly graphics-oriented book, so if the pictures do not pique your interest, that's probably a strong indication of a "no-buy" decision. Our ultimate goal is satisfied customers, even above total book sales. On the other hand, if this book meets or exceeds your expectations, we certainly appreciate your telling other people about your experience with this book.

This book is not simply an enhanced version of online documentation or tutorials, some of which you have probably read already. We have no desire to pad the page count of this book by discussing mainly basic concepts, or to provide unnecessarily detailed and repetitive explanations. In other words, this book is not merely a thin additional layer on top of an abbreviated listing of the HTML5 Canvas Application Programming Interfaces (APIs), nor is it a rehash of the new CSS3 features. As you will soon discover, many code samples in this book show you how to combine HTML5 Canvas APIs and CSS3 graphics effects in the same HTML pages in order to create novel and interesting visual effects.

As you will see, many CSS3 code samples in this book are visually intense (usually because of the linear or radial gradients) because the intent of the code samples is to illustrate the capabilities of CSS3 and also to show you how to use the powerful features of CSS3. In fact, some of the code samples create visual effects that you are unlikely to find elsewhere. If you need to use patterns that are similar to the code samples but with more muted visual effects, you can modify the code samples to "tone down" their visual intensity.

In addition, please view the code samples in a browser as you read the code and the accompanying explanation. The rendered graphics will make it easier to understand the code, thereby enabling you to grasp the concepts more quickly and read the material at a faster pace, and hopefully also stimulate your creativeness to come up with your own interesting variations of the graphics samples. In addition, the images in the printed book are in black and white, so if you launch the HTML pages in a browser, you will experience the visually rich color effects in these code samples.

Although every attempt has been made to present the material in a logical and sequential fashion, the techniques for creating graphics effects do not exist in isolation from each other, which means that concepts are sometimes introduced prematurely (almost like forward referencing a variable in a program). When those situations arise, however, you will often find a follow-up section, later in the same chapter, that provides a more in-depth discussion of those out-of-sequence concepts.

Many of the CSS3 code samples in this chapter are drawn from an open source project (*http://code.google.com/p/css3-graphics*) containing more than 1,000 code samples that render properly on both Windows Vista and MacBook operating systems. You can replace the CSS3 stylesheets in the code samples with the additional CSS3 stylesheets that are provided on the DVD that accompanies this book, or you can experiment with the many CSS3 code samples that are available in the open source project. Hopefully this assortment of code samples will enable you to create suitable visual effects for your Web site.

The code samples in the open source project render correctly on iPod Touch®, iPhone®, iPad®, and Samsung Galaxy Tab™ 10.1 mobile devices. At this writing, the B&N NOOK Color™ does not provide hardware acceleration, so many of the 2D animation samples were very slow, and some of the 3D animation samples were essentially inoperable. These CSS3 code samples ought to work correctly on any tablets that provide hardware acceleration.

Note that a comprehensive coverage of the aspects and features of HTML5 Canvas and CSS3 could easily double or even triple the size of this book. Some important topics, such as performance and best practices for CSS3, are covered in a cursory manner, but links to other resources that can provide additional details and useful information are provided. Of course, you are always able to perform an Internet search for any of the topics that are covered in this book.

The main purpose of the code samples is to present techniques for creating aesthetically pleasing visual effects using the HTML5 Canvas APIs and the new features of CSS3. Clarity is deemed more important than optimized code that is less clear, so the JavaScript code and the CSS3 selectors can be refactored in order to make both more efficient. We recommend making performance-related improvements prior to using any portions of the code samples in a production system.

After experimenting with the interactive samples (those with a Redraw button), you can easily modify the existing code to programmatically create the effects that are generated by multiple mouseclicks. After all, those code samples invoke the same functions but with a slight offset, thereby creating a cumulative visual effect.

Performance is obviously important, especially for mobile devices. Learn performance enhancement techniques from experts, including Paul Irish and Steve Souders. Paul is a Googler and a frequent blogger and he creates videos about performance techniques for HTML5 and CSS3. Steve is also a Googler and he has written several performance-based O'Reilly books. Paul and Steve are frequent speakers at various events, and you can use Google™ search for videos of their presentations.

You have probably purchased books whose code samples continuously "build" on concepts that are discussed in previous chapters of those books. Although there are merits to this approach, sometimes this approach can be problematic; specifically, if you do not understand a particular concept in a code sample, it will be difficult to understand any subsequent code samples that use that concept. You need to study the earlier concept until it becomes clear, otherwise all the examples that rely on that concept will remain unclear. Although various code samples in this book do use concepts that are introduced in earlier chapters, there is no cumulative chapter project. At the same time, we have endeavored to provide code samples that create compelling visual effects.

We have made an effort to be consistent in the terminology, but there are some slight variations. For instance, you might see "method abc ()" as well as "function abc ()"; or "HTML <div> element" as well as "<div> element"; and sometimes you will see "CSS property" replaced with "CSS attribute." The former terminology is preferable over the latter, and in each case, if you keep this liberty in mind, there will not be any confusion regarding the intended usage.

ACKNOWLEDGMENTS

This is my first book about HTML5 graphics, and my previous five books gave me the technical background to appreciate the capabilities of CSS3 and HTML5 Canvas. I always aspire to under-promise yet over-deliver regarding book content, and I genuinely hope that my "concept code" style gives other people a similar level of satisfaction that I have enjoyed from HTML5 graphics.

I'm blessed with a highly supportive family and relatives, including Andrea, his wife Gianna, and his sons Pietro, Marco, and Luca, who always unabashedly express their admiration for my books, and I feel fortunate and grateful to receive such genuine and unsolicited praise from them.

Other relatives who have influenced me include Lia Campesato, whose house was like a second home for me when I lived in Milan; Elda Grisostolo, for cooking six-at-a-time quail dinners for me; Carlo Grisostolo, for his cellar filled with cheese, wine barrels, and a plethora of multi-berried wines. My thanks also extend to my lifelong friends and soulmates Laurie Dresser and Farid Sharifi.

I'm always grateful for the people who have supported me in my endeavors or influenced me in my life, sometimes in subliminal ways, and I've found such people in many parts of the world, even in an uber-competitive place such as Silicon Valley. I've met many wicked smart people in San Francisco, whose positive energy inspires me and brings out the best in me.

Finally, I would be remiss if I did not thank Dave Pallai, publisher of Mercury Learning, Melissa Ray, technical reviewer, and Kate Stein, copy editor, who made valuable contributions to improve the quality of this book. As always, I take responsibility for any errors or omissions that you might find in any of the chapters.

CHAPTER 1

INTRODUCTION TO CSS3

C hapter 1 is the first of two chapters that discusses CSS3, with a focus on CSS3 features that enable you to create vivid graphics effects. The first part of this chapter contains a short section that discusses the structure of a minimal HTML5 document, followed by a brief discussion regarding browser support for CSS3 and online tools that can be helpful in this regard. CSS3 stylesheets are referenced in HTML5 pages; therefore, it's important to understand the limitations that exist with respect to browser support for CSS3.

The second part of this chapter contains various code samples that illustrate how to create shadow effects, how to render rectangles with rounded corners, and also how to use linear and radial gradients. The third part of this chapter covers CSS3 transforms (scale, rotate, skew, and translate), along with code samples that illustrate how to apply transforms to HTML elements and to JPG files.

When you have completed this chapter, you will know how to use the CSS3 methods `translate()`, `rotate()`, `skew()`, and `scale()`. This will prepare you for the material in Chapter 2, "CSS3 2D/3D Animation and CSS Frameworks," which contains code samples with additional new CSS3 features (e.g., 2D/3D animation), as well as an overview of some CSS frameworks. Before you read this chapter, please keep in mind the following points. First, the CSS3 code samples in this book are for WebKit-based browsers, so the code will work on Microsoft® Windows®, Macintosh®, and Linux®. In addition, there are tools for generating the CSS3 code for other non-WebKit browsers, which streamline the process of maintaining CSS3 stylesheets for different types of browsers.

Second, several chapters mention performing an Internet search to obtain more information about a specific topic. The rationale for doing so is that the relevance of online information depends on the knowledge level of the reader, so it's virtually impossible to find a one-size-fits-all link that is suitable for everyone's needs. In addition, there is a gap between the time that a book is written and the time that it is published, which means that newer links are continually made available. Furthermore, topics that are less relevant to the theme or beyond the scope of this book will be covered more lightly, thereby maintaining a reasonable balance between the number of topics and the depth of explanation of the relevant details. With these points in mind, please be assured that referring you to the Internet is never intended to be "user unfriendly" in any manner.

Third, virtually all of the links in this book refer to open source projects, but you can also find very good commercial products; the choice of tools depends on the features that they support, the requirements for your project, and the size of your budget.

TERMINOLOGY IN THIS BOOK

Although this book makes every attempt to be consistent, there are times when terminology is not 100% correct. For example, WebKit is an engine and not a browser. Therefore, "WebKit-based browser" is correct, whereas "WebKit browser" is incorrect, but you will see both used (even though only the former is technically correct). Second, you will see "HTML Web page" and "HTML page" used interchangeably. Third, sometimes references to HTML elements do not specify "HTML", so you will see "<p> element" and "HTML <p> element" (or some other HTML element) in the discussion that precedes or follows a code sample.

Please keep the preceding points in mind, and that way there won't be any confusion as you read this book.

HTML5 AND `<!DOCTYPE>`

In addition to introducing many new semantic tags, HTML5 has simplified the `<!DOCTYPE>` declaration for Web pages. This book does not contain a discussion of new HTML5 tags, but the HTML pages in this book do use the HTML5 `<!DOCTYPE>` declaration. The typical structure of the HTML pages in this book looks like this:

```
<!DOCTYPE html>

<html lang="en">

<head>

...

</head>


<body>
  <div id="outer">

   ...

  </div>
</body>
</html>
```

Most of the "action" in the CSS3-based code samples takes place in the CSS3 selectors. In addition, the code for rendering 2D shapes in the HTML5 `Canvas` code samples consists of JavaScript code inside a `<script>` element. Consequently, you do not need any knowledge of the new HTML5 tags in order to follow the examples in this book. The only exception is Chapter 2, which contains `MultiColumns1.html` (with a few semantic tags) and the CSS stylesheet `MultiColumns1.css` with CSS3 selectors that render text in multiple columns. You will be able understand the HTML page even without knowing the semantics of the HTML5 tags in that example (and if need be, you can perform an Internet search for articles that explain the purpose of those tags).

CSS3 FEATURES AND BROWSER SUPPORT

There are two important details about defining CSS3-based selectors for HTML pages. First, different browsers (and different browser versions) support different CSS3 features. One of the best Web sites for finding this detailed level of information is here: *http://caniuse.com/*. This Web site

contains tabular information regarding CSS3 support in Internet Explorer®
(IE), Firefox®, Safari®, Chrome™, and Opera™ browsers.

The second detail is that many CSS3 properties currently require
browser-specific prefixes in order for them to work correctly. The prefixes -ie-,
-moz-, and -o- are for Internet Explorer, Firefox, and Opera, respectively. As
an illustration, the following code block shows examples of these prefixes:

```
-ie-webkit-border-radius: 8px;

-moz-webkit-border-radius: 8px;

-o-webkit-border-radius: 8px;

border-radius: 8px;
```

In your CSS selectors, specify the attributes with browser-specific prefixes
before the "generic" attribute, which serves as a default choice in the event
that the browser-specific attributes are not selected. The CSS3 code samples
in this book contain Webkit-specific prefixes, which helps us keep the CSS
stylesheets manageable in terms of size. If you need CSS stylesheets that work
on multiple browsers, there are essentially two options available. One option
involves manually adding the CSS3 code with all the required browser-specific
prefixes, which can be tedious to maintain and is also error prone. Another
option is to use CSS frameworks (discussed in Chapter 2) that can programmatically generate the CSS3 code that contains all browser-specific prefixes.

MODERNIZR

Modernizr (*http://www.modernizr.com/*) is a very useful tool for
HTML5-related feature detection in various browsers.

At some point, you will start using JavaScript in your HTML5 pages
(indeed, you probably do so already), and Modernizr provides a programmatic way to check for many HTML5 and CSS3 features in different browsers.

As a simple example, you can write the following type of code block
when you include Modernizr in an HTML page:

```
if(Modernizr.canvas) {
  // canvas is available
```

```
    // do something here
} else {
    // canvas is not available
    // do something else here
}
```

Note that the code samples in this book are written specifically for Webkit-based browsers, which provide support for HTML5 `Canvas`.

Navigate to the Modernizr home page where you can read the documentation, tutorials, and details regarding the set of feature detection.

SUPPORT FOR IE-BASED BROWSERS

Remy Sharp provides a JavaScript file `html5.js` for IE 6/7/8 that you can download here: *http://html5shim.googlecode.com/svn/trunk/html5.js*. When you navigate to this Web page, simply save the link as `html5.js`. Include this JavaScript file in the `<head>` element of your HTML5 Web pages using this code fragment that conditionally includes the JavaScript file:

```
<!–[if lt IE 9]>
<script>
http://html5shim.googlecode.com/svn/trunk/html5.js
<![endif]-->
```

Remy provides a Web page with this information, along with other content that could prove useful, that is available here: *http://remysharp.com/2009/01/07/html5-enabling-script/*.

IE 9 and IE 10 provide much-improved support for HTML5 (compared to earlier versions of IE), including CSS3 features and support for SVG (Scalable Vector Graphics). When in doubt, check the Modernizr Web site discussed earlier in this chapter for information regarding support for CSS3 features for the browser version in question.

A QUICK OVERVIEW OF CSS3 FEATURES

CSS3 adopts a modularized approach for extending existing CSS2 functionality as well as supporting new functionality. As such, CSS3 can be logically divided into the following categories:

- Backgrounds/borders
- Color
- Media queries
- Multicolumn layout
- Selectors

With CSS3 you can create boxes with rounded corners and shadow effects; create rich graphics effects using linear and radial gradients; switch between portrait and landscape mode and detect the type of mobile device using media query selectors; produce multicolumn text rendering and formatting; and specify sophisticated node selection rules in selectors using first-child, last-child, first-of-type, and last-of-type.

CSS3 SHADOW EFFECTS AND ROUNDED CORNERS

CSS3 shadow effects are useful for creating vivid visual effects with simple selectors. You can use shadow effects for text as well as rectangular regions. CSS3 also enables you to easily render rectangles with rounded corners, so you do not need JPG files in order to create this effect.

CSS3 and Text Shadow Effects

A shadow effect for text can make a Web page look more vivid and appealing. Listing 1.1 displays the contents of the HTML5 page TextShadow1.html, illustrating how to render text with a shadow effect, and Listing 1.2 displays the contents of the CSS stylesheet TextShadow1.css that is referenced in Listing 1.1.

Listing 1.1 TextShadow1.html

```
<!DOCTYPE html>

<html lang="en">
```

```
<head>
  <title>CSS Text Shadow Example</title>
  <meta charset="utf-8" />
  <link href="TextShadow1.css" rel="stylesheet"
        type="text/css">
</head>

<body>
  <div id="text1">
    Line One Shadow Effect
  </div>
  <div id="text2">
    Line Two Shadow Effect
  </div>
  <div id="text3">
    Line Three Vivid Effect
  </div>

  <div id="text4">
    <span id="dd">13</span>
    <span id="mm">August</span>
    <span id="yy">2011</span>
  </div>

  <div id="text5">
    <span id="dd">13</span>
    <span id="mm">August</span>
    <span id="yy">2011</span>
  </div>
```

```
<div id="text6">
  <span id="dd">13</span>
  <span id="mm">August</span>
  <span id="yy">2011</span>
</div>
</body>
</html>
```

The code in Listing 1.1 is straightforward: there is a reference to the CSS stylesheet `TextShadow1.css` that contains two CSS selectors. One selector specifies how to render the HTML `<div>` element whose `id` attribute has value `text1`, and the other selector is applied to the HTML `<div>` element whose `id` attribute is `text2`. The CSS3 `rotate()` function is included in this example; however, a more detailed discussion of this function will be included later in this chapter.

Listing 1.2 `TextShadow1.css`

```
#text1 {
  font-size: 24pt;
  text-shadow: 2px 4px 5px #00f;
}


#text2 {
  font-size: 32pt;
  text-shadow: 0px 1px 6px #000,
               4px 5px 6px #f00;
}


#text3 {
  font-size: 40pt;
  text-shadow: 0px 1px 6px  #fff,
```

```
                        2px  4px  4px   #0ff,
                        4px  5px  6px   #00f,
                        0px  0px  10px  #444,
                        0px  0px  20px  #844,
                        0px  0px  30px  #a44,
                        0px  0px  40px  #f44;
}

#text4 {
   position: absolute;
   top: 200px;
   right: 200px;
   font-size: 48pt;
   text-shadow: 0px  1px  6px   #fff,
                        2px  4px  4px   #0ff,
                        4px  5px  6px   #00f,
                        0px  0px  10px  #000,
                        0px  0px  20px  #448,
                        0px  0px  30px  #a4a,
                        0px  0px  40px  #fff;
   -webkit-transform: rotate(-90deg);
}

#text5 {
   position: absolute;
   left: 0px;
   font-size: 48pt;
   text-shadow: 2px 4px 5px #00f;
   -webkit-transform: rotate(-10deg);
}
```

```
#text6 {
  float: left;
  font-size: 48pt;
  text-shadow: 2px 4px 5px #f00;
  -webkit-transform: rotate(-170deg);
}


/* 'transform' is explained later */
#text1:hover, #text2:hover, #text3:hover,
#text4:hover, #text5:hover, #text6:hover {
-webkit-transform : scale(2) rotate(-45deg);
-transform : scale(2) rotate(-45deg);
}
```

The first selector in Listing 1.2 specifies a `font-size` of 24 and a `text-shadow` that renders text with a blue background (represented by the hexadecimal value `#00f`). The attribute `text-shadow` specifies (from left to right) the x-coordinate, the y-coordinate, the blur radius, and the color of the shadow. The second selector specifies a `font-size` of 32 and a red shadow background (`#f00`). The third selector creates a richer visual effect by specifying multiple components in the `text-shadow` property, which were chosen by experimenting with effects that are possible with different values in the various components.

The final CSS3 selector creates an animation effect when users hover over any of the six text strings; the details of the animation will be deferred until later in this chapter. Figure 1.1 displays the result of applying the CSS stylesheet `TextShadow1.css` to the HTML `<div>` elements in the HTML page `TextShadow1.html`.

CSS3 and Box Shadow Effects

You can also apply a shadow effect to a box that encloses a text string, which can be effective in terms of drawing attention to specific parts of

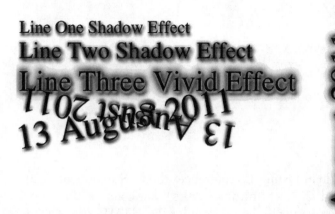

FIGURE 1.1 CSS3 text shadow effects.

a Web page. The same caveat regarding over-use applies to box shadows. Listing 1.3 displays the contents of the HTML page `BoxShadow1.html` that renders a box shadow effect, and Listing 1.4 displays the contents of `BoxShadow1.css` that contains the associated CSS3 selectors.

Listing 1.3 `BoxShadow1.html`

```
<!DOCTYPE html>

<html lang="en">

<head>

  <title>CSS Box Shadow Example</title>

  <meta charset="utf-8" />

  <link href="BoxShadow1.css" rel="stylesheet"
        type="text/css">

</head>
```

```
<body>
  <div id="box1"> Line One with a Box Effect </div>
  <div id="box2"> Line Two with a Box Effect </div>
  <div id="box3"> Line Three with a Box Effect </div>
</body>
</html>
```

The code in Listing 1.3 references the CSS stylesheet BoxShadow1. css (instead of TextShadow1.css) that contains three CSS selectors. These selectors specify how to render the HTML <div> elements whose id attribute has value box1, box2, and box3, respectively (and all three <div> elements are defined in BoxShadow1.html).

Listing 1.4 BoxShadow1.css

```
#box1 {
  position:relative;top:10px;
  width: 50%;
  height: 30px;
  font-size: 20px;
  -moz-box-shadow: 10px 10px 5px #800;
  -webkit-box-shadow: 10px 10px 5px #800;
  box-shadow: 10px 10px 5px #800;
}

#box2 {
  position:relative;top:20px;
  width: 80%;
  height: 50px;
  font-size: 36px;
  padding: 10px;
```

```
   -moz-box-shadow: 14px 14px 8px #008;

   -webkit-box-shadow: 14px 14px 8px #008;

   box-shadow: 14px 14px 8px #008;

}


#box3 {

   position:relative;top:30px;

   width: 80%;

   height: 60px;

   font-size: 52px;

   padding: 10px;

   -moz-box-shadow: 14px 14px 8px #008;

   -webkit-box-shadow: 14px 14px 8px #008;

   box-shadow: 14px 14px 8px #008;

}
```

The first selector in Listing 1.4 specifies the attributes `width`, `height`, and `font-size`, which control the dimensions of the associated HTML `<div>` element and also the enclosed text string. The next three attributes consist of a Mozilla-specific `box-shadow` attribute, followed by a WebKit-specific `box-shadow` property, and finally the "generic" `box-shadow` attribute. Figure 1.2 displays the result of applying the CSS stylesheet `BoxShadow1.css` to the HTML page `BoxShadow1.html`.

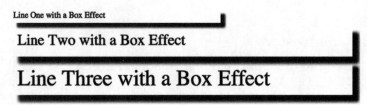

FIGURE 1.2 CSS3 box shadow effect.

CSS3 and Rounded Corners

Web developers have waited a long time for rounded corners in CSS, and CSS3 makes it very easy to render boxes with rounded corners. Listing 1.5 displays the contents of the HTML page `RoundedCorners1.html` that renders text strings in boxes with rounded corners, and Listing 1.6 displays the CSS file `RoundedCorners1.css`.

Listing 1.5 `RoundedCorners1.html`

```
<!DOCTYPE html>

<html lang="en">

<head>

  <title>CSS Text Shadow Example</title>

  <meta charset="utf-8" />

  <link href="RoundedCorners1.css" rel="stylesheet"
      type="text/css">

</head>


<body>

  <div id="outer">

    <a href="#" class="anchor">Text Inside a Rounded
      Rectangle</a>

  </div>


  <div id="text1">

    Line One of Text with a Shadow Effect

  </div>


  <div id="text2">

    Line Two of Text with a Shadow Effect

  </div>

</body>

</html>
```

Listing 1.5 contains a reference to the CSS stylesheet Rounded-Corners1.css that contains three CSS selectors that are applied to the elements whose id attribute has value anchor, text1, and text2, respectively. The CSS selectors defined in RoundedCorners1.css create visual effects, and as you will see, the hover pseudo-selector enables you to create animation effects.

Listing 1.6 RoundedCorners1.css

```
a.anchor:hover {
background: #00F;
}

a.anchor {
background: #FF0;
font-size: 24px;
font-weight: bold;
padding: 4px 4px;
color: rgba(255,0,0,0.8);
text-shadow: 0 1px 1px rgba(0,0,0,0.4);
-webkit-transition: all 2.0s ease;
-transition: all 2.0s ease;
-webkit-border-radius: 8px;
border-radius: 8px;
}

#text1 {
  font-size: 24pt;
  text-shadow: 2px 4px 5px #00f;
}
```

```css
#text2 {
  font-size: 32pt;
  text-shadow: 4px 5px 6px #f00;
}

#round1 {
  -moz-border-radius-bottomleft: 20px;
  -moz-border-radius-bottomright: 20px;
  -moz-border-radius-topleft: 20px;
  -moz-border-radius-topright: 20px;
  -moz-box-shadow: 2px 2px 10px #ccc;
  -webkit-border-bottom-left-radius: 20px;
  -webkit-border-bottom-right-radius: 20px;
  -webkit-border-top-left-radius: 20px;
  -webkit-border-top-right-radius: 20px;
  -webkit-box-shadow: 2px 2px 10px #ccc;
  background-color: #f00;
  margin: 25px auto 0;
  padding: 25px 10px;
  text-align: center;
  width: 260px;
}
```

Listing 1.6 contains the selector a.anchor:hover that changes the text color from yellow (#FF0) to blue (#00F) during a two-second interval when users hover over any anchor element with their mouse.

The selector a.anchor contains various attributes that specify the dimensions of the box that encloses the text in the <a> element, along with two new pairs of attributes. The first pair specifies the transition attribute (and a WebKit-specific prefix), which we will discuss later in this chapter. The second pair specifies the border-radius attribute (and the

WebKit-specific attribute) whose value is 8px, which determines the radius (in pixels) of the rounded corners of the box that encloses the text in the <a> element. The last two selectors are identical to the selectors in Listing 1.1. Figure 1.3 displays the result of applying the CSS stylesheet RoundedCorners1.css to the elements in the HTML page Rounded Corners1.html.

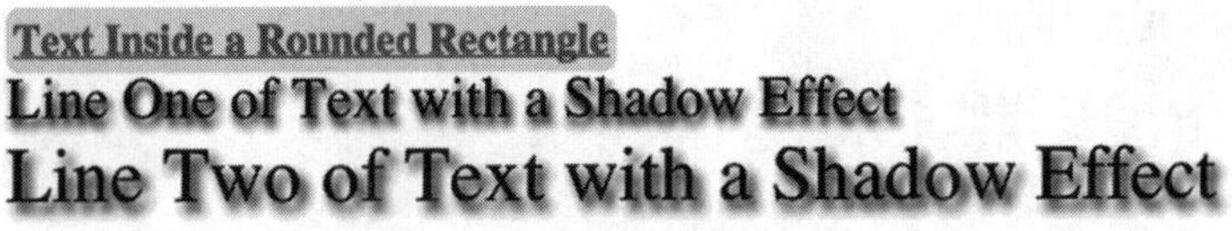

Text Inside a Rounded Rectangle
Line One of Text with a Shadow Effect
Line Two of Text with a Shadow Effect

FIGURE 1.3 CSS3 rounded corners effect.

CSS3 GRADIENTS

CSS3 supports linear gradients and radial gradients, which enable you to create gradient effects that are as visually rich as gradients in other technologies such as SVG and Silverlight. The code samples in this section illustrate how to define linear gradients and radial gradients in CSS3 and then apply them to HTML elements.

Linear Gradients

CSS3 linear gradients require you to specify one or more "color stops," each of which specifies a start color, and end color, and a rendering pattern. WebKit-based browsers support the following syntax to define a linear gradient:

- a start point
- an end point
- a start color using from()
- zero or more stop-colors
- an end color using to()

A start point can be specified as an (x,y) pair of numbers or percentages. For example, the pair (100, 25%) specifies the point that is 100 pixels to the right of the origin and 25% of the way down from the top of the pattern. Recall that the origin is located in the upper-left corner of the screen. Listing 1.7 displays the contents of `LinearGradient1.html` and Listing 1.8 displays the contents of `LinearGradient1.css`, which illustrate how to apply linear gradients to text strings that are enclosed in <p> elements and an <h3> element.

Listing 1.7 `LinearGradient1.html`

```
<!doctype html>
<html lang="en">
<head>
  <title>CSS Linear Gradient Example</title>
  <meta charset="utf-8" />
  <link href="LinearGradient1.css" rel="stylesheet"
        type="text/css">
</head>

<body>
  <div id="outer">
    <p id="line1">line 1 with a linear gradient</p>
    <p id="line2">line 2 with a linear gradient</p>
    <p id="line3">line 3 with a linear gradient</p>
    <p id="line4">line 4 with a linear gradient</p>
    <p id="outline">line 5 with Shadow Outline</p>
    <h3><a href="#">A Line of Gradient Text</a></h3>
  </div>
</body>
</html>
```

Listing 1.7 is a simple Web page containing four <p> elements and one <h3> element. Listing 1.7 also references the CSS stylesheet `Linear-Gradient1.css` that contains CSS selectors that are applied to the four <p> elements and the <h3> element in Listing 1.7.

Listing 1.8 `LinearGradient1.css`

```
#line1 {
width: 50%;
font-size: 32px;
background-image: -webkit-gradient(linear, 0% 0%, 0% 100%,
                                   from(#fff), to(#f00));
background-image: -gradient(linear, 0% 0%, 0% 100%,
                            from(#fff), to(#f00));
-webkit-border-radius: 4px;
border-radius: 4px;
}

#line2 {
width: 50%;
font-size: 32px;
background-image: -webkit-gradient(linear, 100% 0%, 0%
                            100%, from(#fff), to(#ff0));
background-image: -gradient(linear, 100% 0%, 0% 100%,
                            from(#fff), to(#ff0));
-webkit-border-radius: 4px;
border-radius: 4px;
}

#line3 {
width: 50%;
font-size: 32px;
background-image: -webkit-gradient(linear, 0% 0%, 0% 100%,
                            from(#f00), to(#00f));
```

```
background-image: -gradient(linear, 0% 0%, 0% 100%,
                            from(#f00), to(#00f));
-webkit-border-radius: 4px;
border-radius: 4px;
}

#line4 {
width: 50%;
font-size: 32px;
background-image: -webkit-gradient(linear, 100% 0%, 0%
                        100%, from(#fff), to(#ff0));
background-image: -gradient(linear, 100% 0%, 0% 100%,
                            from(#f00), to(#00f));
-webkit-border-radius: 4px;
border-radius: 4px;
}

#outline {
font-size: 2.0em;
font-weight: bold;
color: #fff;
text-shadow: 1px 1px 1px rgba(0,0,0,0.5);
}

h3 {
width: 50%;
position: relative;
margin-top: 0;
font-size: 32px;
font-family: helvetica, ariel;
}
```

```
h3 a {

position: relative;

color: red;

text-decoration: none;

-webkit-mask-image:  -webkit-gradient(linear, left top,
                     left bottom, from(rgba(0,0,0,1)),
                     color-stop(50%, rgba(0,0,0,0.5)),
                     to(rgba(0,0,0,0)));

}

h3:after {

content:"This is a Line of Gradient Text";

color: blue;

}
```

The first selector in Listing 1.8 specifies a `font-size` of 32 for text, a `border-radius` of 4 (which renders rounded corners), and a linear gradient that varies from white to blue, as shown here:

```
#line1 {

width: 50%;

font-size: 32px;

background-image: -webkit-gradient(linear, 0% 0%, 0% 100%,
                                   from(#fff), to(#f00));

background-image: -gradient(linear, 0% 0%, 0% 100%,
                            from(#fff), to(#f00));

-webkit-border-radius: 4px;

border-radius: 4px;

}
```

As you can see, the first selector contains two attributes with a -webkit-prefix and two standard attributes without this prefix. Because the next three selectors in Listing 1.8 are similar to the first selector, we will not discuss their content.

The next CSS selector creates a text outline with a nice shadow effect by rendering the text in white with a thin black shadow, as shown here:

```
color: #fff;

text-shadow: 1px 1px 1px rgba(0,0,0,0.5);
```

The final portion of Listing 1.8 contains three selectors that affect the rendering of the <h3> element and its embedded <a> element: the h3 selector specifies the width and font size; the h3 a selector specifies a linear gradient; and the h3:after selector specifies the text string to display. Note that other attributes are specified, but these are the main attributes for these selectors. Figure 1.4 displays the result of applying the selectors in the CSS stylesheet LinearGradient1.css to the HTML page LinearGradient1.html.

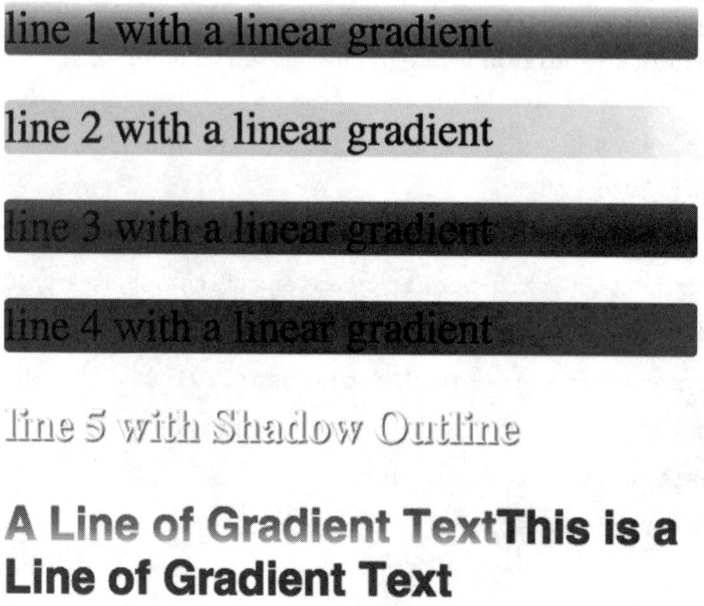

FIGURE 1.4 CSS3 linear gradient effect.

Radial Gradients

CSS3 radial gradients are more complex than CSS3 linear gradients, but you can use them to create more complex gradient effects. WebKit-based browsers support the following syntax to define a radial gradient:

- a start point
- a start radius
- an end point
- an end radius
- a start color using from()
- zero or more stop-colors
- an end color using to()

Notice that the syntax for a radial gradient is similar to the syntax for a linear gradient, except that you also specify a start radius and an end radius. Listing 1.9 displays the contents of RadialGradient1.html and Listing 1.10 displays the contents of RadialGradient1.css, which illustrate how to render various circles with radial gradients.

Listing 1.9 RadialGradient1.html

```
<!doctype html>
<html lang="en">
<head>
  <title>CSS Radial Gradient Example</title>
  <meta charset="utf-8" />
  <link href="RadialGradient9.css" rel="stylesheet"
        type="text/css">
</head>

<body>

<div id="outer">
<div id="radial3">Text3</div>
```

```
<div id="radial2">Text2</div>

<div id="radial4">Text4</div>

<div id="radial1">Text1</div>

</div>

</body>

</html>
```

Listing 1.9 contains five DIV elements whose id attribute has value outer, radial1, radial2, radial3, and radial4, respectively. Listing 1.9 also references the CSS stylesheet RadialGradient1.css that contains five CSS selectors that are applied to the five DIV elements.

Listing 1.10 RadialGradient1.css

```
#outer {
position: relative; top: 10px; left: 0px;
}
#radial1 {
font-size: 24px;
width:  300px;
height: 300px;
position: absolute; top: 300px; left: 300px;

background: -webkit-gradient(
  radial, 500 40%, 0, 301 25%, 360, from(red),
  color-stop(0.05, orange), color-stop(0.4, yellow),
  color-stop(0.6, green), color-stop(0.8, blue),
  to(#fff)
);
}
```

```
#radial2 {
font-size: 24px;
width:  500px;
height: 500px;
position: absolute; top: 100px; left: 100px;

background: -webkit-gradient(
   radial, 500 40%, 0, 301 25%, 360, from(red),
   color-stop(0.05, orange), color-stop(0.4, yellow),
   color-stop(0.6, green), color-stop(0.8, blue),
   to(#fff)
 );
}

#radial3 {
font-size: 24px;
width:  600px;
height: 600px;
position: absolute; top: 0px; left: 0px;

background: -webkit-gradient(
   radial, 500 40%, 0, 301 25%, 360, from(red),
   color-stop(0.05, orange), color-stop(0.4, yellow),
   color-stop(0.6, green), color-stop(0.8, blue),
   to(#fff)
 );
-webkit-box-shadow:  0px 0px 8px #000;
}
```

```
#radial4 {
font-size: 24px;
width:   400px;
height: 400px;
position: absolute; top: 200px; left: 200px;

background: -webkit-gradient(
  radial, 500 40%, 0, 301 25%, 360, from(red),
  color-stop(0.05, orange), color-stop(0.4, yellow),
  color-stop(0.6, green), color-stop(0.8, blue),
  to(#fff)
 );
}
```

The first part of the #radial1 selector in Listing 1.10 contains the attributes width and height that specify the dimensions of a rendered rectangle, and also a position attribute that is similar to the position attribute in the #outer selector. The #radial1 also contains a back-ground attribute that defines a radial gradient using the -webkit- prefix, as shown here:

```
background: -webkit-gradient(
  radial, 100 25%, 20, 100 25%, 40, from(blue), to(#fff)
 );
```

The preceding radial gradient specifies the following:

- a start point of (100, 25%)
- a start radius of 20
- an end point of (100, 25%)
- an end radius of 40
- a start color of blue
- an end color of white (#fff)

Notice that the start point and end point are the same, which renders a set of concentric circles that vary from blue to white.

The other four selectors in Listing 1.10 have the same syntax as the first selector, but the rendered radial gradients are significantly different. You can create these and other effects by specifying different start points and end points, and by specifying a start radius that is larger than the end radius.

The `#radial4` selector creates a ringed effect by means of two `stop-color` attributes, as shown here:

```
color-stop(0.2, orange), color-stop(0.4, yellow),
color-stop(0.6, green), color-stop(0.8, blue),
```

You can add additional stop-color attributes to create more complex radial gradients.

Figure 1.5 displays the result of applying the selectors in the CSS stylesheet `RadialGradient1.css` to the HTML page `Radial-Gradient1.html`.

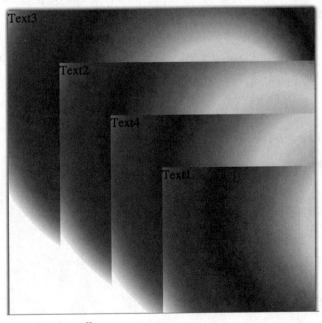

FIGURE 1.5 CSS3 radial gradient effect.

CSS3 2D TRANSFORMS

In addition to transitions, CSS3 supports four transforms that you can apply to 2D shapes and also to JPG files. The four CSS3 transforms are `scale`, `rotate`, `skew`, and `translate`. The following sections contain code samples that illustrate how to apply each of these CSS3 transforms to a set of JPG files. The animation effects occur when users hover over any of the JPG files; moreover, you can create partial animation effects by moving your mouse quickly between adjacent JPG files.

Zoom In/Out Effects with Scale Transforms

The CSS3 `transform` attribute allows you to specify the `scale()` function in order to create zoom in/out effects, and the syntax for the `scale()` method looks like this:

```
scale(someValue);
```

You can replace `someValue` with any nonzero number. When `someValue` is between 0 and 1, you will reduce the size of the 2D shape or JPG file, creating a "zoom out" effect; values greater than 1 for `someValue` will increase the size of the 2D shape or JPG file, creating a "zoom in" effect; and a value of 1 does not perform any changes.

Listing 1.11 displays the contents of `Scale1.html` and Listing 1.12 displays the contents of `Scale1.css`, which illustrate how to scale JPG files to create a "hover box" image gallery.

Listing 1.11 `Scale1.html`

```
<!DOCTYPE html>
<html lang="en">
<head>
  <title>CSS Scale Transform Example</title>
  <meta charset="utf-8" />
  <link href="Scale1.css" rel="stylesheet"
        type="text/css">
</head>
```

```
<body>
  <header>
   <h1>Hover Over any of the Images:</h1>
  </header>

  <div id="outer">
    <img src="Laurie1.jpeg" class="scaled" width="150"
         height="150"/>
    <img src="Laurie2.jpeg" class="scaled" width="150"
         height="150"/>
    <img src="Laurie1.jpeg" class="scaled" width="150"
         height="150"/>
    <img src="Laurie2.jpeg" class="scaled" width="150"
         height="150"/>
  </div>
</body>
</html>
```

Listing 1.11 references the CSS stylesheet Scale1.css, which contains selectors for creating scaled effects, and four HTML <img> elements that reference the JPG files Laurie1.jpeg and Laurie2.jpeg. The remainder of Listing 1.12 is straightforward, with simple boilerplate text and HTML elements.

Listing 1.12 Scale1.css

```
#outer {
float: left;
position: relative; top: 50px; left: 50px;
}

img {
-webkit-transition: -webkit-transform 1.0s ease;
-transition: transform 1.0s ease;
}
```

```
img.scaled {
  -webkit-box-shadow: 10px 10px 5px #800;
  box-shadow: 10px 10px 5px #800;
}
img.scaled:hover {
-webkit-transform : scale(2);
-transform : scale(2);
}
```

The img selector in Listing 1.12 specifies a transition property that contains a transform effect that occurs during a one-second interval using the ease function, as shown here:

```
-transition: transform 1.0s ease;
```

Next, the selector img.scaled specifies a box-shadow property that creates a reddish shadow effect (seen in Figure 1.2), as shown here:

```
img.scaled {
  -webkit-box-shadow: 10px 10px 5px #800;
  box-shadow: 10px 10px 5px #800;
}
```

Finally, the selector img.scaled:hover specifies a transform attribute that uses the scale() function in order to double the size of the associated JPG file when users hover over any of the <img> elements with their mouse, as shown here:

```
-transform : scale(2);
```

Because the img selector specifies a one-second interval using an ease function, the scaling effect will last for one second. Experiment with different values for the CSS3 scale() function and also different values for the time interval to create the animation effects that suit your needs.

Another point to remember is that you can scale both horizontally and vertically:

```
img {
-webkit-transition: -webkit-transform 1.0s ease;
-transition: transform 1.0s ease;
}


img.mystyle:hover {
-webkit-transform : scaleX(1.5) scaleY(0.5);
-transform : scaleX(1.5) scaleY(0.5);
}
```

Figure 1.6 displays the result of applying the selectors in the CSS stylesheet Scale1.css to the HTML page Scale1.html.

Hover Over any of the Images:

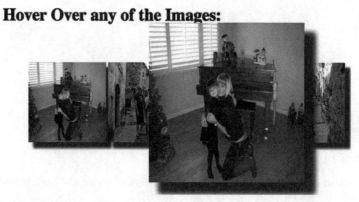

FIGURE 1.6 CSS3 scaling effect.

Rotate Transforms

The CSS3 transform attribute allows you to specify the rotate() function in order to create scaling effects, and its syntax looks like this:

```
rotate(someValue);
```

You can replace someValue with any number. When someValue is positive, the rotation is clockwise; when someValue is negative, the rotation is counterclockwise; and when someValue is zero, there is no rotation effect. In all cases the initial position for the rotation effect is the positive horizontal axis. Listing 1.13 displays the contents of Rotate1.html and Listing 1.14 displays the contents of Rotate1.css, which illustrate how to rotate JPG files in opposite directions.

Listing 1.13 Rotate1.html

```
<!DOCTYPE html>

<html lang="en">

<head>

  <title>CSS Rotate Transform Example</title>

  <meta charset="utf-8" />

  <link href="Rotate1.css" rel="stylesheet"
        type="text/css">

</head>


<body>

  <header>

    <h1>Hover Over any of the Images:</h1>

  </header>


  <div id="outer">

    <img src="Laurie1.jpeg" class="imageL" width="150"
        height="150"/>

    <img src="Laurie2.jpeg" class="imageR" width="150"
        height="150"/>

    <img src="Laurie1.jpeg" class="imageL" width="150"
        height="150"/>
```

```
<img src="Laurie2.jpeg" class="imageR" width="150"
    height="150"/>
</div>
</body>
</html>
```

Listing 1.13 references the CSS stylesheet `Rotate1.css`, which contains selectors for creating rotation effects, and an HTML `<img>` element that references the JPG files `Laurie1.jpeg` and `Laurie2.jpeg`. The remainder of Listing 1.13 consists of simple boilerplate text and HTML elements.

Listing 1.14 `Rotate1.css`

```
#outer {
float: left;
position: relative; top: 100px; left: 150px;
}

img {
  -webkit-transition: -webkit-transform 1.0s ease;
  -transition: transform 1.0s ease;
}

img.imageL {
  -webkit-box-shadow: 14px 14px 8px #800;
  box-shadow: 14px 14px 8px #800;
}

img.imageR {
  -webkit-box-shadow: 14px 14px 8px #008;
  box-shadow: 14px 14px 8px #008;
}
```

```
img.imageL:hover {
  -webkit-transform : scale(2) rotate(-45deg);
  -transform : scale(2) rotate(-45deg);
}


img.imageR:hover {
  -webkit-transform : scale(2) rotate(360deg);
  -transform : scale(2) rotate(360deg);
}
```

Listing 1.14 contains the img selector that specifies a transition attribute that creates an animation effect during a one-second interval using the ease timing function, as shown here:

```
-transition: transform 1.0s ease;
```

Next, the selectors img.imageL and img.imageR contain a property that renders a reddish and bluish background shadow, respectively.

The selector img.imageL:hover specifies a transform attribute that performs a counterclockwise scaling effect (doubling the original size) and a rotation effect (45-degrees counterclockwise) when users hover over the <img> element with their mouse, as shown here:

```
-transform : scale(2) rotate(-45deg);
```

The selector img.imageR:hover is similar, except that it performs a clockwise rotation of 360 degrees. Figure 1.7 displays the result of applying the selectors in the CSS stylesheet Rotate1.css to the elements in the HTML page Rotate1.html.

Hover Over any of the Images:

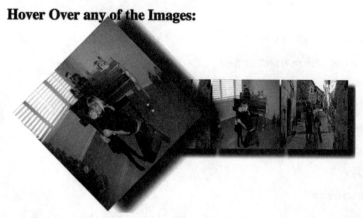

FIGURE 1.7 CSS3 rotation effect.

Skew Transforms

The CSS3 transform attribute allows you to specify the `skew()` function in order to create skewing effects, and its syntax looks like this:

```
skew(xAngle, yAngle);
```

You can replace `xAngle` and `yAngle` with any number. When `xAngle` and `yAngle` are positive, the skew effect is clockwise; when `xAngle` and `yAngle` are negative, the skew effect is counterclockwise; and when `xAngle` and `yAngle` are zero, there is no skew effect. In all cases the initial position for the skew effect is the positive horizontal axis. Listing 1.15 displays the contents of `Skew1.html` and Listing 1.16 displays the contents of `Skew1.css`, which illustrate how to skew a JPG file.

Listing 1.15 `Skew1.html`

```
<!DOCTYPE html>
<html lang="en">
```

```
<head>
  <title>CSS Skew Transform Example</title>
  <meta charset="utf-8" />
  <link href="Skew1.css" rel="stylesheet"
        type="text/css">
</head>

<body>
  <header>
   <h1>Hover Over any of the Images:</h1>
  </header>

  <div id="outer">
    <img src="Laurie1.jpeg" class="skewed1" width="150"
        height="150"/>
    <img src="Laurie2.jpeg" class="skewed2" width="150"
        height="150"/>
    <img src="Laurie1.jpeg" class="skewed3" width="150"
        height="150"/>
    <img src="Laurie2.jpeg" class="skewed4" width="150"
        height="150"/>
  </div>
</body>
</html>
```

Listing 1.15 references the CSS stylesheet Skew1.css, which contains selectors for creating skew effects, and an <img> element that references the JPG files Laurie1.jpeg and Laurie2.jpeg. The remainder of Listing 1.15 consists of simple boilerplate text and HTML elements.

Listing 1.16 Skew1.css

```css
#outer {
float: left;
position: relative; top: 100px; left: 100px;
}

img {
  -webkit-transition: -webkit-transform 1.0s ease;
  -transition: transform 1.0s ease;
}

img.skewed1 {
  -webkit-box-shadow: 14px 14px 8px #800;
  box-shadow: 14px 14px 8px #800;
}

img.skewed2 {
  -webkit-box-shadow: 14px 14px 8px #880;
  box-shadow: 14px 14px 8px #880;
}

img.skewed3 {
  -webkit-box-shadow: 14px 14px 8px #080;
  box-shadow: 14px 14px 8px #080;
}
```

```
img.skewed4 {
  -webkit-box-shadow: 14px 14px 8px #008;
  box-shadow: 14px 14px 8px #008;
}


img.skewed1:hover {
  -webkit-transform : scale(2) skew(-10deg, -30deg);
  -transform : scale(2) skew(-10deg, -30deg);
}


img.skewed2:hover {
  -webkit-transform : scale(2) skew(10deg, 30deg);
  -transform : scale(2) skew(10deg, 30deg);
}


img.skewed3:hover {
  -webkit-transform : scale(0.4) skew(-10deg, -30deg);
  -transform : scale(0.4) skew(-10deg, -30deg);
}


img.skewed4:hover {
  -webkit-transform : scale(0.5, 1.5) skew(10deg, -30deg);
  -transform : scale(0.5, 1.5) skew(10deg, -30deg);
opacity:0.5;
}
```

Listing 1.16 contains the img selector that specifies a transition attribute that creates an animation effect during a one-second interval using the ease timing function, as shown here:

```
-transition: transform 1.0s ease;
```

The four selectors `img.skewed1`, `img.skewed2`, `img.skewed3`, and `img.skewed4` create background shadow effects with darker shades of red, yellow, green, and blue, respectively (all of which you have seen in earlier code samples). The selector `img.skewed1:hover` specifies a transform attribute that performs a skew effect when users hover over the first `<img>` element with their mouse, as shown here:

```
-transform : scale(2) skew(-10deg, -30deg);
```

The other three CSS3 selectors also use a combination of the CSS functions `skew()` and `scale()` to create distinct visual effects. Notice that the fourth hover selector also sets the `opacity` property to `0.5`, which is applied in parallel with the other effects in this selector. Figure 1.8 displays the result of applying the selectors in the CSS stylesheet `Skew1.css` to the elements in the HTML page `Skew1.html`.

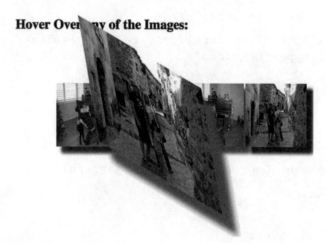

FIGURE 1.8 CSS3 skew effect.

Translate Transforms

The CSS3 transform attribute allows you to specify the `translate()` function in order to create translation or "shifting" effects, and its syntax looks like this:

```
translate(xDirection, yDirection);
```

The translation is in relation to the origin, which is the upper-left corner of the screen. Thus, positive values for xDirection and yDirection produce a shift toward the right and a shift downward, respectively, whereas negative values for xDirection and yDirection produce a shift toward the left and a shift upward; zero values for xDirection and yDirection do not cause any translation effect. Listing 1.17 displays the contents of Translate1.html and Listing 1.18 displays the contents of Translate1.css, which illustrate how to apply a translation effect to a JPG file.

Listing 1.17 Translate1.html

```
<!DOCTYPE html>

<html lang="en">

<head>

  <title>CSS Translate Transform Example</title>

  <meta charset="utf-8" />

  <link href="Translate1.css" rel="stylesheet"
        type="text/css">

</head>


<body>

  <header>

   <h1>Hover Over any of the Images:</h1>

  </header>


  <div id="outer">

    <img src="Laurie1.jpeg" class="trans1" width="150"
        height="150"/>

    <img src="Laurie2.jpeg" class="trans2" width="150"
        height="150"/>

    <img src="Laurie1.jpeg" class="trans3" width="150"
        height="150"/>
```

```
    <img src="Laurie2.jpeg" class="trans4" width="150"
        height="150"/>
  </div>
</body>
</html>
```

Listing 1.17 references the CSS stylesheet `Translate1.css`, which contains selectors for creating translation effects, and an `<img>` element that references the JPG files `Laurie1.jpeg` and `Laurie2.jpeg`. The remainder of Listing 1.17 consists of straightforward boilerplate text and HTML elements.

Listing 1.18 `Translate1.css`

```
#outer {
float: left;
position: relative; top: 100px; left: 100px;
}

img {
  -webkit-transition: -webkit-transform 1.0s ease;
  -transition: transform 1.0s ease;
}

img.trans1 {
  -webkit-box-shadow: 14px 14px 8px #800;
  box-shadow: 14px 14px 8px #800;
}

img.trans2 {
  -webkit-box-shadow: 14px 14px 8px #880;
  box-shadow: 14px 14px 8px #880;
}
```

```
img.trans3 {
  -webkit-box-shadow: 14px 14px 8px #080;
  box-shadow: 14px 14px 8px #080;
}

img.trans4 {
  -webkit-box-shadow: 14px 14px 8px #008;
  box-shadow: 14px 14px 8px #008;
}

img.trans1:hover {
  -webkit-transform : scale(2) translate(100px, 50px);
  -transform : scale(2) translate(100px, 50px);
}

img.trans2:hover {
  -webkit-transform : scale(0.5) translate(-50px, -50px);
  -transform : scale(0.5) translate(-50px, -50px);
}

img.trans3:hover {
  -webkit-transform : scale(0.5,1.5) translate(0px, 0px);
  -transform : scale(0.5,1.5) translate(0px, 0px);
}

img.trans4:hover {
  -webkit-transform : scale(2) translate(50px, -50px);
  -transform : scale(2) translate(100px, 50px);
}
```

Listing 1.17 contains the `img` selector that specifies a transform effect during a one-second interval using the `ease` timing function, as shown here:

```
-transition: transform 1.0s ease;
```

The four selectors `img.trans1`, `img.trans2`, `img.trans3`, and `img.trans4` create background shadow effects with darker shades of red, yellow, green, and blue, respectively, just as you saw in the previous section.

The selector `img.trans1:hover` specifies a `transform` attribute that performs a scale effect and a translation effect when users hover over the first `<img>` element with their mouse, as shown here:

```
-webkit-transform : scale(2) translate(100px, 50px);
transform : scale(2) translate(100px, 50px);
```

The other three selectors contain similar code involving a combination of a translate and a scaling effect, each of which creates a distinct visual effect. Figure 1.9 displays the result of applying the selectors defined in the CSS3 stylesheet `Translate1.css` to the elements in the HTML page `Translate1.html`.

Hover Over any of the Images:

FIGURE 1.9 JPG files with CSS3 scale and translate effects.

SUMMARY

This chapter showed you how to create graphics effects, shadow effects, and how to use CSS3 transforms in CSS3. You learned how to create animation effects that you can apply to HTML elements. You saw how to define CSS3 selectors to do the following:

- render rounded rectangles

- create shadow effects for text and 2D shapes

- create linear and radial gradients

- use the methods `translate()`, `rotate()`, `skew()`, and `scale()`

- create CSS3-based animation effects

Chapter 2 shows you how to create CSS3 animation effects using keyframes and also discusses how to use CSS frameworks to create CSS stylesheets.

CSS3 2D/3D ANIMATION AND CSS FRAMEWORKS

In Chapter 2, we continue the discussion of CSS3, starting with an example of applying CSS3 transforms to a CSS3-based cube. You will see examples of CSS3 transitions for creating simple animation effects, such as glow effects and bouncing effects, and how to create 3D effects. This part of the chapter also contains code samples that show you how to define CSS3 selectors that perform more sophisticated effects with text, such as rendering multicolumn text.

In the second part of this chapter, you will learn how to define CSS3 selectors to create 3D effects and 3D animation effects. Specifically, you will learn how to use CSS3 `keyframes` and the CSS3 functions `scale3d()`, `rotate3d()`, and `translate3d()` that enable you to create 3D animation effects.

The third part of this chapter briefly discusses CSS3 media queries, which enable you to render a given HTML page based on the properties of the device. The fourth and final portion of this chapter introduces you to CSS-based frameworks (e.g., SASS, Compass, CSS Scaffold) that can help you develop code more quickly and also simplifies the task of code maintenance. Although you can create CSS stylesheets manually, keep in mind that CSS frameworks provide powerful functionality that is not available in pure CSS3.

Although the HTML pages in the first three chapters of this book use only CSS3, you can also use JavaScript in order to create visual effects that are easier than using CSS3 alone. Moreover, you can use CSS3 media queries for rendering HMTL5 pages differently on different mobile devices. Neither of these topics is covered in this book, but an Internet search will provide various links and tutorials that contain information on these topics.

A CSS3-BASED CUBE

You can use the CSS3 transforms rotate(), scale(), and skew() in order to create and render a 3D cube with gradient shading. Listing 2.1 displays the contents of 3DCube1.html and Listing 2.2 displays the contents of 3DCube1.css, which illustrate how to simulate a cube in CSS3.

Listing 2.1 3DCube1.html

```
<!DOCTYPE html>

<html lang="en">

<head>

<title>CSS 3D Cube Example</title>

<meta charset="utf-8" />

<link href="3DCSS1.css" rel="stylesheet"
      type="text/css">

</head>


<body>

<header>

<h1>Hover Over the Cube Faces:</h1>

</header>

<div id="outer">

<div id="top">Text1</div>

<div id="left">Text2</div>

<div id="right">Text3</div>

</div>

</body>

</html>
```

Listing 2.1 is a straightforward HTML page that references the CSS stylesheet 3DCSS1.css that contains the CSS3 selectors for styling the HTML <div> elements in this Web page.

Listing 2.2 3DCSS1.css

```
/* animation effects */
#right:hover {
-webkit-transition: -webkit-transform 3.0s ease;
-transition: transform 3.0s ease;

-webkit-transform : scale(1.2) skew(-10deg, -30deg)
                    rotate(-45deg);
-transform : scale(1.2) skew(-10deg, -30deg) rotate(-
            45deg);
}


#left:hover {
-webkit-transition: -webkit-transform 2.0s ease;
-transition: transform 2.0s ease;

-webkit-transform : scale(0.8) skew(-10deg, -30deg)
                    rotate(-45deg);
-transform : scale(0.8) skew(-10deg, -30deg)
            rotate(-45deg);
}


#top:hover {
-webkit-transition: -webkit-transform 2.0s ease;
-transition: transform 2.0s ease;

-webkit-transform : scale(0.5) skew(-20deg, -30deg)
                    rotate(45deg);
```

```
-transform : scale(0.5) skew(-20deg, -30deg)
            rotate(45deg);

}


/* size and position */
#right, #left, #top {
position:relative;  padding: 0px;  width: 200px;
        height: 200px;

}
#left {

  font-size: 48px;

  left: 20px;


background-image:

    -webkit-radial-gradient(red 4px, transparent 28px),

    -webkit-repeating-radial-gradient(red 0px, yellow 4px,
            green 8px, red 12px, transparent 26px,
            blue 20px, red 24px, transparent 28px,
            blue 12px),

    -webkit-repeating-radial-gradient(red 0px,
            yellow 4px, green 8px, red 12px,
            transparent 26px, blue 20px, red 24px,
            transparent 28px, blue 12px);

background-size: 100px 40px, 40px 100px;
background-position: 0 0;

  -webkit-transform: skew(0deg, 30deg);

}

#right {
font-size: 48px;
width:  170px;
```

```
top: -192px;

left: 220px;


background-image:

    -webkit-radial-gradient(red 4px, transparent 48px),

    -webkit-repeating-linear-gradient(0deg, red 5px,
            green 4px, yellow 8px, blue 12px,
            transparent 16px, red 20px, blue 24px,
            transparent 28px, transparent 32px),

    -webkit-radial-gradient(blue 8px, transparent 68px);

background-size: 120px 120px, 24px 24px;

background-position: 0 0;


  -webkit-transform: skew(0deg, -30deg);
}


#top {

font-size: 48px;

top: 50px;

left: 105px;


background-image:

    -webkit-radial-gradient(white 2px, transparent 8px),

    -webkit-repeating-linear-gradient(45deg, white 2px,
            yellow 8px, green 4px, red 12px,
            transparent 26px, blue 20px, red 24px,
            transparent 28px, blue 12px),

    -webkit-repeating-linear-gradient(-45deg, white 2px,
            yellow 8px, green 4px, red 12px, transparent
            26px, blue 20px, red 24px, transparent 28px,
            blue 12px);

background-size: 100px 30px, 30px 100px;

background-position: 0 0;
```

```
    -webkit-transform: rotate(60deg) skew(0deg, -30deg);
                       scale(1, 1.16);
}
```

The first three selectors in Listing 2.2 define the animation effects when users hover on the top, left, or right faces of the cube. In particular, the `#right:hover` selector performs an animation effect during a three-second interval when users hover over the right face of the cube, as shown here:

```
#right:hover {

-webkit-transition: -webkit-transform 3.0s ease;

-transition: transform 3.0s ease;


-webkit-transform : scale(1.2) skew(-10deg, -30deg)
                    rotate(-45deg);

-transform : scale(1.2) skew(-10deg, -30deg)
             rotate (-45deg);

}
```

The transition attribute is already familiar to you, and notice that the `transform` property specifies the CSS3 transform functions `scale()`, `skew()`, and `rotate()`, all of which you have seen already in this chapter. These three functions are applied simultaneously, which means that you will see a scaling, skewing, and rotating effect happening at the same time instead of sequentially.

The last three selectors in Listing 2.2 define the properties of each face of the cube. For example, the `#left` selector specifies the font size for some text and also positional attributes for the left face of the cube. The most complex portion of the `#left` selector is the value of the `background-image` attribute, which consists of a WebKit-specific combination of a radial gradient, a repeating radial gradient, and another radial gradient. Notice that the left face is a rectangle that is transformed into a parallelogram using this line of code:

```
-webkit-transform: skew(0deg, -30deg);
```

The `#top` selector and `#right` selector contain code that is comparable to the `#left` selector, and you can experiment with their values in order to create other visual effects. Figure 2.1 displays the result of applying the CSS selectors in `3DCube1.css` to the `<div>` elements in the HTML page `3DCube1.html`.

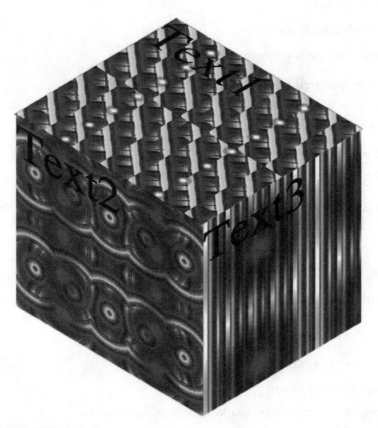

FIGURE 2.1 A CSS3-based cube.

CSS3 TRANSITIONS

CSS3 transitions involve changes to CSS values in a smooth fashion, and they are initiated by user gestures, such as mouse clicks, focus, or hover effects. WebKit originally developed CSS3 transitions, and they are also supported in Safari, Chrome (3.2 or higher), Opera (10.5 or higher), and Firefox (4.0 or higher) by using browser-specific prefixes. Keep in mind that there are toolkits (such as jQuery and Prototype) that support transitions effects similar to their CSS3-based counterparts.

The basic syntax for creating a CSS transition is a "triple" that specifies:

- a CSS property
- a duration (in seconds)
- a transition timing function

Here is an example of a WebKit-based transition:

```
-webkit-transition-property: background;

-webkit-transition-duration: 0.5s;

-webkit-transition-timing-function: ease;
```

Fortunately, you can also combine these transitions in one line, as shown here:

```
-webkit-transition: background 0.5s ease;
```

Here is an example of a CSS3 selector that includes these transitions:

```
a.foo {
padding: 3px 6px;
background: #f00;
-webkit-transition: background 0.5s ease;
}

a.foo:focus, a.foo:hover {
background: #00f;
}
```

Transitions currently require browser-specific prefixes in order for them to work correctly in browsers that are not based on WebKit. Here is an example for Internet Explorer (IE), Firefox, and Opera:

```
-ie-webkit-transition: background 0.5s ease;

-moz-webkit-transition: background 0.5s ease;

-o-webkit-transition: background 0.5s ease;
```

Currently, you can specify one of the following transition timing functions (using browser-specific prefixes):

- ease

- ease-in

- ease-out

- ease-in-out

- cubic-bezier

If these transition functions do not meet your needs, you can create custom functions using this on-line tool: *www.matthewlein.com/ceaser*. You can specify many properties with `-webkit-transition-property`, and an extensive list of properties is here:

https://developer.mozilla.org/en/CSS/CSS_transitions.

SIMPLE CSS3 ANIMATION EFFECTS

The CSS3-based code samples that you have seen so far involved primarily static visual effects (although you did see how to use the hover pseudoselector to create an animation effect). The CSS3 code samples in this section illustrate how to create "glowing" effects and "bouncing" effects for form-based elements.

Glowing Effects

You can combine keyframes and the hover pseudoselector in order to create an animation effect when users hover with their mouse on a specific element in an HTML page. Listing 2.3 displays the contents of `Transition1.html` and Listing 2.4 displays the contents of `Transition1.css`, which contains CSS3 selectors that create a glowing effect on an input field.

Listing 2.3 `Transition1.html`

```
<!DOCTYPE html>

<html lang="en">

<head>

<title>CSS Animation Example</title>

<meta charset="utf-8" />

<link href="Transition1.css" rel="stylesheet"
      type="text/css">

</head>


<body>

<div id="outer">

<input id="input" type="text" value="This is an input
       line"</input>

</div>

</body>

</html>
```

Listing 2.3 is a simple HTML page that contains a reference to the CSS stylesheet `Transition1.css` and one HTML `<div>` element that contains an `<input>` field element. As you will see, an animation effect is created when users hover over the `<input>` element with their mouse.

Listing 2.4 `Transition1.css`

```
#outer {
position: relative; top: 20px; left: 20px;
}


@-webkit-keyframes glow {
  0% {
    -webkit-box-shadow: 0 0 24px rgba(255, 255, 255, 0.5);
  }
```

```
50% {

  -webkit-box-shadow: 0 0 24px rgba(255, 0, 0, 0.9);

}

100% {

  -webkit-box-shadow: 0 0 24px rgba(255, 255, 255, 0.5);

}

}


#input {

font-size: 24px;

-webkit-border-radius: 4px;

border-radius: 4px;

}


#input:hover {

 -webkit-animation: glow 2.0s 3 ease;

}
```

Listing 2.4 contains a @keyframes rule (called "glow") that specifies three shadow effects. The first shadow effect (which occurs at time 0 of the animation effect) renders a white color with whose opacity is 0.5. The second shadow effect (at the midway point of the animation effect) renders a red color whose opacity is 0.9. The third shadow effect (which occurs at the end of the animation effect) is the same as the first animation effect.

The #input selector is applied to the input field in Transition1. html in order to render a rounded rectangle. The #input:hover selector uses the glow keyframes in order to create an animation effect for a two-second interval, repeated three times, using an ease function, as shown here:

```
-webkit-animation: glow 2.0s 3 ease;
```

Figure 2.2 displays the result of applying the selectors in Transition1.css to the elements in the HTML page Transition1.html.

This is an input line

FIGURE 2.2 CSS3 glowing transition effect.

Image Fading and Rotating Effects with CSS3

This section shows you how to create a fading effect with JPG images. Listing 2.5 displays the contents of FadeRotateImages1.html and Listing 2.6 displays the contents of FadeRotateImages1.css, which illustrate how to create a "fading" effect on a JPG file and a glowing effect on another JPG file.

Listing 2.5 FadeRotateImages1.html

```
<!DOCTYPE html>

<html lang="en">

<head>

<title>CSS3 Fade and Rotate Images</title>

<meta charset="utf-8" />

<link href="FadingImages1.css" rel="stylesheet"
     type="text/css">

</head>


<body>

<div id="outer">

<img class="lower" width="200" height="200" src="Ellen1.
     jpg" />

<img class="upper" width="200" height="200" src="Ellen2.
     jpg" />

</div>


<div id="third">

<img width="200" height="200" src="Lauriel.jpg" />

</div>

</body>
```

Listing 2.5 contains a reference to the CSS stylesheet `FadingImages1.css` that contains CSS selectors for creating a fading effect and a glowing effect. The first HTML `<div>` element in Listing 2.5 contains two `<img>` elements; when users hover over the rendered JPG file, it will "fade" and reveal another JPG file. The second HTML `<div>` element contains one `<img>` element, and when users hover over this JPG, a CSS3 selector will rotate the referenced JPG file about the vertical axis.

Listing 2.6 `FadingImages1.css`

```css
#outer {
position: absolute; top: 20px; left: 20px;
margin: 0 auto;
}

#outer img {
position:absolute; left:0;
 -webkit-transition: opacity 1s ease-in-out;
transition: opacity 1s ease-in-out;
}

#outer img.upper:hover {
opacity:0;
}

#third img {
position: absolute; top: 20px; left: 250px;
}

#third img:hover {
 -webkit-animation: rotatey 2.0s 3 ease;
}
```

```
@-webkit-keyframes rotatey {
  0% {
   -webkit-transform: rotateY(45deg);
  }
  50% {
   -webkit-transform: rotateY(90deg);
  }
  100% {
    -webkit-transform: rotateY(0);
  }
}
```

We will skip the details of the code in Listing 2.6 that is already familiar to you. The key point for creating the fading effect is to set the opacity value to 0 when users hover over the leftmost image, and the one line of code in the CSS selector is shown here:

```
#outer img.upper:hover {
opacity:0;
}
```

As you can see, this code sample shows you that it's possible to create attractive visual effects without complicated code or logic.

Next, Listing 2.6 defines a CSS3 selector that creates a rotation effect about the vertical axis by invoking the CSS3 function `rotateY()` in the keyframe `rotatey`. Note that you can create a rotation effect about the other two axes by replacing `rotateY()` with the CSS3 function `rotateX()` or the CSS3 function `rotateZ()`. You can even use these three functions in the same keyframe to create 3D effects. CSS3 3D effects are discussed in more detail later in this chapter. Figure 2.3 displays the result of applying the selectors in the CSS stylesheet `FadeRotateIm-ages1.css` to `FadeRotateImages1.html`.

FIGURE 2.3 CSS3 fade and rotate JPG effects.

Bouncing Effects

This section shows you how to create a "bouncing" animation effect. Listing 2.7 displays the contents of `Bounce2.html` and Listing 2.8 displays the contents of `Bounce2.css`, which illustrate how to create a bouncing effect on an input field.

Listing 2.7 `Bounce2.html`

```
<!DOCTYPE html>
<html lang="en">
<head>
<title>CSS Animation Example</title>
<meta charset="utf-8" />
<link href="Bounce2.css" rel="stylesheet" type="text/css">
</head>

<body>
<div id="outer">
```

```
<input id="input" type="text" value="An input line"/ >
</div>
</body>
</html>
```

Listing 2.7 is another straightforward HTML page that contains a reference to the CSS stylesheet `Bounce2.css` and one HTML `<div>` element that contains an `<input>` field element. The CSS stylesheet creates a bouncing animation effect when users hover over the `<input>` element with their mouse.

Listing 2.8 `Bounce2.css`

```
#outer {
position: relative; top: 50px; left: 100px;
}

@-webkit-keyframes bounce {
  0% {
left: 50px;
top: 100px;
background-color: #ff0000;
  }
  25% {
left: 100px;
top: 150px;
background-color: #ffff00;
  }
  50% {
left: 50px;
top: 200px;
```

```
background-color: #00ff00;

    }

   75% {

left: 0px;

top: 150px;

background-color: #0000ff;

    }

   100% {

left: 50px;

top: 100px;

background-color: #ff0000;

    }

}

#input {

font-size: 24px;

-webkit-border-radius: 4px;

border-radius: 4px;

}

#outer:hover {

 -webkit-animation: bounce 2.0s 4 ease;

}
```

Listing 2.8 contains a @keyframes rule (called "bounce") that specifies five time intervals: the 0%, 25%, 50%, 75%, and 100% points of the duration of the animation effect. Each time interval specifies values for the attributes left, top, and background color of the <input> field. Despite the simplicity of this keyframes selector, it creates a pleasing animation effect.

The #input selector is applied to the input field in Bounce2.html in order to render a rounded rectangle. The #input:hover selector uses the bounce @keyframes rule in order to create an animation effect for a two-second interval, repeated four times, using an ease function, as shown here:

```
-webkit-animation: bounce 2.0s 4 ease;
```

Figure 2.4 displays the result of applying the selectors in the CSS stylesheet Bounce2.css to the elements in the HTML page Bounce2.html.

An input line

FIGURE 2.4 CSS3 bouncing animation effect.

Page Flipping with CSS3

The following Web sites create a page-flipping effect using either pure CSS3 (the first Web site) or a combination of CSS3 and JavaScript:

http://romancortes.com/ficheros/page-flip.html

http://jpageflipper.codeplex.com/

http://10k.aneventapart.com/Entry/325

The second Web site provides downloadable code so you can learn the code-specific details of creating a page-flipping effect.

CSS3 EFFECTS FOR TEXT

You have seen examples of rendering text strings as part of several code samples in the previous chapter, and in this section we discuss a new feature of CSS3 that enables you to render text in multiple columns.

Rendering Multicolumn Text

CSS3 supports multicolumn text, which can create a nice visual effect when a Web page contains significant amounts of text. Listing 2.9 displays the contents of MultiColumns1.html and Listing 2.10 displays the contents of MultiColumns1.css, which illustrate how to render multicolumn text.

Listing 2.9 `MultiColumns1.html`

```
<!doctype html>
<html lang="en">
<head>
<title>CSS Multi Columns Example</title>
<meta charset="utf-8" />
<link href="MultiColumns1.css" rel="stylesheet"
     type="text/css">
</head>

<body>
<header>
<h1>Hover Over the Multi-Column Text:</h1>
</header>

<div id="outer">
<p id="line1">.</p>
<article>
<div id="columns">

<p> CSS enables you to define selectors that specify
the style or the manner in which you want to render
elements in an HTML page.  CSS helps you modularize
your HTML content and since you can place your CSS
definitions in a separate file, you can also re-use
the same CSS definitions in multiple HTML files.
</p>

<p> Moreover, CSS also enables you to simplify the
updates that you need to make to elements in HTML
pages.  For example, suppose that multiple HTML
table elements use a CSS rule that specifies the
color red.  If you later need to change the color to
```

```
blue, you can effect such a change simply by making
one change (i.e., changing red to blue) in one CSS
rule.

</p>

<p> Without a CSS rule, you would be forced to man-
ually update the color attribute in every HTML table
element that is affected, which is error-prone, time-
consuming, and extremely inefficient.

<p>

</div>

</article>

<p id="line1">.</p>

</div>

</body>

</html>
```

The HTML5 page in Listing 2.9 contains semantic tags (which are discussed in Chapter 1, "Introduction to CSS3") that render the text in several HTML <p> elements. As you can see, this HTML5 page is straightforward, and the multicolumn effects are defined in the CSS stylesheet `MultiColumns1.css` that is displayed in Listing 2.10.

Listing 2.10 MultiColumns1.css

```
/* animation effects */

#columns:hover {

-webkit-transition: -webkit-transform 3.0s ease;

-transition: transform 3.0s ease;


-webkit-transform : scale(0.5) skew(-20deg, -30deg)
                    rotate(45deg);

-transform : scale(0.5) skew(-20deg, -30deg)
             rotate(45deg);
```

```
}


#line1:hover {

-webkit-transition: -webkit-transform 3.0s ease;

-transition: transform 3.0s ease;


-webkit-transform : scale(0.5) skew(-20deg, -30deg)
                    rotate(45deg);

-transform : scale(0.5) skew(-20deg, -30deg)
             rotate(45deg);

background-image: -webkit-gradient (linear, 0% 0%,
                   0% 100%, from(#fff), to(#00f));

background-image: -gradient(linear, 0% 0%, 0% 100%,
                   from(#fff), to(#00f));

-webkit-border-radius: 8px;border-radius: 8px;}


#columns {

-webkit-column-count : 3;

-webkit-column-gap : 80px;

-webkit-column-rule : 1px solid rgb(255,255,255);

column-count : 3;

column-gap : 80px;

column-rule : 1px solid rgb(255,255,255);

}


#line1 {

color: red;

font-size: 24px;

background-image: -webkit-gradient (linear, 0% 0%,
                   0% 100%, from(#fff), to(#f00));
```

```
background-image: -gradient(linear, 0% 0%, 0% 100%,
                    from(#fff), to(#f00));

-webkit-border-radius: 4px;border-radius: 4px;

}
```

The first two selectors in Listing 2.10 create an animation effect when users hover over the `<div>` elements whose `id` attribute is `columns` or `line1`. Both selectors create an animation effect during a three-second interval using the CSS3 functions `scale()`, `skew()`, and `rotate()`, as shown here:

```
-webkit-transition: -webkit-transform 3.0s ease;

-transition: transform 3.0s ease;

-webkit-transform : scale(0.5) skew(-20deg, -30deg)
                    rotate(45deg);
```

The second selector also defines a linear gradient background effect.

The `#columns` selector in Listing 2.10 contains 3 layout-related attributes. The `column-count` attribute is 3, so the text is displayed in 3 columns; the `column-gap` attribute is `80px`, so there is a space of 80 pixels between adjacent columns; the `column-rule` attribute specifies a white background.

The `#line1` selector specifies a linear gradient that creates a nice visual effect above and below the multicolumn text. Figure 2.5 displays the result of applying the CSS selectors in `MultiColumns1.css` to the text in the HTML page `MultiColumns1.html`.

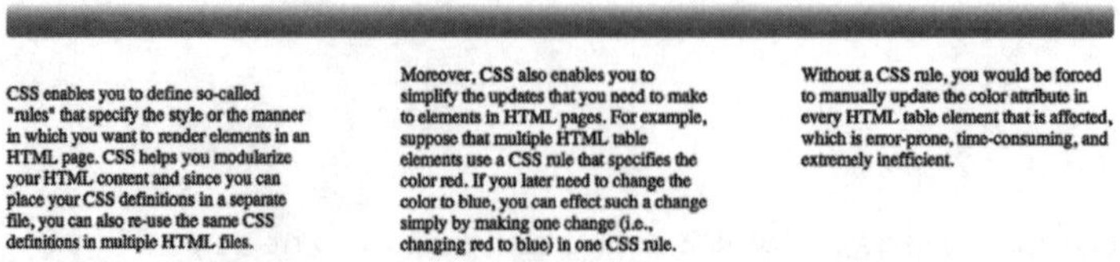

Hover Over the Multi-Column Text:

CSS enables you to define so-called "rules" that specify the style or the manner in which you want to render elements in an HTML page. CSS helps you modularize your HTML content and since you can place your CSS definitions in a separate file, you can also re-use the same CSS definitions in multiple HTML files.

Moreover, CSS also enables you to simplify the updates that you need to make to elements in HTML pages. For example, suppose that multiple HTML table elements use a CSS rule that specifies the color red. If you later need to change the color to blue, you can effect such a change simply by making one change (i.e., changing red to blue) in one CSS rule.

Without a CSS rule, you would be forced to manually update the color attribute in every HTML table element that is affected, which is error-prone, time-consuming, and extremely inefficient.

FIGURE 2.5 Rendering multicolumn text in CSS3.

CSS3 MEDIA QUERIES

CSS3 media queries determine the following attributes of a device:

- browser window width and height
- device width and height
- orientation (landscape or portrait)
- resolution

CSS3 media queries enable you to write mobile applications that will render differently on devices with differing width, height, orientation, and resolution. As a simple example, consider this media query that loads the CSS stylesheet `mystuff.css` only if the device is a screen and the maximum width of the device is 480px:

```
<link rel="stylesheet" type="text/css"
      media="screen and (max-device-width: 480px)"
            href="mystuff.css" />
```

As you can see, this media query contains a media attribute that specifies two components:

- a media type (`screen`)
- a query (`max-device-width: 480px`)

The preceding example is a very simple CSS3 media query; fortunately, you can combine multiple components in order to test the values of multiple attributes, as shown in the following pair of CSS3 selectors:

```
@media screen and (max-device-width: 480px) and
      (resolution: 160dpi) {

  #innerDiv {

    float: none;

  }

}
```

```
@media screen and (min-device-width: 481px) and
        (resolution: 160dpi) {

  #innerDiv {

float: left;

  }

}
```

In the first CSS3 selector, the HTML element whose `id` attribute has the value `innerDiv` will have a `float` property whose value is `none` on any device whose maximum screen width is `480px`. In the second CSS3 selector, the HTML element whose `id` attribute has the value `innerDiv` will have a `float` property whose value is `left` on any device whose minimum screen width is `481px`.

3D EFFECTS IN CSS3

CSS3 provides support for creating 3D effects, but currently these 3D effects are only supported in WebKit (Chrome and Safari) on Windows Vista® operating systems and MacBook® computers, but support will probably be available soon in other browsers. Listing 2.11 displays the contents of `Threed2.html` that creates 3D effects with CSS3 selectors.

Listing 2.11 `Threed2.html`

```
<!DOCTYPE html>

<html lang="en">

<head>

<title>CSS 3D Effects Example</title>

<meta charset="utf-8" />

<link href="Threed2.css" rel="stylesheet" type="text/css">

</head>
```

```
<body>
<div id="outer">
<div id="radial1">Text1</div>
<div id="radial2">Text2</div>
</div>
</body>
</html>
```

Listing 2.11 is a simple Web page that references the CSS stylesheet `Threed2.css` in the HTML `<head>` element. The top-level `<div>` element contains two more `<div>` elements, each of which contains an HTML `<iframe>` element that references the Google™ home page. The CSS selectors in Listing 2.12 create animation effects when they are applied to the HTML elements in Listing 2.11.

Listing 2.12 `Threed2.css`

```
#outer {
  position: relative; top: 10px; left: 0px;
}

#radial1 {
opacity: 0.8;
font-size: 24px;
width:  200px;
height: 200px;
position: absolute; top: 0px; left: 0px;

background: -webkit-gradient(
  radial, 300 40%, 0, 301 25%, 360, from(blue),
  color-stop(0.05, orange), color-stop(0.4, yellow),
```

```
   color-stop(0.6, green), color-stop(0.8, red),
   to(#fff)
 );
}


#radial2 {
opacity: 0.6;
font-size: 24px;
width:  200px;
height: 200px;
position: absolute; top: 200px; left: 200px;

background: -webkit-gradient(
   radial, 300 40%, 0, 301 25%, 360, from(red),
   color-stop(0.05, orange), color-stop(0.4, yellow),
   color-stop(0.6, green), color-stop(0.8, blue),
   to(#fff)
 );
}


#radial1:hover {
   -webkit-transform: rotate3d(20,30,40, 50deg)
                      translate3d(50px,50px,50px)
                      skew(-15deg,0);
transform: rotate3d(20,30,40, 50deg)
           translate3d(50px,50px,50px) skew(-15deg,0);
}


#radial2:hover {
   -webkit-transform: rotate3d(1,0,0, 60deg)
                      scale3d (1.5, 0.5, 0.75);
```

```
transform: rotate3d(1,0,0, 60deg)
           scale3d (1.5, 0.5, 0.75);

}
```

The #outer selector in Listing 2.12 contains simple position proper-ties, followed by the definitions for the #radial1 and #radial2 selec-tors, both of which specify radial gradient patterns that are similar to those that you have seen in Chapter 1.

The #radial1:hover selector contains the -webkit-trans-form property that specifies the rotate3d() function that takes a vector (20,30,40), as well as an angle of rotation of 50 degrees. The relative values of these numbers will determine the rotation. For example, you can replace the vector (20,30,40) with the vector (2,3,4), or (200,300,400), or any other multiple of the specified vector, and the rotation effect will be the same. The second part of the -webkit-trans-form property of this selector also contains the translate3d() func-tion (analogous to the 2D translate() function), which specifies the destination point in pixels, and in this case the destination point is (50px,50px,50px). The third and final part of the -webkit-trans-form property of this selector specifies the 2D function skew(-15deg,0) because there is no 3D counterpart for this function.

The #radial2:hover selector also contains the -webkit-trans-form property that specifies the rotate3d() function that takes a vector (1,0,0), as well as an angle of rotation of 50 degrees. In this case the rotation will be about the x-axis because (1,0,0) specifies the positive x-axis. You can rotate about the y-axis or the z-axis by specifying the vectors (0,1,0) or (0,0,1), respectively.

The second part of the -webkit-transform property of this selec-tor also contains the function scale3d(), which is the 3D counterpart of the 2D function scale(). The values specified in this function are (1.5,0.5,0.75), which creates a scaling effect of 1.5, 0.5, and 0.75 along the x-, y-, and z-axis, respectively.

This simple example illustrates how to use the three 3D transform functions that are available, and you can experiment with this code to create some interesting visual effects of your own. Figure 2.6 displays the result of applying the selectors in the stylesheet ThreeD2.css to the elements in the HTML page ThreeD2.html.

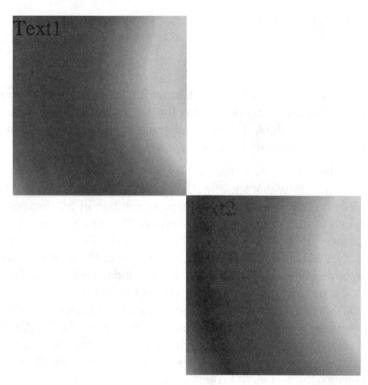

FIGURE 2.6 CSS3 3D effect.

CSS3 3D ANIMATION EFFECTS

As you know by now, CSS3 supports keyframes for creating animation effects (and the duration of those effects) at various points in time. The example in this section uses a CSS3 `keyframe` and various combinations of the CSS3 functions `scale3d()`, `rotate3d()`, and `translate3d()` in order to create an animation effect that lasts for four minutes. Listing 2.13 displays the contents of `Anim240Flicker3DLGrad4.html`, which is a very simple HTML page that contains four `<div>` elements.

Listing 2.13 `Anim240Flicker3DLGrad4.html`

```
<!DOCTYPE html>

<html lang="en">
```

```
<head>

<title>CSS3 Animation Example</title>

<meta charset="utf-8" />

<link href="Anim240Flicker3DLGrad4.css" rel="stylesheet"
      type="text/css">

</head>


<body>

<div id="outer">

<div id="linear1">Text1</div>

<div id="linear2">Text2</div>

<div id="linear3">Text3</div>

<div id="linear4">Text4</div>

</div>

</body>

</html>
```

Listing 2.13 is a very simple HTML5 page with corresponding CSS selectors (shown in Listing 2.14). As usual, the real complexity occurs in the CSS selectors that contain the code for creating the animation effects. Because `Anim240Flicker3DLGrad4.css` is such a lengthy code sample, only a portion of the code is displayed in Listing 2.14. However, the complete code is available on the DVD for this book.

Listing 2.14 `Anim240Flicker3DLGrad4.css`

```
@-webkit-keyframes upperLeft {

0% {

    -webkit-transform: matrix(1.5, 0.5,  0.0, 1.5, 0, 0)
                       matrix(1.0, 0.0,  1.0, 1.0,
                       0, 0);

    }
```

```
10% {

   -webkit-transform: translate3d(50px,50px,50px)
                      rotate3d(50,50,50,-90deg)
                      skew(-15deg,0) scale3d(1.25,
                      1.25, 1.25);

}

// similar code omitted

90% {

   -webkit-transform: matrix(2.0, 0.5, 1.0, 2.0, 0, 0)
                      matrix(1.5, 0.0, 0.5, 2.5,
                      0, 0);

}

95% {

   -webkit-transform: translate3d(-50px,-50px,-50px)
                      rotate3d(-50,-50,-50, 120deg)
                      skew(135deg,0) scale3d(0.3,
                      0.4, 0.5);

}

96% {

   -webkit-transform: matrix(0.2, 0.3, -0.5, 0.5,
                      100, 200) matrix(0.4, 0.5, 0.5,
                      0.2, 200, 50);

}

97% {

   -webkit-transform: translate3d(50px,-50px,50px)
                      rotate3d(-50,50,-50, 120deg)
                      skew(315deg,0) scale3d(0.5,
                      0.4, 0.3);

}

98% {

   -webkit-transform: matrix(0.4, 0.5,  0.5, 0.3,
              200, 50) matrix(0.3, 0.5, -0.5, 0.4,
              50, 150);

}
```

```
    99% {

       -webkit-transform: translate3d(150px,50px,50px)
                          rotate3d(60,80,100, 240deg)
                          skew(315deg,0) scale3d(1.0,
                          0.7, 0.3);

    }

    100% {

       -webkit-transform: matrix(1.0, 0.0, 0.0, 1.0, 0, 0)
                          matrix(1.0, 0.5, 1.0, 1.5, 0, 0);

    }

}

// code omitted for brevity

#linear1 {

font-size: 96px;

text-stroke: 8px blue;

text-shadow: 8px 8px 8px #FF0000;

width:  400px;

height: 250px;


position: relative; top: 0px; left: 0px;


background-image: -webkit-gradient(linear, 100% 50%,
                   0% 100%, from(#f00), color-stop
                   (0.2, orange), color-stop(0.4,
                   yellow), color-stop(0.6, blue),
                   color-stop (0.8, green), to(#00f));

// similar code omitted

-webkit-border-radius: 4px;

border-radius: 4px;

-webkit-box-shadow:  30px 30px 30px #000;

-webkit-animation-name: lowerLeft;

-webkit-animation-duration: 240s;

}
```

Listing 2.14 contains a WebKit-specific @keyframes rule called upperLeft that starts with the following line:

```
@-webkit-keyframes upperLeft {

// percentage-based definitions go here

}
```

The #linear selector contains properties that you have seen already, along with a property that references the keyframes identified by lower-Left, and a property that specifies a duration of 240 seconds, as shown here:

```
#linear1 {

// code omitted for brevity

-webkit-animation-name: lowerLeft;

-webkit-animation-duration: 240s;

}
```

Now that you know how to associate a keyframes definition to a selector (which, in turn, is applied to an HTML element), let's look at the details of the definition of lowerLeft, which contains 19 elements that specify various animation effects. Each element of lowerLeft occurs during a specific stage during the animation. For example, the eighth element in lowerLeft specifies the value 50%, which means that it will occur at the halfway point of the animation effect. Because the #linear selector contains a -webkit-animation-duration property whose value is 240s (shown in bold in Listing 2.14), the animation will last for four minutes, starting from the point in time when the HTML5 page is launched.

The eighth element of lowerLeft specifies a translation, rotation, skew, and scale effect (all of which are in three dimensions), an example of which is shown here:

```
50% {

    -webkit-transform: translate3d(250px,250px,250px)
            rotate3d(250px,250px,250px,-120deg)
            skew (-65deg,0) scale3d(0.5, 0.5, 0.5);

}
```

The animation effect occurs in a sequential fashion, starting with the translation, and finishing with the scale effect, which is also the case for the other elements in `lowerLeft`.

Figure 2.7 displays the initial view of applying the CSS3 selectors defined in the CSS3 stylesheet `Anim240Flicker3DLGrad4.css` to the HTML elements in the HTML page `Anim240Flicker3DLGrad4.html`.

FIGURE 2.7 CSS3 3D animation effects.

CSS FRAMEWORKS

CSS3 provides powerful functionality, but you need to include browser-specific code in your selectors if you want your code to work in multiple browsers. Maintenance can be a tedious and error-prone process, especially when you have many CSS stylesheets, and enhancing the functionality in your CSS stylesheets can become a nontrivial task. There are limitations to CSS, such as lack of support for variables or for "mixins" (discussed later in this section).

Fortunately, there are numerous open source CSS frameworks available that extend the features of CSS in a manner that simplifies maintenance of your CSS stylesheets. This section contains a condensed overview of several well-known CSS frameworks, along with code samples that illustrate how to use some of their features. After you have finished this section, you will have a rudimentary understanding of the functionality that CSS frameworks provide in terms of creating and maintaining CSS stylesheets.

A deeper understanding of the relative strengths of these CSS frameworks obviously requires that you perform a more detailed analysis, which you can do by reading the corresponding documentation and also by reading various articles available through an Internet search, some of which discuss other people's experiences with these and other CSS frameworks.

As you can surmise, CSS stylesheets can become very lengthy, even without the inclusion of browser-specific prefixes. For example, some of the CSS stylesheets in this CSS3 project (*http://code.google.com/p/css3-graphics*) are 600 lines or more. Consequently, the task of maintaining and enhancing CSS stylesheets can become quite time-consuming (as you can imagine). Open source CSS frameworks, including Compass/SASS, Blueprint, and LESS, can help simplify the task of maintaining CSS stylesheets. One commercial tool for Mac-based users (with a 15-day trial period download) that is very good for developing Web applications in HTML5 and CSS3 is Espresso, and its home page is here:

http://macrabbit.com/espresso/.

Note that you need to have Ruby installed on your machine in order to use the Blueprint validator and the LESS framework. If you have a Macintosh computer, then Ruby should already be preinstalled on your machine. If you need to manually install Ruby on a Windows machine, a self-contained Windows-based installer is available here:

http://rubyinstaller.org/.

If Ruby is not already installed on your Linux machine, instructions for different flavors of Linux are available here:

http://ruby.about.com/od/tutorials/ht/installrubylin.htm.

Please keep in mind that you need to have Node.js installed if you want to use the server-side functionality that is supported by the LESS framework.

The Compass/Sass Framework

Compass is a framework that enables you to create CSS stylesheets using Sass instead of pure CSS, and its home page is here:

http://compass-style.org/.

The link for the Sass language (which you will use with Compass) is here:

http://sass-lang.com/.

Sass supports the following features:

- @import
- arguments
- arithmetic operations and functions
- mixins
- nesting
- parent referencing
- variables

If you want to use the Sass-based code samples, you need to install Ruby if you have a Windows machine or a Linux machine (search the Internet for instructions), and if you're using an OS X® machine, you already have Ruby installed.

After installing Ruby, install Sass by invoking the following command:

```
gem install sass
```

The next several subsections contain simple code samples that illustrate some of the features of the Sass framework.

Sass Variables

Sass supports the use of variables, which are useful for modifying CSS stylesheets quickly and easily. Listing 2.15 displays the contents of Sass1. scss and Listing 2.16 displays the generated CSS stylesheet Sass1.css. The content of both files is straightforward and self-explanatory, so we will not provide further details.

Listing 2.15 Sass1.scss

```
$theColor1: #ff0000;
$theColor2: #0000ff;
```

```
$theWidth: 400;
$theHeight: 300;

#linear1 {
width: $theWidth;
height: $theHeight;
color: $theColor1;
}

a {
color: $theColor1;
&:hover: { background: $theColor2; }
}
```

Listing 2.16 `Sass1.css`

```
#linear1 {
width: 400;
height: 300;
color: #ff0000;
}
a {
color: #ff0000;
a:hover: { background: #0000ff; }
}
```

Sass Mixins

Sass mixins enable you to reuse styles in multiple CSS selectors, and they are defined using the @mixin directive. As an example of Sass mixins, Listing 2.17 displays the contents of Sass2.scss and Listing 2.18 displays the generated CSS stylesheet Sass2.css.

Listing 2.17 `Sass2.scss`

```
@mixin rounded-top {
  $side: top;
  $radius: 10px;

  border-#{$side}-radius: $radius;
  -moz-border-radius-#{$side}: $radius;
  -webkit-border-#{$side}-radius: $radius;
}


#navbar li { @include rounded-top; }
#footer { @include rounded-top; }
```

Notice that the two selectors at the bottom of Listing 2.17 reference the `rounded-top` mixin via an `@include` statement, which will have the effect of replacing this statement with the contents of `rounded-top` after replacing the specified variables with their values when they are referenced.

Listing 2.18 `Sass2.css`

```
#navbar li {
  border-top-radius: 10px;
  -moz-border-radius-top: 10px;
  -webkit-border-top-radius: 10px;
}


#footer {
  border-top-radius: 10px;
  -moz-border-radius-top: 10px;
  -webkit-border-top-radius: 10px;
}
```

Listing 2.18 displays the contents of the CSS selectors that are generated from the Sass file in Listing 2.17 after performing the specified substitutions.

The preceding sections illustrate how easy it is to use variables and mixins with Sass. For more information, navigate to the Sass reference guide (*http://sass-lang.com/docs/yardoc/file.SASS_REFERENCE.html*), which provides an extensive list of features and code snippets, and the Sass tutorial (*http://sass-lang.com/tutorial.html*).

The Blueprint Framework

The Blueprint CSS framework provides an extensive set of features, and its home page is here:

http://www.blueprintcss.org.

Blueprint supports the following features:

- a CSS reset stylesheet
- form styles
- print styles
- plugins for buttons, tabs, and sprites
- editors, templates, and tools

You need to include the following three CSS stylesheets in your HTML5 pages in order to use Blueprint: `screen.css`, `print.css`, and `ie.css`. For example, you can include these three stylesheets with the following HTML fragment:

```
<link rel="stylesheet" href="css/blueprint/screen.css"
    type="text/css" media="screen, projection">

<link rel="stylesheet" href="css/blueprint/print.css"
    type="text/css" media="print">

<!-[if lt IE 8]>

<link rel="stylesheet" href="css/blueprint/ie.css"
    type="text/css" media="screen, projection">

<! [endif]-->
```

Notice that the third stylesheet listed above uses conditional logic to determine whether to include the stylesheet (only for Internet Explorer versions earlier than 8).

One of the important features of Blueprint is its support for grids. Consult the online documentation to learn about Blueprint grid and its other features.

The LESS Framework

The LESS CSS framework runs on both the client side (IE 6+, WebKit, and Firefox) and server side (with `Node.js`), and its home page is here:

http://lesscss.org/.

LESS supports the following features:

- functions
- mixins
- operations
- variables

You can put LESS code in a text file (typically with an extension of "less") and then compile that file into CSS code from the command line as follows:

```
lessc mylessfile.less >mycssfile.css
```

The following subsections show you how to use variables and mixins in the LESS framework.

LESS Variables

The following example illustrates how to use variables in LESS code:

```
@color: #FF0000;

#header {

color: @color;
}
p {
color: @color;
}
```

The preceding code block defines the variable @color and references this variable in two selectors. The content of the generated CSS code is shown here:

```
#header {
color: #FF0000;
}
p {
color: #FF0000;
}
```

As you can see, the variable @color is replaced by its value #FF0000 in both CSS selectors.

LESS Mixins

The following example illustrates how to use a mixin in LESS:

```
#rounded-corners (@radius:4px) {
border-radius: @radius;
  -webkit-border-radius: @radius;
  -moz-border-radius: @radius;
}
#header {
  #rounded-corners;
}
#footer {
  #rounded-corners(10px);
}
```

The preceding code block contains the #rounded-corners mixin that defines the variable radius whose default value is 4px, along with three attributes that are assigned the value of the variable radius. The generated CSS code is shown here:

```
#header {
border-radius: 4px;
  -webkit-border-radius: 4px;
  -moz-border-radius: 4px;
}
#footer {
border-radius: 10px;
  -webkit-border-radius: 10px;
  -moz-border-radius: 10px;
}
```

Notice that the attribute `border-radius` in the #header selector has the value 4px, which is the default value for the `radius` variable in the `rounded-corners` mixin, whereas `border-radius` in the #footer selector has the value 10px. You can also use operators and functions in LESS to create sophisticated mixins, which are illustrated in the online documentation for LESS.

Using LESS in Client-Side and Server-Side Code

This is a straightforward process that involves the inclusion of a LESS CSS stylesheet and the LESS JavaScript file. Include the following link to a LESS stylesheet:

```
<link rel="stylesheet/less" type="text/css"
    href="styles/less" />
```

Download the JavaScript file `less.js` from the LESS home page and then include the following line of code that references the LESS JavaScript file:

```
<script src="less.js" type="text/javascript" />
```

A detailed discussion of Node.js is beyond the scope of this book, and if you do not plan to use the server-side functionality of LESS, you can omit this section without loss of continuity. On the other hand, if you do intend to use `Node.js`, download the distribution onto your machine from the `Node.js` home page: *http://nodejs.org*. After you have installed `Node.js` and `npm` (the Node package manager), install LESS with the following command:

```
npm install less
```

The latest version of LESS can be installed with the following command:

```
npm install less@latest
```

This concludes our brief discussion of CSS frameworks, and despite the simplicity of the code samples, you can see the power of the functionality that these frameworks provide for writing and maintaining CSS stylesheets.

CSS3 PERFORMANCE

Although this topic is covered briefly here, CSS3 performance is obviously important. Many of the CSS3 stylesheets in this book contain selectors with 2D/3D animation effects, and hardware acceleration will significantly improve performance. In fact, some tablet devices do not provide good hardware acceleration, and stylesheets with many 2D or 3D animation effects are almost impossible on those devices.

Fortunately, there is a technique for triggering hardware acceleration for CSS3 selectors (using `translateZ(0)` or `translate3d(0,0,0)`) for devices with a GPU, and also debugging techniques for WebKit (Safari and Chrome). The following video by Paul Irish (a developer advocate at Google) discusses these and other techniques in this 30-minute video:

http://paulirish.com/2011/dom-html5-css3-performance/.

An article that provides information for writing more efficient CSS selectors is here:

http://www.pubnub.com/blog/css3-performance-optimizations.

Information regarding best practices for writing CSS3 selectors is provided at

http://webdesignerwall.com/trends/css3-examples-and-best-practices
http://www.impressivewebs.com/css3-best-practices/.

Perform an Internet search to find other online videos and tutorials regarding CSS3 performance and best practices for CSS3 as well as HTML5 `Canvas`.

SENCHA ANIMATOR

Sencha Animator is a desktop application for developing CSS3 animations for WebKit browsers and mobile devices, and its home page (with a download link) is here: *http://www.sencha.com/products/animator*. Sencha Animator enables you to create various 2D shapes, with support for transitions, 2D/3D transforms, animation effects, and property panels for modifying the properties of shapes. In addition, Sencha Animator allows you to define custom CSS effects, and supported devices include iPhone®, iPad®, iPod Touch®, Blackberry® Torch™, and Android™ devices, as well as Google Chrome.

You can get more detailed information in this blog post: *http://www.sencha.com/blog/rocking-the-boat-of-flash-with-css3-animations/*.

Several videos that can give you an overview of how to use the features of Sencha Animator are also available: *http://notes.sencha.com/post/1416864756/sencha-animator-introduction-video-19-47*.

After performing the download and installation, launch Sencha Animator and create a new project to experiment with the various features. There is an export feature that enables you to export the contents of your project as an HTML5 page. Listing 2.19 shows an example of the HTML page `index.html` generated after creating a Sencha Animator project with a circle, rectangle (with simple animation), line segment, and text, and then exporting this project.

Listing 2.19 `index.html`

```
<!DOCTYPE html>

<html lang="en">

<head>

<meta http-equiv="Content-Type" content="text/html;
    charset=utf-8">

<title>SenchaAnimator1 &middot; Made with Sencha
    Animator</title>
```

```
<script type="text/javascript">
function setConfig(configObject) {
config = configObject;


    //get ol list and children
var ol = document.body.getElementsByTagName('ol')[0];
scenes = ol.children;

currentSceneIndex = -1;
}

function start() {
goToScene(0);
}

function goToSceneID(id) {
for (var i=0; i < config.length; i++) {
if (config[i].id === id) {
goToScene(i);
return;
    }
  }
}


//function to go directly to any scene
function goToScene(index) {
    //go to scene
startScene(index);
```

```
    //set up timer if jumping on done
if (config[index].jump !== -1) {
applyTimeout(config[index].jump, config[index].duration);
    }
}


function startScene(index) {
    //restart current scene without flicker
if (index === currentSceneIndex) {
scenes[index].setAttribute('class','run restart');
setTimeout(function(){
scenes[index].setAttribute('class','run');
        },0);
return;
    }

    //add the class "run" to the scene currently running
and remove it from anybody else
var scene;
for (var i=0; i < scenes.length; i++) {
scene = scenes[i];
if (i === index) {
scene.setAttribute('class','run');
        } else {
scene.setAttribute('class','');
        }
    }

currentSceneIndex = index;
}
```

```
//set timeout
function applyTimeout(index,time) {
setTimeout(function(){
goToScene(index);
    },time);
}
</script>
// sections omitted for brevity
#rect1{
 -webkit-transform: translate3d(333px, 31px, 0px);
width: 100px;
height: 100px;
border-top: 1px solid rgba(1,14,13,1);
border-right: 1px solid rgba(1,14,13,1);
border-bottom: 1px solid rgba(1,14,13,1);
border-left: 1px solid rgba(1,14,13,1);
-webkit-border-radius: 10px;
background-color: rgba(78,78,78,1);
top:0;
left:0;
background-image: -webkit-gradient(linear, 0% 0%,0% 100%,
                  color-stop (0, rgba(255,255,255,1)),
                  color-stop(0.426, rgba(255,255,255,1)),
                  color-stop(1, rgba(0,0,0,1)));
 }

#circle1{
 -webkit-transform: translate3d(66px, 29px, 0px);
width: 100px;
height: 100px;
```

```
border-top: 1px solid rgba(1,14,13,1);

border-right: 1px solid rgba(1,14,13,1);

border-bottom: 1px solid rgba(1,14,13,1);

border-left: 1px solid rgba(1,14,13,1);

-webkit-border-radius: 50px;

background-color: rgba(194,194,194,1);

top:0;

left:0;

background-image: -webkit-gradient(linear, 0% 0%,0%
100%,color-stop(0, rgba(255,255,255,1)),color-stop(0.42,
rgba(255,255,255,1)),color-stop(1, rgba(0,0,0,1)));
 }

// portions omitted for brevity

<body>

<ol>

<li id="scene-0">

<div class="AN-sObj-stage" id="ext-gen3480">

<div id="circle1"></div>

<div id="AN-sObj-3"></div>

<div id="AN-sObj-5"></div>

<div id="rect1"></div>

<div id="AN-sObj-7"><span>Some text</span></div>

</div>

</li>

</ol>

</body>

</html>
```

Sencha Animator generates the code in Listing 2.19 after exporting a project that consists of a circle, a rectangle, a line segment, and a default text string. The linear gradients called `circle1` and `rectangle1` were added to the circle and the rectangle by simple point-and-click operations, and you can see the corresponding CSS selectors in Listing 2.19. An animation effect was also added (based on a keyframe), and Sencha Animator provides a live preview so that you can adjust the objects you have created, along with their properties, in your project in order to create the effects that meet your requirements.

FURTHER READING

The following list of links is certainly not exhaustive, but it contains links with very good information; you can always perform your own Internet search as well. Note that as this book goes to print, the links listed below are functional.

http://caniuse.com

http://CSS3generator.com

http://CSS3please.com

http://diveintohtml5.org/detect.html

http://ecsstender.org

http://gradients.glrzad.com

http://html5readiness.com

http://selectivizr.com

http://www.CSS3.info

http://www.modernizr.com

http://www.quirksmode.org

These links provide a wealth of information and useful techniques, so there's a very good chance that you can find the information you need to create the visual effects that you want for your Web site.

SUMMARY

This chapter showed you how to create graphics effects, including shadow effects, and how to use CSS3 transforms in CSS3 to define CSS3 selectors. You learned how to create 2D/3D animation effects that you can apply to HTML elements. You saw how to define CSS3 selectors to do the following:

- create simple animation effects

- display multicolumn text

- create 2D/3D effects with CSS3 selectors

- use CSS frameworks to create CSS stylesheets

- use variables and mixins to generate stylesheets

The next chapter gives you an introduction to Scalable Vector Graphics (SVG), with various code samples, and you will also learn how to combine CSS3 selectors with SVG.

SVG AND CSS3

This chapter gives you an overview of Scalable Vector Graphics (SVG), along with examples of how to reference SVG documents in CSS3 selectors. Keep in mind that the CSS3 examples in this book are for WebKit-based browsers, but you can insert the code for other browsers by using browser-specific prefixes, which were discussed briefly in Chapter 1, "Introduction to CSS3."

The majority of Chapter 3 delves into SVG, which is an XML-based technology for rendering 2D shapes. SVG supports linear gradients, radial gradients, filter effects, transforms(translate, scale, skew, and rotate), and animation effects using an XML-based syntax. Although SVG does not support 3D effects, SVG provides functionality that is unavailable in CSS3, such as support for arbitrary polygons, elliptic arcs, quadratic and cubic Bezier curves, and filters.

Fortunately, you can reference SVG documents in CSS selectors via the CSS url() function, and the third part of this chapter contains examples of combining CSS3 and SVG in an HTML page. As you will see, the combination of CSS3 and SVG gives you a powerful mechanism for leveraging the functionality of SVG in CSS3 selectors. After reading this chapter you can learn more about SVG by performing an Internet search and then choosing from the many online tutorials that provide many SVG code samples.

Note that many of the SVG-based samples (lines, circles, ellipses, Bezier curves, etc.) in SVG in this chapter have HTML5 Canvas counterparts that are discussed in Chapters 4, 5, 6, 7, and 8 in a much less compressed manner. This chapter follows Chapter 2, "CSS3 2D/3D Animation and CSS Frameworks," because the material is logically related, even though it may be out of sequence with respect to the Canvas-based chapters. As an alternative (and depending on your level of knowledge), you might find it easier to return to this chapter after you have finished reading the Canvas-related chapters.

OVERVIEW OF SVG

This section contains various examples that illustrate some of the 2D shapes and effects that you can create with SVG. This section gives you a compressed overview, and if you want to learn more about SVG, you can perform an Internet search for details about books and many online tutorials.

Basic 2D Shapes in SVG

SVG supports a <line> element for rendering line segments, and its syntax looks like this:

```
<line x1="20" y1="20" x2="100" y2="150".../>
```

SVG <line> elements render line segments that connect the two points (x1, y1) and (x2, y2).

SVG also supports a <rect> element for rendering rectangles, and its syntax looks like this:

```
<rect width="200" height="50" x="20" y="50".../>
```

The SVG <rect> element renders a rectangle whose width and height are specified in the width and height attributes. The upper-left vertex of the rectangle is specified by the point with coordinates (x, y). Listing 3.1 displays the contents of BasicShapes1.svg, which illustrates how to render line segments and rectangles.

Listing 3.1 BasicShapes1.svg

```
<?xml version="1.0" encoding="iso-8859-1"?>
<!DOCTYPE svg PUBLIC "-//W3C//DTD SVG 20001102//EN"
```

```
"http://www.w3.org/TR/2000/CR-SVG-20001102/DTD/
      svg-20001102.dtd">

<svg xmlns="http://www.w3.org/2000/svg"
      xmlns:xlink="http://www.w3.org/1999/xlink"
      width="100%" height="100%">
<g>
<!-- left-side figures -->
<line x1="20" y1="20" x2="220" y2="20"
        stroke="blue" stroke-width="4"/>

<line x1="20" y1="40" x2="220" y2="40"
        stroke="red" stroke-width="10"/>

<rect width="200" height="50" x="20" y="70"
        fill="red" stroke="black" stroke-width="4"/>

<path d="M20,150 l200,0 10,50 l-200,0 z"
        fill="blue" stroke="red" stroke-width="4"/>

<!-- right-side figures -->
<path d="M250,20 l200,0 l-100,50 z"
        fill="blue" stroke="red" stroke-width="4"/>

<path d="M300,100 l100,0 150,50 l-50,50 l-100,0 l-50,-50 z"
        fill="yellow" stroke="red" stroke-width="4"/>
</g>
</svg>
```

The first SVG <line> element in Listing 3.1 specifies the color blue and a stroke-width (i.e., line width) of 4, whereas the second SVG <line> element specifies the color red and a stroke-width of 10.

Notice that the first SVG <rect> element renders a rectangle that looks the same (except for the color) as the second SVG <line> element, which shows you that you can use more than one SVG element to render a rectangle (or a line segment).

The SVG <path> element is probably the most flexible and powerful element, because you can create arbitrarily complex shapes, based on a concatenation of other SVG elements. Later in this chapter you will see an example of how to render multiple Bezier curves in an SVG <path> element.

An SVG <path> element contains a d attribute that specifies the points in the desired path. For example, the first SVG <path> element in Listing 3.1 contains the following d attribute:

```
d="M20,150 l200,0 10,50 l-200,0 z"
```

This is how to interpret the contents of the d attribute:

- move to the absolute point (20, 150)
- draw a horizontal line segment 200 pixels to the right
- draw a line segment 10 pixels to the right and 50 pixels down
- draw a horizontal line segment 200 pixels toward the left
- draw a line segment to the initial point (z)

Similar comments apply to the other two <path> elements in Listing 3.1. One thing to keep in mind is that uppercase letters (C, L, M, and Q) refer to absolute positions, whereas lowercase letters (c, l, m, and q) refer to relative positions with respect to the element that is to the immediate left. Experiment with the code in Listing 3.1 by using combinations of lowercase and uppercase letters to gain a better understanding of how to create different visual effects. Figure 3.1 displays the result of rendering the SVG document BasicShapes1.svg.

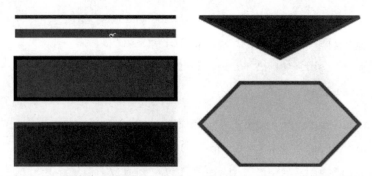

FIGURE 3.1 SVG line segments and rectangles.

SVG Gradients

As you have probably surmised, SVG supports linear gradients as well as radial gradients that you can apply to 2D shapes. For example, you can use the SVG <path> element to define elliptic arcs (using the d attribute) and then specify gradient effects. Note that SVG supports the stroke-dasharray attribute and the <polygon> element, neither of which is available in HTML5 Canvas. Listing 3.2 displays the contents of Basic-ShapesLRG1.svg, which illustrates how to render 2D shapes with linear gradients and with radial gradients.

Listing 3.2 BasicShapesLRG1.svg

```
<?xml version="1.0" encoding="iso-8859-1"?>
<!DOCTYPE svg PUBLIC "-//W3C//DTD SVG 20001102//EN"
 "http://www.w3.org/TR/2000/CR-SVG-20001102/DTD/
        svg-20001102.dtd">

<svg xmlns="http://www.w3.org/2000/svg"
    xmlns:xlink="http://www.w3.org/1999/xlink"
    width="100%" height="100%">
<defs>
<linearGradient id="pattern1"
                x1="0%" y1="100%" x2="100%" y2="0%">
```

```
<stop offset="0%"    stop-color="yellow"/>
<stop offset="40%"   stop-color="red"/>
<stop offset="80%"   stop-color="blue"/>
</linearGradient>

<radialGradient id="pattern2">
<stop offset="0%"    stop-color="yellow"/>
<stop offset="40%"   stop-color="red"/>
<stop offset="80%"   stop-color="blue"/>
</radialGradient>
</defs>

<g>
<ellipse cx="120" cy="80" rx="100" ry="50"
         fill="url(#pattern1)"/>

<ellipse cx="120" cy="200" rx="100" ry="50"
         fill="url(#pattern2)"/>

<ellipse cx="320" cy="80" rx="50" ry="50"
         fill="url(#pattern2)"/>

<path d="M 505,145 v -100 a 250,100 0 0,1 -200,100"
      fill="black"/>

<path d="M 500,140 v -100 a 250,100 0 0,1 -200,100"
      fill="url(#pattern1)"
      stroke="black" stroke-thickness="8"/>

<path d="M 305,165 v  100 a 250,100 0 0,1  200,-100"
      fill="black"/>
```

```
<path d="M 300,160 v  100 a 250,100 0 0,1  200,-100"
        fill="url(#pattern1)"
        stroke="black" stroke-thickness="8"/>

<ellipse cx="450" cy="240" rx="50" ry="50"
        fill="url(#pattern1)"/>
</g>
</svg>
```

Listing 3.2 contains an SVG `<defs>` element that specifies a `<linearGradient>` element (whose `id` attribute has value `pattern1`) with three stop values using an XML-based syntax, followed by a `<radialGradient>` element with three `<stop>` elements and an `id` attribute whose value is `pattern2`.

The SVG `<g>` element contains four `<ellipse>` elements, the first of which specifies the point `(120,80)` as its center `(cx,cy)`, with a major radius of `100`, a minor radius of `50`, filled with the linear gradient `pattern1`, as shown here:

```
<ellipse cx="120" cy="80" rx="100" ry="50"
        fill="url(#pattern1)"/>
```

Similar comments apply to the other three SVG `<ellipse>` elements.

The SVG `<g>` element also contains four `<path>` elements that render elliptic arcs. The first `<path>` element specifies a black background for the elliptic arc defined with the following d attribute:

```
d="M 505,145 v -100 a 250,100 0 0,1 -200,100"
```

Unfortunately, the SVG syntax for elliptic arcs is nonintuitive, and it's based on the notion of major arcs and minor arcs that connect two points on an ellipse. This example is only for illustrative purposes, so we won't delve into a detailed explanation of elliptic arcs work in SVG. If you need to learn the details, you can perform an Internet search and read the information found at the various links (be prepared to spend some time experimenting with how to generate various types of elliptic arcs).

The second SVG <path> element renders the same elliptic arc with a slight offset, using the linear gradient pattern1, which creates a shadow effect. Similar comments apply to the other pair of SVG <path> elements, which render an elliptic arc with the radial gradient pattern2 (also with a shadow effect). Figure 3.2 displays the result of rendering Basic-ShapesLRG1.svg.

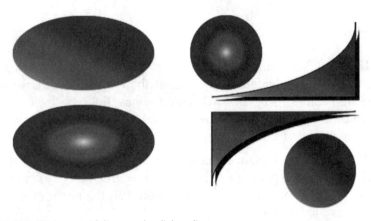

FIGURE 3.2 SVG elliptic arcs with linear and radial gradients.

SVG <polygon> **Element**

The SVG <polygon> element contains a polygon attribute in which you can specify points that represent the vertices of a polygon. The SVG <polygon> element is most useful when you want to create polygons with an arbitrary number of sides, but you can also use this element to render line segments and rectangles. Listing 3.3 displays the contents of Svg-Cube1.svg, which illustrates how to render a cube in SVG.

Listing 3.3 SvgCube1.svg

```
<?xml version="1.0" encoding="iso-8859-1"?>
<!DOCTYPE svg PUBLIC "-//W3C//DTD SVG 20001102//EN"
  "http://www.w3.org/TR/2000/CR-SVG-20001102/DTD/
      svg-20001102.dtd">
```

```
<svg xmlns="http://www.w3.org/2000/svg"
    xmlns:xlink="http://www.w3.org/1999/xlink"
    width="100%" height="100%">
<defs>
<linearGradient id="pattern1">
<stop offset="0%"    stop-color="yellow"/>
<stop offset="40%"   stop-color="red"/>
<stop offset="80%"   stop-color="blue"/>
</linearGradient>

<radialGradient id="pattern2">
<stop offset="0%"    stop-color="yellow"/>
<stop offset="40%"   stop-color="red"/>
<stop offset="80%"   stop-color="blue"/>
</radialGradient>

<radialGradient id="pattern3">
<stop offset="0%"    stop-color="red"/>
<stop offset="30%"   stop-color="yellow"/>
<stop offset="60%"   stop-color="white"/>
<stop offset="90%"   stop-color="blue"/>
</radialGradient>
</defs>

<!-- top face (counter clockwise) -->
<polygon fill="url(#pattern1)"
            points="50,50 200,50 240,30 90,30"/>

<!-- front face -->
<rect width="150" height="150" x="50" y="50"
        fill="url(#pattern2)"/>
```

```
<!-- right face (counter clockwise) -->

<polygon fill="url(#pattern3)"

            points="200,50 200,200 240,180 240,30"/>

</svg>
```

Listing 3.3 contains an SVG `<defs>` element that defines a linear gradient and two radial gradients. Next, the SVG `<g>` element contains the three faces of a cube: an SVG `<polygon>` element renders the top face (which is a parallelogram), an SVG `<rect>` element renders the front face, and another SVG `<polygon>` element renders the right face (which is also a parallelogram). The three faces of the cube are rendered with the linear gradient and the two radial gradients defined in the SVG `<defs>` element at the beginning of Listing 3.3. Figure 3.3 displays the result of rendering the SVG document `SvgCube1.svg`.

FIGURE 3.3 An SVG cube with gradient shading.

Bezier Curves

SVG supports quadratic and cubic Bezier curves that you can render with linear gradients or radial gradients. You can also concatenate multiple Bezier curves using an SVG `<path>` element. Listing 3.4 displays the contents of `BezierCurves1.svg`, which illustrates how to render various Bezier curves.

Listing 3.4 `BezierCurves1.svg`

```
<?xml version="1.0" encoding="iso-8859-1"?>
<!DOCTYPE svg PUBLIC "-//W3C//DTD SVG 20001102//EN"
 "http://www.w3.org/TR/2000/CR-SVG-20001102/DTD/
        svg-20001102.dtd">

<svg xmlns="http://www.w3.org/2000/svg"
     xmlns:xlink="http://www.w3.org/1999/xlink"
     width="100%" height="100%">
<defs>
<linearGradient id="pattern1"
                  x1="0%" y1="100%" x2="100%" y2="0%">
<stop offset="0%"    stop-color="yellow"/>
<stop offset="40%"   stop-color="red"/>
<stop offset="80%"   stop-color="blue"/>
</linearGradient>

<linearGradient id="pattern2"
                  gradientTransform="rotate(90)">
<stop offset="0%"    stop-color="#C0C040"/>
<stop offset="30%"   stop-color="#303000"/>
<stop offset="60%"   stop-color="#FF0F0F"/>
<stop offset="90%"   stop-color="#101000"/>
</linearGradient>
</defs>

<g transform="scale(1.5,0.5)">
<path d="m 0,50 C 400,200 200,-150 100,350"
        stroke="black" stroke-width="4"
        fill="url(#pattern1)"/>
</g>
```

```
<g transform="translate(50,50)">
<g transform="scale(0.5,1)">
<path d="m 50,50 C 400,100 200,200 100,20"
          fill="red" stroke="black" stroke-width="4"/>
</g>

<g transform="scale(1,1)">
<path d="m 50,50 C 400,100 200,200 100,20"
          fill="yellow" stroke="black" stroke-width="4"/>
</g>
</g>

<g transform="translate(-50,50)">
<g transform="scale(1,2)">
<path d="M 50,50 C 400,100 200,200 100,20"
          fill="blue" stroke="black" stroke-width="4"/>
</g>
</g>

<g transform="translate(-50,50)">
<g transform="scale(0.5, 0.5) translate(195,345)">
<path d="m20,20 C20,50 20,450 300,200 s-150,-250
      200,100" fill="blue" style="stroke:#880088;
                  stroke-width:4;"/>
</g>

<g transform="scale(0.5, 0.5) translate(185,335)">
<path d="m20,20 C20,50 20,450 300,200 s-150,-250 200,100"
          fill="url(#pattern2)"
```

```
style="stroke:#880088;stroke-width:4;"/>
</g>

<g transform="scale(0.5, 0.5) translate(180,330)">
<path d="m20,20 C20,50 20,450 300,200 s-150,-250 200,100"
      fill="blue" style="stroke:#880088;stroke-width:4;"/>
</g>

<g transform="scale(0.5, 0.5) translate(170,320)">
<path d="m20,20 C20,50 20,450 300,200 s-150,-250 200,100"
        fill="url(#pattern2)" style="stroke:black;
            stroke-width:4;"/>
</g>
</g>

<g transform="scale(0.8,1) translate(380,120)">
<path d="M0,0 C200,150 400,300 20,250"
        fill="url(#pattern2)" style="stroke:blue;
            stroke-width:4;"/>
</g>

<g transform="scale(2.0,2.5) translate(150,-80)">
<path d="M200,150 C0,0 400,300 20,250"
        fill="url(#pattern2)" style="stroke:blue;stroke-
            width:4;"/>
</g>
</svg>
```

Listing 3.4 contains an SVG `<defs>` element that defines two linear gradients, followed by 10 SVG `<path>` elements, each of which renders a cubic Bezier curve. The SVG `<path>` elements are enclosed in SVG `<g>` elements whose transform attributes contain the SVG `scale()` function or the SVG `translate()` functions (or both).

The first SVG `<g>` element invokes the SVG `scale()` function to scale the cubic Bezier curve that is specified in an SVG `<path>` element, as shown here:

```
<g transform="scale(1.5,0.5)">
<path d="m 0,50 C 400,200 200,-150 100,350"
        stroke="black" stroke-width="4"
        fill="url(#pattern1)"/>
</g>
```

The cubic Bezier curve has an initial point `(0,50)`, with control points `(400,200)` and `(200,-150)`, followed by the second control point `(100,350)`. The Bezier curve is black, with a width of 4, and its fill color is defined in the `<linearGradient>` element (whose `id` attribute is `pattern1`) that is contained in the SVG `<defs>` element. The remaining SVG `<path>` elements are similar to the first SVG `<path>` element, so they will not be described. Figure 3.4 displays the result of rendering the Bezier curves that are defined in the SVG document `BezierCurves1.svg`.

FIGURE 3.4 SVG Bezier curves.

SVG Filters, Shadow Effects, and Text Paths

You can create filter effects that you can apply to 2D shapes and also to text strings; this section contains three SVG-based examples of creating such effects. Listing 3.5, Listing 3.6, and Listing 3.7 display the contents of the SVG documents BlurFilterText1.svg, ShadowFilterText1.svg, and TextOnQBezierPath1.svg, respectively.

Listing 3.5 BlurFilterText1.svg

```
<?xml version="1.0" encoding="iso-8859-1"?>
<!DOCTYPE svg PUBLIC "-//W3C//DTD SVG 20001102//EN"
  "http://www.w3.org/TR/2000/CR-SVG-20001102/DTD/
        svg20001102.dtd">

<svg xmlns="http://www.w3.org/2000/svg"
     xmlns:xlink="http://www.w3.org/1999/xlink"
     width="100%" height="100%">
<defs>
<filter
     id="blurFilter1"
     filterUnits="objectBoundingBox"
     x="0" y="0"
     width="100%" height="100%">
<feGaussianBlur stdDeviation="4"/>
</filter>
</defs>

<g transform="translate(50,100)">
<text id="normalText" x="0" y="0"
        fill="red" stroke="black" stroke-width="4"
        font-size="72">
     Normal Text
</text>
```

```
<text id="horizontalText" x="0" y="100"
        filter="url(#blurFilter1)"
        fill="red" stroke="black" stroke-width="4"
        font-size="72">
     Blurred Text
</text>
</g>
</svg>
```

The SVG `<defs>` element in Listing 3.5 contains an SVG `<filter>` element that specifies a Gaussian blur with the following line:

```
<feGaussianBlur stdDeviation="4"/>
```

You can specify larger values for the `stdDeviation` attribute if you want to create more-diffuse filter effects.

The first SVG `<text>` element that is contained in the SVG `<g>` element renders a normal text string, whereas the second SVG `<text>` element contains a `filter` attribute that references the filter (defined in the SVG `<defs>` element) in order to render the same text string, as shown here:

```
filter="url(#blurFilter1)"
```

Figure 3.5 displays the result of rendering `BlurFilterText1.svg`, which creates a filter effect.

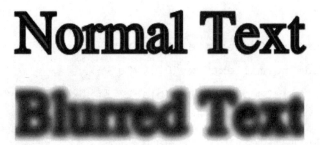

FIGURE 3.5 SVG filter effect.

Listing 3.6 ShadowFilterText1.svg

```
<?xml version="1.0" encoding="iso-8859-1"?>
<!DOCTYPE svg PUBLIC "-//W3C//DTD SVG 20001102//EN"
 "http://www.w3.org/TR/2000/CR-SVG-20001102/DTD/
        svg20001102.dtd">

<svg xmlns="http://www.w3.org/2000/svg"
     xmlns:xlink="http://www.w3.org/1999/xlink"
     width="100%" height="100%">
<defs>
<filter
     id="blurFilter1"
     filterUnits="objectBoundingBox"
     x="0" y="0"
     width="100%" height="100%">
<feGaussianBlur stdDeviation="4"/>
</filter>
</defs>

<g transform="translate(50,150)">
<text id="horizontalText" x="15" y="15"
        filter="url(#blurFilter1)"
        fill="red" stroke="black" stroke-width="2"
        font-size="72">
     Shadow Text
</text>

<text id="horizontalText" x="0" y="0"
        fill="red" stroke="black" stroke-width="4"
```

```
        font-size="72">
    Shadow Text
</text>
</g>
</svg>
```

Listing 3.6 is very similar to the code in Listing 3.5, except that the relative offset for the second SVG `<text>` element is slightly different, thereby creating a shadow effect.

Figure 3.6 displays the result of rendering `ShadowFilterText1.svg`, which creates a shadow effect.

FIGURE 3.6 SVG text with a shadow effect.

Listing 3.7 `TextOnQBezierPath1.svg`

```
<?xml version="1.0" encoding="iso-8859-1"?>
<!DOCTYPE svg PUBLIC "-//W3C//DTD SVG 20001102//EN"
  "http://www.w3.org/TR/2000/CR-SVG-20001102/DTD/
        svg-20001102.dtd">

<svg xmlns="http://www.w3.org/2000/svg"
     xmlns:xlink="http://www.w3.org/1999/xlink"
     width="100%" height="100%">
<defs>
<path id="pathDefinition"
        d="m0,0 Q100,0 200,200 T300,200 z"/>
</defs>
```

```
<g transform="translate(100,100)">
<text id="textStyle" fill="red"
      stroke="blue" stroke-width="2"
      font-size="24">

<textPath xlink:href="#pathDefinition">
      Sample Text that follows a path specified by a
                  Quadratic Bezier curve
</textPath>
</text>
</g>
</svg>
```

The SVG <defs> element in Listing 3.7 contains an SVG <path> element that defines a quadratic Bezier curve (note the Q in the d attribute). This SVG <path> element has an id attribute whose value is pathDefinition, which is referenced later in this code sample.

The SVG <g> element contains an SVG <text> element that specifies a text string to render, as well as an SVG <textPath> element that specifies the path along which the text is rendered, as shown here:

```
<textPath xlink:href="#pathDefinition">
      Sample Text that follows a path specified by a
                  Quadratic Bezier curve
</textPath>
```

Notice that the SVG <textPath> element contains the attribute xlink:href whose value is pathDefinition, which is also the id of the SVG <path> element that is defined in the SVG <defs> element. As a result, the text string is rendered along the path of a quadratic Bezier curve instead of rendering the text string horizontally (which is the default behavior). Figure 3.7 displays the result of rendering TextOnQBezier-Path1.svg, which renders a text string along the path of a quadratic Bezier curve.

FIGURE 3.7 SVG text on a quadratic Bezier curve.

SVG Transforms

Earlier in this chapter you saw some examples of SVG transform effects. In addition to the SVG functions `scale()`, `translate()`, and `rotate()`, SVG provides the `skew()` function to create skew effects. Listing 3.8 displays the contents of `TransformEffects1.svg`, which illustrates how to apply transforms to rectangles and circles in SVG.

Listing 3.8 `TransformEffects1.svg`

```
<?xml version="1.0" encoding="iso-8859-1"?>
<!DOCTYPE svg PUBLIC "-//W3C//DTD SVG 20001102//EN"
  "http://www.w3.org/TR/2000/CR-SVG-20001102/DTD/
      svg20001102.dtd">
```

```
<svg xmlns="http://www.w3.org/2000/svg"
    xmlns:xlink="http://www.w3.org/1999/xlink"
    width="100%" height="100%">
<defs>
<linearGradient id="gradientDefinition1"
    x1="0" y1="0" x2="200" y2="0"
    gradientUnits="userSpaceOnUse">
<stop offset="0%"   style="stop-color:#FF0000"/>
<stop offset="100%" style="stop-color:#440000"/>
</linearGradient>

<pattern id="dotPattern" width="8" height="8"
        patternUnits="userSpaceOnUse">

<circle id="circle1" cx="2" cy="2" r="2"
        style="fill:red;"/>
</pattern>
</defs>

<!-- full cylinder -->
<g id="largeCylinder" transform="translate(100,20)">
<ellipse cx="0"  cy="50" rx="20" ry="50"
        stroke="blue" stroke-width="4"
        style="fill:url(#gradientDefinition1)"/>

<rect x="0" y="0" width="300" height="100"
        style="fill:url(#gradientDefinition1)"/>

<rect x="0" y="0" width="300" height="100"
        style="fill:url(#dotPattern)"/>

<ellipse cx="300" cy="50" rx="20"  ry="50"
```

```
                        stroke="blue" stroke-width="4"
                        style="fill:yellow;"/>
</g>

<!-- half-sized cylinder -->
<g transform="translate(100,100) scale(.5)">
<use xlink:href="#largeCylinder" x="0" y="0"/>
</g>

<!-- skewed cylinder -->
<g transform="translate(100,100) skewX(40) skewY(20)">
<use xlink:href="#largeCylinder" x="0" y="0"/>
</g>

<!-- rotated cylinder -->
<g transform="translate(100,100) rotate(40)">
<use xlink:href="#largeCylinder" x="0" y="0"/>
</g>
</svg>
```

The SVG `<defs>` element in Listing 3.8 contains a `<linearGradient>` element that defines a linear gradient, followed by an SVG `<pattern>` element that defines a custom pattern, which is shown here:

```
<pattern id="dotPattern" width="8" height="8"
         patternUnits="userSpaceOnUse">

<circle id="circle1" cx="2" cy="2" r="2"
         style="fill:red;"/>
</pattern>
```

As you can see, the SVG `<pattern>` element contains an SVG `<circle>` element that is repeated in a grid-like fashion inside an 8 × 8 rectangle (note the values of the width attribute and the height attribute).

The SVG <pattern> element has an id attribute whose value is dot-Pattern because, as you will see, this element creates a "dotted" effect.

Listing 3.8 contains four SVG <g> elements, each of which renders a cylinder that references the SVG <pattern> element that is defined in the SVG <defs> element. The first SVG <g> element in Listing 3.8 contains two <ellipse> elements and two SVG <rect> elements. The first <ellipse> element renders the left-side "cover" of the cylinder with the linear gradient that is defined in the SVG <defs> element. The first <rect> element renders the "body" of the cylinder with a linear gradient, and the second <rect> element renders the "dot pattern" on the body of the cylinder. Finally, the second <ellipse> element renders the right-side "cover" of the ellipse.

The other three cylinders are easy to create: they simply reference the first cylinder and apply a transformation to change the size, shape, and orientation. Specifically, these three cylinders reference the first cylinder with the following code:

```
<use xlink:href="#largeCylinder" x="0" y="0"/>
```

and then they apply scale, skew, and rotate functions in order to render scaled, skewed, and rotated cylinders. Figure 3.8 displays the result of rendering TransformEffects1.svg.

FIGURE 3.8 SVG transform effects.

SVG Animation

SVG supports animation effects that you can specify as part of the declaration of SVG elements. Listing 3.9 displays the contents of the SVG document `AnimateMultiRect1.svg`, which illustrates how to create an animation effect with four rectangles.

Listing 3.9 AnimateMultiRect1.svg

```
<?xml version="1.0" encoding="iso-8859-1"?>
<!DOCTYPE svg PUBLIC "-//W3C//DTD SVG 20010904//EN"
   "http://www.w3.org/TR/2001/REC-SVG-20010904/DTD/
        svg10.dtd">

<svg xmlns="http://www.w3.org/2000/svg"
     xmlns:xlink="http://www.w3.org/1999/xlink"
     width="100%" height="100%">
<defs>
<rect id="rect1" width="100" height="100"
      stroke-width="1" stroke="blue"/>
</defs>

<g transform="translate(10,10)">
<rect width="500" height="400"
      fill="none" stroke-width="4" stroke="black"/>
</g>

<g transform="translate(10,10)">
<use xlink:href="#rect1" x="0" y="0" fill="red">
<animate attributeName="x" attributeType="XML"
              begin="0s" dur="4s"
              fill="freeze" from="0" to="400"/>
</use>
```

```
<use xlink:href="#rect1" x="400" y="0" fill="green">
<animate attributeName="y" attributeType="XML"
                begin="0s" dur="4s"
                fill="freeze" from="0" to="300"/>
</use>

<use xlink:href="#rect1" x="400" y="300" fill="blue">
<animate attributeName="x" attributeType="XML"
                begin="0s" dur="4s"
                fill="freeze" from="400" to="0"/>
</use>

<use xlink:href="#rect1" x="0" y="300" fill="yellow">
<animate attributeName="y" attributeType="XML"
                begin="0s" dur="4s"
                fill="freeze" from="300" to="0"/>
</use>
</g>
</svg>
```

The SVG <defs> element in Listing 3.9 contains an SVG <rect> element that defines a blue rectangle, followed by an SVG <g> element that renders the border of a large rectangle that "contains" the animation effect, which involves the movement of four rectangles in a clockwise fashion along the perimeter of an outer rectangle.

The second SVG <g> element contains four <use> elements that perform a parallel animation effect on four rectangles. The first <use> element references the rectangle defined in the SVG <defs> element and then animates the x attribute during a four-second interval as shown here:

```
<use xlink:href="#rect1" x="0" y="0" fill="red">
<animate attributeName="x" attributeType="XML"
```

```
                        begin="0s" dur="4s"
                        fill="freeze" from="0" to="400"/>
</use>
```

Notice that the x attribute varies from 0 to 400, which moves the rectangle horizontally from left to right. The second SVG <use> element also references the rectangle defined in the SVG <defs> element, except that the animation involves changing the y attribute from 0 to 300 in order to move the rectangle downward, as shown here:

```
<use xlink:href="#rect1" x="400" y="0" fill="green">
<animate attributeName="y" attributeType="XML"
                        begin="0s" dur="4s"
                        fill="freeze" from="0" to="300"/>
</use>
```

In a similar fashion, the third SVG <use> element moves the referenced rectangle horizontally from right to left, and the fourth SVG <use> element moves the referenced rectangle vertically and upward.

If you want to create a sequential animation effect (or a combination of sequential and parallel), then you need to modify the values of the begin attribute (and possibly the dur attribute) in order to achieve your desired animation effect. Figure 3.9 displays the result of rendering AnimateMultiRect1.svg.

Listing 3.10 displays the contents of the SVG document AnimateText1.svg, which illustrates how to animate a text string.

Listing 3.10 AnimateText1.svg

```
<?xml version="1.0" encoding="iso-8859-1"?>
<!DOCTYPE svg PUBLIC "-//W3C//DTD SVG 20010904//EN"
"http://www.w3.org/TR/2001/REC-SVG-20010904/DTD/svg10.dtd">

<svg xmlns="http://www.w3.org/2000/svg"
     xmlns:xlink="http://www.w3.org/1999/xlink"
     width="100%" height="100%">
```

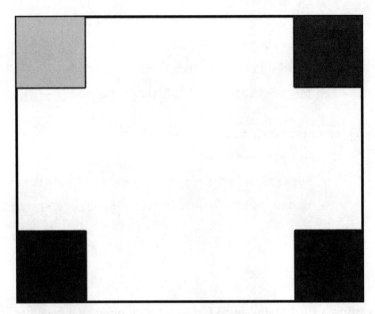

FIGURE 3.9 SVG animation effect with four rectangles.

```
<g transform="translate(100,100)">
<text x="0" y="0" font-size="48" visibility="hidden"
        stroke="black" stroke-width="2">
    Animating Text in SVG
<set attributeName="visibility"
        attributeType="CSS" to="visible"
        begin="2s" dur="5s" fill="freeze"/>

<animateMotion path="M0,0 L50,150"
        begin="2s" dur="5s" fill="freeze"/>

<animateColor attributeName="fill"
        attributeType="CSS"
        from="yellow" to="red"
        begin="2s" dur="8s" fill="freeze"/>
```

```
<animateTransform attributeName="transform"
          attributeType="XML"
          type="rotate" from="-90" to="0"
          begin="2s" dur="5s" fill="freeze"/>

<animateTransform attributeName="transform"
          attributeType="XML"
          type="scale" from=".5" to="1.5" additive="sum"
          begin="2s" dur="5s" fill="freeze"/>
</text>
</g>
</svg>
```

Listing 3.10 contains an SVG <text> element that specifies four different effects. The <set> element specifies the visibility of the text string for a five-second interval with an initial offset of two seconds.

The SVG <animateMotion> element shifts the upper-left corner of the text string from the point (0,0) to the point (50,150) in a linear fashion. This effect is combined with two other motion effects: rotation and scaling.

The SVG <animateColor> element changes the text color from yellow to red, and because the dur attribute has value 8s, this effect lasts three seconds longer than the other animation effects, whose dur attributes have values 5s. Note that all the animation effects start at the same time.

The first SVG <animateTransform> element performs a clockwise rotation of 90 degrees from vertical to horizontal. The second SVG <animateTransform> element performs a scaling effect that occurs in parallel with the first SVG <animateTransform> element because they have the same values for the begin attribute and the dur attribute. Figure 3.10 displays the result of rendering AnimateText1.svg.

Animating Text in SVG

FIGURE 3.10 SVG text animation effect.

SVG and JavaScript

SVG allows you to embed JavaScript in a CDATA section, which means that you can programmatically create SVG elements. Listing 3.11 displays the contents of the SVG document `ArchEllipses1.svg`, which illustrates how to render a set of ellipses that follow the path of an Archimedean spiral.

Listing 3.11 `ArchEllipses1.svg`

```
<?xml version="1.0" standalone="no"?>
<!DOCTYPE svg PUBLIC "-//W3C//DTD SVG 20010904//EN"
   "http://www.w3.org/TR/2001/REC-SVG-20010904/DTD/
        svg10.dtd">

<svg xmlns="http://www.w3.org/2000/svg"
    xmlns:xlink="http://www.w3.org/1999/xlink"
    onload="init(evt)"
    width="100%" height="100%">

<script type="text/ecmascript">
<![CDATA[
    var basePointX    = 250;
    var basePointY    = 200;
```

```
var currentX        = 0;
var currentY        = 0;
var offsetX         = 0;
var offsetY         = 0;
var radius          = 0;
var minorAxis       = 60;
var majorAxis       = 30;
var spiralCount     = 4;
var Constant        = 0.25;
var angle           = 0;
var maxAngle        = 720;
var angleDelta      = 2;
var strokeWidth     = 1;
var redColor        = "rgb(255,0,0)";

var ellipseNode     = null;
var svgDocument     = null;
var target          = null;
var gcNode          = null;

var svgNS           = "http://www.w3.org/2000/svg";

function init(event)
{
    svgDocument = event.target.ownerDocument;
    gcNode = svgDocument.getElementById("gc");

    drawSpiral(event);
}
```

```
function drawSpiral(event)
{
    for(angle=0; angle<maxAngle; angle+=angleDelta)
    {
        radius   = Constant*angle;
        offsetX  = radius*Math.cos(angle*Math.PI/180);
        offsetY  = radius*Math.sin(angle*Math.PI/180);
        currentX = basePointX+offsetX;
        currentY = basePointY-offsetY;

        ellipseNode =
                svgDocument.createElementNS(svgNS,
                            "ellipse");

        ellipseNode.setAttribute("fill", redColor);
        ellipseNode.setAttribute("stroke-width",
                strokeWidth);

        if( angle % 3 == 0 ) {
            ellipseNode.setAttribute("stroke",
                    "yellow");
        } else {
            ellipseNode.setAttribute("stroke", "green");
        }

        ellipseNode.setAttribute("cx", currentX);
        ellipseNode.setAttribute("cy", currentY);
        ellipseNode.setAttribute("rx", majorAxis);
        ellipseNode.setAttribute("ry", minorAxis);

        gcNode.appendChild(ellipseNode);
    }
```

```
    } // drawSpiral
  ]]></script>
<!-- ============================= -->
<g id="gc" transform="translate(10,10)">
<rect x="0" y="0"
        width="800" height="500"
        fill="none" stroke="none"/>
</g>
</svg>
```

Notice that the SVG <svg> element in Listing 3.11 contains an onload attribute that references the JavaScript function init(), and as you can surmise, the init() function is executed when you launch this SVG document in a browser. In this example, the purpose of the init() function is to reference the graphics context that is defined in the SVG <g> element at the bottom of Listing 3.11, and then to invoke the drawSpiral() function.

Whenever you want to include JavaScript in an SVG document, you need to place the JavaScript code inside a CDATA section that is embedded in a <script> element. The CDATA section in Listing 3.11 initializes some variables, along with the definition of the init() function and the drawSpiral() function.

The code in the drawSpiral() function consists of a loop that renders a set of dynamically created SVG <ellipse> elements. Each SVG <ellipse> element is created in the SVG namespace that is specified in the variable svgNS, after which values are assigned to the required attributes of an ellipse, as shown here:

```
ellipseNode =
        svgDocument.createElementNS(svgNS,
                        "ellipse");

ellipseNode.setAttribute("fill", redColor);
ellipseNode.setAttribute("stroke-width",
        strokeWidth);
```

```
// conditional logic omitted
ellipseNode.setAttribute("cx", currentX);
ellipseNode.setAttribute("cy", currentY);
ellipseNode.setAttribute("rx", majorAxis);
ellipseNode.setAttribute("ry", minorAxis);
```

After each SVG <ellipse> element is dynamically created, the element is appended to the DOM with one line of code, as shown here:

```
gcNode.appendChild(ellipseNode);
```

Finally, the SVG <g> element at the bottom of Listing 3.11 acts as a canvas on which the dynamically generated ellipses are rendered. Figure 3.11 displays the result of rendering ArchEllipses1.svg.

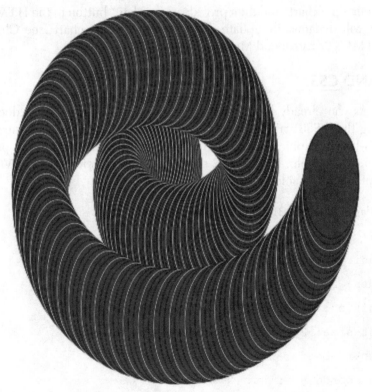

FIGURE 3.11 Dynamically generated SVG <ellipse> elements.

SVG and XSLT

The previous example showed you how to use JavaScript in order to dynamically generate an SVG document, but the contents of the SVG document are in the browser's memory space. If you need to programmatically generate SVG documents and store them on the file system, one option is to create XSL stylesheets and apply them to XML documents, which contain values for constants that are referenced in the XSL stylesheet, in order to generate dynamic SVG documents.

The XSLT-based example involves the XML file `SineR2Ellipses1.xml` and the XSL stylesheet `SineR2Ellipses1.xsl`. XSLT is beyond the scope of this book, so the details of the stylesheet will be omitted, but the entire source code for both files is available on the DVD for this book. If you want to learn about XSLT, you can perform an Internet search and read the various tutorials that are available.

A second option is to create an SVG document that uses JavaScript to render a pie chart, and then provide an "update" button in the HTML page that will dynamically update the values of the pie chart (see Chapter 8, "HTML5 `Canvas` and Mouse Events").

SVG AND CSS3

As you already know, CSS3 selectors can reference SVG documents using the CSS3 `url()` function, which means that you can incorporate SVG-based graphics effects (including animation) in your HTML pages. As a simple example, Listing 3.12 shows you how to reference an SVG document in a CSS3 selector.

Listing 3.12 `Blue3DCircle1.css`

```
#circle1 {
opacity: 0.5;color: red;
width: 250px;height: 250px;
position: absolute; top: 0px; left: 0px;
font-size: 24px;
-webkit-border-radius: 4px;
-moz-border-radius: 4px;
```

```
border-radius: 4px;
-webkit-background: url(Blue3DCircle1.svg) top right;
-moz-background: url(Blue3DCircle1.svg) top right;
background: url(Blue3DCircle1.svg) top right;
}
```

Listing 3.11 contains various attribute/value pairs, and the portion containing the CSS `url()` function is shown here:

```
-webkit-background: url(Blue3DCircle1.svg) top right;
-moz-background: url(Blue3DCircle1.svg) top right;
background: url(Blue3DCircle1.svg) top right;
```

This name/value pair specifies the SVG document `Blue3DCircle1.svg` as the background for an HTML `<div>` element in an HTML5 page whose `id` attribute is `circle1`. Note that the inclusion of a `-moz-` prefix and a `-webkit-` prefix means that this code will work in WebKit-based browsers (such as Safari and Chrome) and also in the Firefox browser. Figure 3.12 displays the result of rendering the HTML page `Blue3DCircle1.html`.

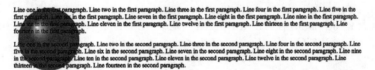

FIGURE 3.12 CSS3 3D effect.

CSS3 and SVG Bar Charts

Now that you know how to reference SVG documents in CSS3 selectors, let's look at an example of referencing an SVG-based bar chart in a CSS3 selector. Listing 3.13 displays the contents of the HTML5 page `CSS3SVGBarChart1.html`, Listing 3.14 displays the contents of the CSS3 stylesheet `CSS3SVGBarChart1.css` (whose selectors are applied to the contents of Listing 3.13), and Listing 3.15 displays the contents of the SVG document `CSS3SVGBarChart1.svg` (referenced in a selector in Listing 3.14), which contains the SVG code for rendering a bar chart.

Listing 3.13 `CSS3SVGBarChart1.html`

```
<!doctype html>

<html en>

<head>

<title>CSS Multi Column Text and SVG Bar Chart</title>

<meta charset="utf-8" />

<link href="CSS3SVGBarChart1.css" rel="stylesheet"
            type="text/css">

</head>


<body>

<div id="outer">

<article>

<p id="line1">.</p>

<div id="columns">

<p>

CSS enables you to define so-called "selectors" that
specify the style or the manner in which you want to
render elements in an HTML page. CSS helps you modular-
ize your HTML content and because you can place your CSS
definitions in a separate file, you can also re-use the
same CSS definitions in multiple HTML files.</p>

<p>

Moreover, CSS also enables you to simplify the updates
that you need to make to elements in HTML pages. For
example, suppose that multiple HTML table elements use
a CSS rule that specifies the color red. If you later
need to change the color to blue, you can effect such a
change simply by making one change (i.e., changing red
to blue) in one CSS rule.</p>

<p>

Without a CSS rule, you would be forced to manually up-
date the color attribute in every HTML table element
```

that is affected, which is error-prone, time-consuming, and extremely inefficient.</p>

<p>

As you can see, it's very easy to reference an SVG document in CSS selectors, and in this example, an SVG-based bar chart is rendered on the left-side of the screen.</p>

</div>

<p id="line1">.</p>

</article>

</div>

<div id="chart1">

</div>

</body>

</html>

In Chapter 2 you saw an example of rendering multicolumn text, and the contents of Listing 3.13 are essentially the same as the contents of that example. There is an additional HTML <div> element (whose id attribute has value chart1), however, that is used for rendering an SVG bar chart via a CSS selector in Listing 3.14.

Listing 3.14 CSS3SVGBarChart1.css

```
#columns {
-webkit-column-count : 4;
-webkit-column-gap : 40px;
-webkit-column-rule : 1px solid rgb(255,255,255);
column-count : 3;
column-gap : 40px;
column-rule : 1px solid rgb(255,255,255);
}
```

```
#line1 {
color: red;
font-size: 24px;
background-image: -webkit-gradient(linear, 0% 0%, 0%
                  100%, from(#fff), to(#f00));
background-image: -gradient(linear, 0% 0%, 0% 100%,
                  from(#fff), to(#f00));
-webkit-border-radius: 4px;
border-radius: 4px;
}

#chart1 {
opacity: 0.5;
color: red;
width: 800px;
height: 50%;
position: absolute; top: 20px; left: 20px;
font-size: 24px;
-webkit-border-radius: 4px;
-moz-border-radius: 4px;
border-radius: 4px;
border-radius: 4px;
-webkit-background: url(CSS3SVGBarChart1.svg) top right;
-moz-background: url(CSS3SVGBarChart1.svg) top right;
background: url(CSS3SVGBarChart1.svg) top right;
}
```

The `#chart` selector contains various attributes, along with a reference to an SVG document that renders an actual bar chart, as shown here:

```
-webkit-background: url(CSS3SVGBarChart1.svg) top right;
-moz-background: url(CSS3SVGBarChart1.svg) top right;
background: url(CSS3SVGBarChart1.svg) top right;
```

Now that you've see the contents of the HTML5 page and the selectors in the CSS stylesheet, let's take a look at the SVG document that renders the bar chart.

Listing 3.15 CSS3SVGBarChart1.svg

```
<?xml version="1.0" encoding="iso-8859-1"?>
<!DOCTYPE svg PUBLIC "-//W3C//DTD SVG 20001102//EN"
  "http://www.w3.org/TR/2000/CR-SVG-20001102/DTD/
        svg20001102.dtd">

<svg xmlns="http://www.w3.org/2000/svg"
    xmlns:xlink="http://www.w3.org/1999/xlink"
    width="100%" height="100%">
<defs>
<linearGradient id="pattern1">
<stop offset="0%"    stop-color="yellow"/>
<stop offset="40%"   stop-color="red"/>
<stop offset="80%"   stop-color="blue"/>
</linearGradient>

<radialGradient id="pattern2">
<stop offset="0%"    stop-color="yellow"/>
<stop offset="40%"   stop-color="red"/>
<stop offset="80%"   stop-color="blue"/>
</radialGradient>
```

```
<radialGradient id="pattern3">
<stop offset="0%"    stop-color="red"/>
<stop offset="30%"   stop-color="yellow"/>
<stop offset="60%"   stop-color="white"/>
<stop offset="90%"   stop-color="blue"/>
</radialGradient>
</defs>

<g id="chart1" transform="translate(0,0) scale(1,1)">
<rect width="30" height="235" x="15"   y="15"   fill="black"/>
<rect width="30" height="240" x="10"   y="10"
     fill="url(#pattern1)"/>

<rect width="30" height="145" x="45"   y="105" fill="black"/>
<rect width="30" height="150" x="40"   y="100"
     fill="url(#pattern2)"/>

<rect width="30" height="195" x="75"   y="55"   fill="black"/>
<rect width="30" height="200" x="70"   y="50"    fill="url
     (#pattern1)"/>
<rect width="30" height="185" x="105"  y="65"   fill="black"/>
<rect width="30" height="190" x="100"  y="60"
     fill="url(#pattern3)"/>

<rect width="30" height="145" x="135"  y="105" fill="black"/>
<rect width="30" height="150" x="130"  y="100"
     fill="url(#pattern1)"/>
```

```
<rect width="30" height="225" x="165" y="25"  fill="black"/>
<rect width="30" height="230" x="160" y="20"
      fill="url(#pattern2)"/>


<rect width="30" height="145" x="195" y="105"
      fill="black"/>
<rect width="30" height="150" x="190" y="100"
      fill="url(#pattern1)"/>
<rect width="30" height="175" x="225" y="75" fill="black"/>
<rect width="30" height="180" x="220" y="70"
      fill="url(#pattern3)"/>
</g>


<g id="chart2" transform="translate(250,125) scale(1,0.5)"
              width="100%" height="100%">
<use xlink:href="#chart1"/>
</g>
</svg>
```

Listing 3.15 contains an SVG `<defs>` element in which three gradients are defined (one linear gradient and two radial gradients), whose `id` attribute has values `pattern1`, `pattern2`, and `pattern3`, respectively. These gradients are referenced by their `id` in the SVG `<g>` element that renders a set of rectangular bars for a bar chart. The second SVG `<g>` element (whose `id` attribute has value `chart2`) performs a transform involving the SVG `translate()` and `scale()` functions, and then renders the actual bar chart, as shown in this code:

```
<g id="chart2" transform="translate(250,125) scale(1,0.5)"
              width="100%" height="100%">
<use xlink:href="#chart1"/>
</g>
```

Figure 3.13 displays the result of applying `CSS3SVGBarChart1.css` to the elements in the HTML page `CSS3SVGBarChart1.html`.

FIGURE 3.13 CSS3 with SVG applied to an HTML page.

SUMMARY

This chapter gave you an introduction to SVG, and you saw several code samples that illustrated the graphics capabilities of SVG. You also learned how to render 2D shapes and how to combine the functionality of SVG with CSS3. In particular you learned how to do the following:

■ create SVG linear gradients and radial gradients

■ apply SVG gradients to ellipses and elliptic arcs

■ render quadratic Bezier curves and cubic Bezier curves in SVG

■ reference SVG documents in CSS3 selectors

CSS3 and SVG support additional features for creating sophisticated effects, and you can perform an Internet search to find links that discuss those features. The next chapter gives you an introduction to HTML5 `Canvas`, along with code samples that illustrate how to render 2D shapes.

CHAPTER 4

RENDERING BASIC 2D SHAPES IN HTML5 CANVAS

T his chapter introduces you to HTML5 Canvas-based APIs, with code samples that illustrate some of the fundamental concepts that underlie many of the Canvas-based code samples in this book. Although many of the examples in this chapter are straightforward, they also provide a foundation for code samples in subsequent chapters, which create graphics effects that might otherwise seem more complex.

A second point to note is that many online Canvas-related and CSS3-related tutorials are available (a quick Internet search will confirm this fact), but relatively few of them provide code examples of using both HTML5 Canvas and CSS3 graphics effects. On the other hand, the code samples in Chapters 5, 6, 7, 8, 9, and 10 of this book contain (sometimes striking) combinations of HTML5 Canvas, CSS3 graphics, and CSS3 2D/3D animation effects that you are unlikely to find in any online resources or topic-related books. These code samples provide a starting point for you to create your own visually compelling graphics effects.

In addition to the comments in the introduction for Chapter 1, "Introduction to CSS3," please keep in mind that the code in this chapter (as well as the other chapters) does not necessarily reflect best practices, so it's possible to refactor the code to follow more current JavaScript idioms, and perhaps also get better performance.

With the preceding points in mind, this chapter starts by showing you techniques for rendering simple 2D shapes in HTML5 Canvas, after which you will learn how to use JavaScript to programmatically create 2D shapes and apply CSS3-based transformation effects to those 2D shapes. The second part of this chapter contains code samples that illustrate how to use the simplest 2D shape (the line segment) as a starting point for creating visually appealing graphics effects. The final portion of this chapter contains an HTML form-based example of dynamically updating the attributes of a text string that is rendered on an HTML5 `<canvas>` element. Incidentally, you might be surprised to discover that the graphics effects in this chapter are created with just three HTML5 `Canvas` APIs: the `fill-Rect()`, `moveTo()`, and `lineTo()` methods.

Although prior graphics experience is not required, familiarity with Scalable Vector Graphics (SVG) or Silverlight will enable you to skim quickly through this chapter as you discern the differences and the similarities among these technologies. If you want to learn more about SVG and Silverlight, there are several books available, including one by the author of this book (*Fundamentals of SVG Programming: Concepts to Source Code*; ISBN 1-58450-298-3).

In addition, if you want to experiment with existing code samples and perhaps get ideas of your own, an extensive set of HTML5 `Canvas`-based graphics code samples is available here: *http://code.google.com/p/html5-canvas-graphics*. The HTML5 `Canvas` code samples that are downloadable from this Web site use HTML5 `Canvas` APIs and techniques that are discussed in Chapters 4, 5, 6, and 7 of this book.

Please keep in mind that the CSS3 code samples in this book are for WebKit-based browsers, so the code will work on Windows, Macintosh, and Linux systems. In addition, there are tools for generating the CSS3 code for other non-WebKit browsers, which streamline the process of maintaining CSS3 stylesheets for different types of browsers.

WHAT IS HTML5 CANVAS?

HTML5 `Canvas` gives you the ability (via JavaScript) to programmatically render graphics in a browser. Several years ago, Apple, Inc. created `Canvas` functionality in the Safari browser, and its popularity grew to the point where HTML5 supports `Canvas` as well. HTML5 `Canvas` uses "immediate mode," which is a write-and-forget approach to rendering graphics. Thus, if you want to write a sketching program and you also want to provide an undo feature, then you must programmatically keep track of everything that users have drawn on the screen. On the other hand, SVG and Silverlight use a "retained mode," which involves a DOM (Document Object Model) structure that keeps track of the rendered objects and their relationship to one another. A good overview of some features/advantages of HTML5 Canvas can be found here: *http://thinkvitamin.com/code/how-to-draw-with-html-5-canvas/*.

One point to consider is when it's advantageous to use HTML5 Canvas instead of another technology, such as SVG or Silverlight. The following short list contains some features to consider when you are making this type of analysis:

- Native versus plug-in browser support

- Level of SVG support in different browsers

- Animation support

- Support for filters (SVG only)

- Built-in support for HTML-like widgets

- Third-party support

Most modern browsers provide varying degrees of built-in support for SVG, and the Adobe® SVG viewer can be used with Internet Explorer. If you need filter-based visual effects, SVG provides a very rich (perhaps even the best) functionality. If you need built-in support for HTML controls, Silverlight is a better choice. Another point to consider is that Adobe no longer supports its SVG viewer. This is a significant decision, because the Adobe SVG viewer had been the *de facto* standard for SVG viewers for many years. Although Firefox and Opera have made significant progress in terms of their support for SVG, and both are enhancing their support for SVG, they still lack the feature support of the Adobe SVG viewer. Thus, you need to weigh the most important factors in order to make the decision that will meet your project-related needs.

The HTML5 Canvas **Coordinate System**

The Cartesian coordinate system identifies any point in the Euclidean plane by means of a pair of numbers. The first number represents the horizontal value and the second number represents the vertical value. The horizontal axis is labeled the x-axis, and positive values on the x-axis are to the right of the vertical axis (i.e., toward the right). The vertical axis is labeled the y-axis, and positive values on the y-axis are above the horizontal axis. The origin is the intersection point of the x-axis and the y-axis.

The Cartesian coordinate system is almost the same as the HTML5 `Canvas` coordinate system. The x-axis is horizontal and the positive direction is toward the right. The y-axis is vertical, but the positive direction is *downward*, which is the opposite direction of most graphs in a typical mathematics textbook. In the HTML5 `Canvas` coordinate system, the origin is the upper-left corner of the screen (not the lower-left corner), and the unit of measurement is the pixel, so the largest visible display is usually 1024 × 728.

Listing 4.1 displays a minimal HTML5 Web page that is ready for rendering HTML5 `Canvas`-based graphics. Every `Canvas`-based code sample in this book uses the code (or some variant) that is displayed in Listing 4.1. Note that this example only provides a template that you can use as a starting point for your code samples, and that nothing is actually rendered, so if you launch this HTML5 page in a Web browser you will see a blank screen.

Listing 4.1 `Canvas1.html`

```
<!DOCTYPE html>
<html lang="en">
<head>
<meta charset="utf-8">
<title>Canvas Drawing Rectangles</title>

  <script type="text/javascript"><!--
    window.addEventListener('load', function () {
      // Get the canvas element
      var elem = document.getElementById('myCanvas');
      if (!elem || !elem.getContext) {
        return;
      }

      // Get the canvas 2d context.
      var context = elem.getContext('2d');
      if (!context) {
```

```
        return;
    }
    // insert your Canvas graphics code here
  // --></script>
</head>

<body>
<p>
  <canvas id="myCanvas" width="300" height="300">No
        support for Canvas.
  </canvas>
 </p>
</body>
</html>
```

Listing 4.1 contains an HTML <head> element that checks for the existence of an HTML <canvas> element inside the HTML <body> element of the Web page, and then gets the 2D context from the HTML <canvas> element. If you skip over the various conditional statements in Listing 4.1, there are two lines of code that enable us to get a reference to the variable context, which represents a drawable surface:

```
var elem = document.getElementById('myCanvas');
var context = elem.getContext('2d');
```

Note that if you launch Listing 4.1 in a browser that does not support HTML5 Canvas, the text message "No support for Canvas." is displayed.

The following code snippet is executed when you launch the Web page because of an anonymous JavaScript function that is added to the load event:

```
window.addEventListener('load', function () {
```

Now that you understand the underlying code for rendering Canvas-based 2D shapes, you can focus on the code that actually draws some 2D shapes, starting with the example in the next section.

RENDERING RECTANGLES IN HTML5 CANVAS

HTML5 Canvas provides the fillRect() method for rendering a rectangle, which requires that you specify four parameters: the upper-left vertex (i.e., the x-coordinate and the y-coordinate) of the rectangle, the width of the rectangle, and the height of the desired rectangle. The Canvas fillRect() API looks like this:

```
context.fillRect(x, y, width, height);
```

One way to set the color of the rendered rectangle is by specifying a hexadecimal triple (R, G, B) of numbers, where each component is a number between the values 0 and 255 (FF in hexadecimal) inclusive. You can also use base 10 instead of base 16 for the components of the triple. As an example, the color red can be represented as (FF, 0, 0) or (255, 0, 0). Among the various ways to set color values, we will use hexadecimal-based numbers for specifying colors in this chapter. A quick Internet search will reveal more alternatives.

Listing 4.2 displays the contents of Rectangles.html, which illustrates how to use this method in order to render three side-by-side rectangles using Canvas, SVG, and CSS.

Listing 4.2 Rectangles.html

```
<!DOCTYPE html>
<html lang="en">
 <head>
  <meta charset="utf-8">
  <title>Canvas/SVG/CSS Rectangles</title>

  <style>
    #outer {
```

```
    position:relative; top:10px; left:0px;
    width:100%;
    height:100%;
}

#canvas {
    position:float; top:0px; left:0px;
    width:50%;
    height:50%;
}

#svg {
    position:absolute; top:0px; left:225px;
    width:50%;
    height:50%;
}

#css {
    position:absolute; top:0px; left:450px;
    width:200px;
    height:200px;
}

#red {
    position:absolute; top:0px; left:0px;
    width:100px;
    height:100px;
    background:red;
}
```

```
    #yellow {
       position:absolute; top:0px; left:100px;
       width:100px;
       height:100px;
       background:yellow;
    }

    #green {
       position:absolute; top:100px; left:0px;
       width:100px;
       height:100px;
       background:green;
    }

    #blue{
       position:absolute; top:100px; left:100px;
       width:100px;
       height:100px;
       background:blue;
    }
</style>

<script type="text/javascript"><!--
  window.addEventListener('load', function () {
    // Get the canvas element
    var elem = document.getElementById('myCanvas');
    if (!elem || !elem.getContext) {
      return;
    }
```

```
// Get the canvas 2d context.
var context = elem.getContext('2d');
if (!context) {
  return;
}

var basePointX = 0;
var basePointY = 0;
var rectWidth  = 100;
var rectHeight = 100;
var fillStyles = ['#f00', '#ff0', '#0f0', '#00f'];

// upper left rectangle
context.fillStyle = fillStyles[0];
context.fillRect(basePointX, basePointY,
                 rectWidth, rectHeight);

// render text in upper left rectangle
context.font = '16px sans-serif';
context.fillStyle = '#000';
context.fillText("Canvas", 0, 14);

// upper right rectangle
context.fillStyle = fillStyles[1];
context.fillRect(basePointX+rectWidth, basePointY,
                 rectWidth, rectHeight);

// lower left rectangle
context.fillStyle = fillStyles[2];
context.fillRect(basePointX, basePointY+rectHeight,
                 rectWidth, rectHeight);
```

```
        // lower right rectangle
        context.fillStyle = fillStyles[3];
        context.fillRect(basePointX+rectWidth,
                         basePointY+rectHeight,
                         rectWidth, rectHeight);
    }, false);
    // --></script>
</head>

<body>
 <div id="outer">
   <!-- Canvas-based rectangles -->
   <div id="canvas">
     <canvas id="myCanvas" width="400" height="200">No
            support for Canvas
     </canvas>
   </div>

   <!-- SVG-based rectangles -->
   <div id="svg">
     <svg width="400" height="200" >
       <!-- upper left: red -->
       <rect width="100" height="100" x="0" y="0"
            fill="red" />
       <text x="0" y="12">SVG</text>

       <!-- upper right: yellow -->
       <rect width="100" height="100" x="100" y="0"
            fill="yellow" />
```

```
   <!-- lower left: green -->
   <rect width="100" height="100" x="0" y="100"
         fill="green" />


   <!-- lower right: blue-->
   <rect width="100" height="100" x="100" y="100"
         fill="blue"/>
 </svg>
</div>


<!-- CSS-based rectangles -->
<div id="css">
   <div id="red">CSS</div>

   <div id="yellow"></div>

   <div id="green"></div>

   <div id="blue"></div>
 </div>
 </div>
 </body>
</html>
```

Listing 4.2 contains all the code from Listing 4.1, and after initializing some variables, there are three code blocks for rendering three rectangles.

One difference between HTML5 Canvas and SVG is that every SVG document *must* contain an XML <svg> element as its root node, which means that the <svg> element is also the parent node of all the other SVG elements in the SVG document.

By way of comparison, SVG uses the attributes x, y, width, and height, which correspond to the upper-left x-coordinate, the upper-left y-coordinate, the width, and the height of the rectangle, respectively. The color of each rectangle is set using a style attribute in each <rect> element.

The third set of rectangles is rendered using CSS selectors whose definitions are similar to examples in Chapter 2, "CSS3 2D/3D Animation and CSS Frameworks," so we won't discuss the details of these selectors. Figure 4.1 displays three rectangles (each of which contains four subrectangles) that are rendered using Canvas, SVG, and CSS, respectively, defined in Listing 4.2.

 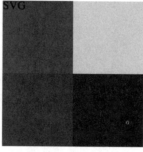 

FIGURE 4.1 Rendering Canvas, SVG, and CSS rectangles in HTML5.

RECTANGLES WITH SHADOW EFFECTS

Shadow effects provide a richer visual experience that is an improvement over the use of nonshadow effects. You create a shadow effect by including values for the three attributes, shadowOffsetX, shadowOffsetY, and shadowBlur, rendering a 2D shape (such as a rectangle). The HTML5 Web page RandRectanglesShadow.html in Listing 4.3 uses this technique in order to render a set of randomly generated rectangles with a shadow effect.

Listing 4.3 RandRectanglesShadow.html

```
<!DOCTYPE html>

<html lang="en">

<head>

  <meta charset="utf-8">

  <title>Canvas Random Rectangles With Shadow Effects</title>
```

```html
<link href="CSS3Background2.css" rel="stylesheet"
      type="text/css">

<style>
  input {
    width:300px;
    font-size:24px;
    background-color:#f00;
  }
</style>

<script type="text/javascript"><!--
  window.addEventListener('load', function() {
    var clickCount = 0;

    // Get the canvas element.
    var elem = document.getElementById('myCanvas');
    if (!elem || !elem.getContext) {
      return;
    }

    // Get the canvas 2d context.
    var context = elem.getContext('2d');
    if (!context) {
      return;
    }

    var basePointX = 10;
    var basePointY = 10;
    var canWidth   = 800;
```

```
var canHeight  = 450;
var shadowX    = 10;
var shadowY    = 10;
var rectCount  = 100;
var rectWidth  = 100;
var rectHeight = 100;
var colorIndex = 0;
var fillStyles = ['#f00', '#ff0', '#0f0', '#00f'];

redrawCanvas = function() {
    // clear the canvas before drawing new set of
              rectangles
   context.clearRect(0, 0, elem.width, elem.height);

   for(var r=0; r<rectCount; r++) {
      basePointX = canWidth*Math.random();
      basePointY = canHeight*Math.random();

      // Define a shadow effect
      if(clickCount % 2 == 0) {
      context.shadowColor   = "rgba(0,0,64,1.0)";
      } else {
      context.shadowColor   = "rgba(64,0,0,1.0)";
      }

      context.shadowOffsetX = shadowX;
      context.shadowOffsetY = shadowY;
      context.shadowBlur    = 4;
      context.lineWidth     = 1;
```

```
        // render a colored rectangle
        colorIndex = Math.floor(basePointX)%
                     fillStyles.length;

        context.fillStyle = fillStyles[colorIndex];


        context.fillRect(basePointX, basePointY,

                         rectWidth, rectHeight);


        ++clickCount;
      }
   }


   // render a set of random rectangles
   redrawCanvas();
 }, false);
 // --></script>
</head>


<body>
 <div>
  <canvas id="myCanvas" width="800" height="450">No
         support for Canvas
  </canvas>
 </div>


 <div>
  <br />
```

```
    <input type="button" onclick="redrawCanvas();return false"
           value="Redraw the Rectangles" />
  </div>
  </body>
</html>
```

The HTML5 code in Listing 4.3 starts by initializing some JavaScript variables and then defining the JavaScript function `redrawCanvas()`, which contains a loop for rendering the rectangles on the screen. The loop calculates the coordinates of the upper-left vertex of each rectangle as shown here:

```
basePointX = canWidth*Math.random();
basePointY = canHeight*Math.random();
```

The next part of the loop assigns the background color (which alternates between a dark blue and dark red shadow), and then creates a shadow effect by specifying values for the attributes `shadowOffsetX`, `shadowOffsetY`, and `shadowBlur`, as shown here:

```
context.shadowOffsetX = shadowX;
context.shadowOffsetY = shadowY;
context.shadowBlur    = 4;
```

The actual rendering of each rectangle is performed by the following code:

```
context.fillRect(basePointX, basePointY,
                 rectWidth, rectHeight);
```

Notice that the `clickCount` variable is incremented each time users click inside the HTML5 `Canvas` element, and its value determines which shadow color is applied to the randomly generated rectangles.

Although shadow effects create a pleasing effect, they also have an impact on performance. If you need shadow-like effects but performance becomes an issue, one alternative is to render a background shape in black (or some other dark color), and then render the same shape (with a small offset) using a different color.

For example, you can create a shadow effect for rectangles by first rendering a black rectangle and then rendering a red rectangle on top of the black rectangle, as shown here:

```
// render a black rectangle
context.fillStyle = '#000';
context.fillRect(50+shadowX, 50+shadowY, 200, 100);

// render a red rectangle
context.fillStyle = '#f00';
context.fillRect(50, 50, 200, 100);
```

The values for shadowX and shadowY determine the size of the background shadow, and the choice of positive versus negative values for shadowX and shadowY will determine the relative position of the black rectangle with respect to the red rectangle.

Listing 4.4 CSS3Background2.css

```
#myCanvas {
position: relative; top: 0px; left: 0px;

background-color:white;
background-image:
  -webkit-radial-gradient(red 4px, transparent 18px),
  -webkit-repeating-radial-gradient(red 0px, green 4px,
                            yellow 8px,
                            blue 12px,
                            transparent 28px,
                            green 20px, red 24px,
                            transparent 28px,
                            transparent 32px),
```

```
            -webkit-repeating-radial-gradient(red 0px,green 4px,
                                    yellow 8px,
                                    blue 12px,
                                    transparent 28px,
                                    green 20px, red 24px,
                                    transparent 28px,
                                    transparent 32px);
background-size: 50px 60px, 70px 80px;
background-position: 0 0;
-webkit-box-shadow:  30px 30px 30px #000;

resize:both;
overflow:auto;
}


#myCanvas:hover {
position: relative; top: 0px; left: 0px;

background-color:white;
background-image:
   -webkit-radial-gradient(red 4px, transparent 48px),
   -webkit-repeating-radial-gradient(red 2px,
                                    green 4px, yellow 8px,
                                    blue 12px,
                                    transparent 16px,
                                    red 20px, blue 24px,
                                    transparent 28px,
                                    transparent 32px),
   -webkit-radial-gradient(blue 8px, transparent 68px);
background-size: 120px 120px, 4px 4px;
background-position: 0 0;
}
}
```

Listing 4.4 contains two similar CSS3 selectors for rendering the HTML5 <canvas> element defined in Listing 4.3, as well as a hover-based selector that changes the background of the HTML5 <canvas> element when users hover over this element with their mouse. The #myCanvas selector defines a radial gradient, followed by two repeating radial gradients that specify various combinations of red, green, yellow, and blue at different pixel locations. A key point involves the use of transparent, which changes the gap between consecutive colors that are rendered.

As you can see in the definition of the #myCanvas selector, there are many possible combinations available for the colors, the gradients (and their types), and the colors for the gradients, along with the values for the background-size attribute. There is no "right" way to define these patterns, so experiment with different combinations, and you might create unexpectedly pleasing results. Figure 4.2 displays a set of randomly generated rectangles with a shadow effect based on the code in Listing 4.3.

FIGURE 4.2 Randomly generated rectangles with a shadow effect.

NESTED RECTANGLES WITH GRADIENT EFFECTS

HTML5 `Canvas` supports linear gradients and radial gradients (both of which are discussed in Chapter 5, "2D Shapes with Linear and Radial Gradients"), and this section shows you a simple technique for creating your own gradient effects. Listing 4.5 displays the contents of the HTML5 page `NestedRectangles1.html`, which illustrates how to use loops to render a set of nested rectangles with a gradient effect.

Listing 4.5 `NestedRectangles1.html`

```
<!DOCTYPE html>
<html lang="en">
<head>
 <meta charset="utf-8">
 <title>Canvas Drawing Rectangles</title>
 <link href="CSS3Background1.css" rel="stylesheet"
       type="text/css">
 <style>
   input {
     width:300px;
     font-size:24px;
     background-color:#f00;
   }
 </style>

<script type="text/javascript"><!--
   window.addEventListener('load', function () {
     // Get the canvas element.
     var elem = document.getElementById('myCanvas');
     if (!elem || !elem.getContext) {
       return;
     }
```

```
// Get the canvas 2d context.
var context = elem.getContext('2d');
if (!context) {
  return;
 }

var basePointX = 10;
var basePointY = 10;
var rectCount  = 256;
var rectWidth  = 256;
var rectHeight = 256;
var lineWidth  = 200;
var clickCount = 0;
var rectColor  = "";
var hexArray   = new
            Array('0','1','2','3','4','5','6','7',
               '8','9','a','b','c','d','e','f');

redrawCanvas = function() {
   // clear the canvas before drawing new set of
            rectangles
    //context.clearRect(0, 0, elem.width, elem.
            height);

   // first set of rectangles...
   context.beginPath();
   for(var r=0; r<rectCount/2; r++) {
      lineColor = '#' + hexArray[r%16] + '00';
        context.fillStyle = lineColor;
```

```
        context.fillRect(basePointX+r, basePointY+r,
                        rectWidth-2*r, rectHeight-2*r);
    }
     context.stroke();

    // second set of rectangles...
    context.beginPath();
    for(var r=0; r<rectCount/2; r++) {
        lineColor = '#' + hexArray[r%16] +
                    hexArray[r%16] + '0';
         context.fillStyle = lineColor;

        context.fillRect(basePointX+rectWidth+r,
                basePointY+r, rectWidth-2*r,
                rectHeight-2*r);
    }
     context.stroke();

    ++clickCount;
    ++basePointX;
    ++basePointY;

  }

    // render nested rectangles
    redrawCanvas();
  }, false);
  // --></script>
</head>
```

```
<body>
 <div>
  <canvas id="myCanvas" width="800" height="350">No
          support for Canvas
          alt="Rendering Nested Rectangles.">
  </canvas>
  </div>

  <div>
  <input type="button" onclick="redrawCanvas();return false"
         value="Redraw the Rectangles" />
  </div>
</body>
</html>
```

Listing 4.5 starts by initializing some variables and then uses two loops to render nested rectangles using the fillRect() method. In the first code block, the loop variable r is used as an index into the array hexArray (which defines 16 colors) in order to create a linear gradient effect, as shown here:

```
lineColor = '#' + hexArray[r%16] + '00';
```

The upper-left vertex of each rectangle is shifted diagonally in the lower-right direction, and the width and height are adjusted accordingly (in order to created a nested effect), as shown here:

```
context.fillRect(basePointX+r, basePointY+r,
        rectWidth-2*r, rectHeight-2*r);
```

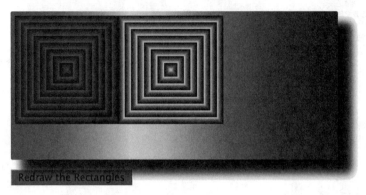

FIGURE 4.3 A set of nested rectangles with a gradient effect.

The other loop uses a similar technique to construct another set of nested rectangles. Figure 4.3 displays a set of nested rectangles with a gradient effect.

LINE SEGMENTS WITH GRADIENT COLOR EFFECTS

HTML5 Canvas allows you to render line segments by specifying the (x, y) coordinates of the two endpoints of the line segments. The two new APIs that are used in the code sample in this section are moveTo() and lineTo(), and they look like this:

```
context.moveTo(x1, y1);
context.lineTo(x2, y2);
```

You can think of a rectangle as a set of adjacent line segments, and if you change the color of each line segment, the result is a rectangle with a gradient effect. Listing 4.6 displays the contents of LineSegments1. html, which illustrates how to render a set of line segments with a gradient effect.

Listing 4.6 LineSegments1.html

```
<!DOCTYPE html>
<html lang="en">
 <head>
  <meta charset="utf-8">
  <title>Canvas Drawing Line Segments</title>
  <link href="CSS3Background6.css" rel="stylesheet"
        type="text/css">

  <style>
    input {
      width:350px;
      font-size:24px;
      background-color:#f00;
    }
  </style>

  <script type="text/javascript"><!--
    window.addEventListener('load', function () {
      // Get the canvas element
      var elem = document.getElementById('myCanvas');
      if (!elem || !elem.getContext) {
        return;
      }

      // Get the canvas 2d context
      var context = elem.getContext('2d');
```

```
if (!context) {
  return;
}
var basePointX = 10;
var basePointY = 10;
var clickCount = 0;
var lineCount  = 256;
var lineLength = 200;
var lineWidth  = 4;
var lineColor  = "";
var hexArray   = new Array('0','1','2','3','4',
                           '5','6','7','8','9','a',
                           'b','c','d','e','f');

redrawCanvas = function() {
  // clear the canvas before drawing new set of
        rectangles
  //context.clearRect(0, 0, elem.width, elem.
        height);

  // first set of line segments...
  for(var y=0; y<lineCount; y++) {
    context.beginPath();

    lineColor = '#' + hexArray[y%16] + '00';
    context.strokeStyle = lineColor;
    context.lineCap  = 'square'; // 'butt'
        'round' 'square'
    context.lineJoin = 'round';  // 'bevel'
        'miter' 'round'
    context.lineWidth = lineWidth;
```

```
    context.moveTo(basePointX, basePointY+y);
    context.lineTo(basePointX+lineLength,
            basePointY+y);
    context.stroke();
}

// second set of line segments...
for(var y=0; y<lineCount; y++) {
    context.beginPath();

    lineColor = '#' + hexArray[y%16] +
            hexArray[y%16] + '0';
    context.strokeStyle = lineColor;

    context.moveTo(basePointX+lineLength,
            basePointY+y);
    context.lineTo(basePointX+2*lineLength,
            basePointY+y);
    context.stroke();
}

// third set of line segments...
for(var y=0; y<lineCount; y++) {
    context.beginPath();

    lineColor = '#00' + hexArray[y%16];
    context.strokeStyle = lineColor;

    context.moveTo(basePointX+2*lineLength,
            basePointY+y);
    context.lineTo(basePointX+3*lineLength,
            basePointY+y);
    context.stroke();
}
```

```
                  ++clickCount;

                  basePointX += 1;

                  basePointY += 1;

          }


          // render the line segments

          redrawCanvas();

     }, false);

     // --></script>

</head>

<body>

  <div>

    <canvas id="myCanvas" width="800" height="350">No
            support for Canvas

            alt="Example rendering of a Pyramid.">

    </canvas>

  </div>


  <div>

    <input type="button" onclick="redrawCanvas();return
            false"

            value="Redraw the Line Segments" />

  </div>

</body>

</html>
```

Listing 4.6 performs the usual initialization and then uses three separate loops to render three adjacent sets of horizontal line segments whose
linear gradient effect is from black to red, black to yellow, and black to blue,
respectively. All three loops use the loop variable as an index into the array
hexArray in order to change the color of each horizontal line segment.
For example, the following code snippet in the first loop defines a linear
gradient that varies from black to red:

```
lineColor = '#' + hexArray[y%16] + '00';
```

In the second loop, this code snippet defines a linear gradient that varies from black to yellow:

```
lineColor = '#' + hexArray[y%16] + hexArray[y%16] + '0';
```

Finally, this code snippet defines a linear gradient that varies from black to blue in the third loop:

```
lineColor = '#00' + hexArray[y%16];
```

When you render a more complex path, such as a contiguous set of line segments, it's more efficient to place the code line `context.begin-Path();` before the loop, and the code line `context.stroke();` outside the loop. Listing 4.6, however, consists of two loops that render individual line segments with different shading effects, so if you change the code, you will significantly alter the visual effect (try it and see).

Listing 4.6 also references the CSS3 stylesheet `CSS3Background6.css` that contains two selectors that use a combination of radial and linear gradients to set the background of the HTML5 `<canvas>` element in Listing 4.6, as well as a selector that changes the background when users hover over the HTML5 `<canvas>` element with their mouse. The CSS3 stylesheet `CSS3Background6.css` contains CSS3 selectors that are structurally similar to the CSS3 stylesheet `CSS3Background2.css`, as well as code that you have seen in earlier chapters, and for the sake of brevity its contents are not included here (but the source code is available on the DVD for this book).

Incidentally, if you want to render a polygon, there is no `fillPolygon()` method available, so you must construct polygons programmatically. One technique involves calculating the vertices of a regular polygon using the built-in JavaScript methods `Math.cos()` and `Math.sin()`, and then rendering a line segment between each pair of consecutive vertices of the polygon.

```
var vertexCount = 6;
var vertexAngle = 360/vertexCount;
var vertexXPts  = new Array();
```

```
var vertexYPts  = new Array();

for(var v=0; v<vertexCount; v++) {
      theAngle = v*vertexAngle*Math.PI/180;

      vertexXPts.push(basePointX+lineLength*Math.
             cos(theAngle));
      vertexYPts.push(basePointY+lineLength*Math.
             sin(theAngle));
}

context.beginPath();
for(var v=0; v<vertexCount; v++) {
    if(v == 0) {
      context.moveTo(2*p+vertexXPts[v],
                     p+vertexYPts[v]);
    } else {
      context.lineTo(2*p+vertexXPts[v],
                     p+vertexYPts[v]);
    }
}

context.closePath();
context.fill();
```

The first loop in the preceding code fragment calculates the coordinates of a regular polygon with six sides because the value of the variable `vertexCount` is 6; you could change this value to increase or decrease the number of sides of the polygon. The second loop renders a polygon using `beginPath()` to start a new path, followed by a set of `moveTo()` invocations to draw the line segments that connect consecutive vertices of the polygon. The `closePath()` function closes the path of the polygon, and then the polygon is rendered by invoking the `fill()` function.

Notice that the preceding code places the code line `context.beginPath();` before the loop, and the code line `context.fill();` outside the loop, which makes this code more efficient than including the code inside the loop. Figure 4.4 displays a set of line segments with a gradient color effect.

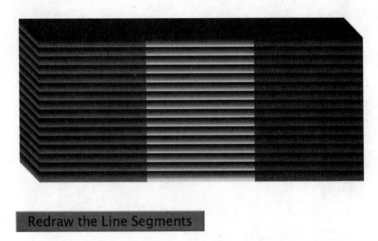

FIGURE 4.4 A set of line segments with a gradient color effect.

DYNAMICALLY UPDATING TEXT STRINGS ON CANVAS

HTML5 `Canvas` allows you to render a text string by specifying the text that you wish to draw, as well as the `(x, y)` coordinates of the start point of the text string, and the API looks like this:

```
context.fillText(textValue, xPos, yPos);
```

The code sample in this section shows you how to create an HTML form with an input field and two drop-down lists so that users can dynamically update the attributes of the text string. Listing 4.7 displays the contents of `Text1Form1.html`, which illustrates how to update a text string (and its attributes) rendered on an HTML5 `<canvas>` element.

Listing 4.7 `Text1Form1.html`

```
<!DOCTYPE html>
<html lang="en">
<head>
  <meta charset="utf-8">
  <title>Rendering Text</title>
  <link href="CSS3Background1.css" rel="stylesheet"
        type="text/css">

  <style>
    input {
      width:300px;
      font-size:24px;
      background-color:#f00;
    }
  </style>

  <script type="text/javascript"><!--
    window.addEventListener('load', function () {
      var fontSize=28, textColor="#ff0",
          textValue="Hello CSS3";
      var xPos=10, yPos=80, theElement, target;
      var elem = document.getElementById('myCanvas');
```

```
if (!elem || !elem.getContext) {
  return;
}

var context = elem.getContext('2d');
if (!context) {
  return;
}

theElement = document.getElementById("fontSize");
theElement.addEventListener('change', font-
          SizeChanged, false);

theElement = document.getElementById("textColor");
theElement.addEventListener('change', textColor-
          Changed, false);

theElement = document.getElementById("textValue");
theElement.addEventListener('change', textVal-
          ueChanged, false);

function fontSizeChanged(e) {
   target = e.target;
   fontSize = target.value;
   drawText();
}

function textColorChanged(e) {
   target = e.target;
   textColor = target.value;
   drawText();
}
```

```
function textValueChanged(e) {
    target = e.target;
    textValue = target.value;
    drawText();
}

drawText = function() {
    // clear the canvas before drawing new set of
            rectangles
    context.clearRect(0, 0, elem.width, elem.height);

    // Define a shadow effect
    context.shadowColor   = "rgba(0,0,255,0.3)";
    context.shadowOffsetX = 3;
    context.shadowOffsetY = 3;
    context.shadowBlur    = 2;
    context.lineWidth     = 1;

    // Define other attributes and text
    context.lineWidth   = 2;
    context.strokeStyle = "#000";
    context.font        = "Bold "+fontSize+"pt
            Helvetica";
    context.fillStyle   = textColor;
    context.fillText(textValue, xPos, yPos);
}
    // render text strings
    drawText();
}, false);
// --></script>
</head>
```

```
<body>
  <div>
   <canvas id="myCanvas" width="800" height="200">No
          support for Canvas
          alt="Rendering Text.">
   </canvas>
  </div>

  <div>
   <br><br>
   <form>
    Text Color:
    <select id="textColor">
      <option value="#ff0">Yellow</option>
      <option value="#f00">Red</option>
      <option value="#00f">Blue</option>
    </select>

    Font Size:
    <select id="fontSize">
      <option value="28">28</option>
      <option value="36">36</option>
      <option value="44">44</option>
      <option value="60">60</option>
    </select>
    <br>

    Text Value:
    <input id="textValue" placeholder="Hello CSS3" />
   </form>
```

```
     </div>
   </body>
</html>
```

Listing 4.7 is conceptually simple: there are two drop-down lists and an input field that enable users to change the font size, the text color, and the text string itself. In particular, there is a drop-down list (whose id attribute has the value fontSize) that allows users to select from the values 28, 36, 44, and 60 for the font size of the rendered text string, as shown here:

```
<select id="fontSize">
  <option value="28">28</option>
  <option value="36">36</option>
  <option value="44">44</option>
  <option value="60">60</option>
</select>
```

An event listener is added in order to detect a change event for this drop-down list, as shown here:

```
theElement = document.getElementById("fontSize");
theElement.addEventListener('change', fontSizeChanged,
          false);
```

Next, the JavaScript function fontSizeChanged() updates the font size of the rendered text string when users select a different value from the drop-down list, as shown here:

```
function fontSizeChanged(e) {
    target = e.target;
    fontSize = target.value;
    drawText();

}
```

Finally, the main JavaScript function `drawText()` redraws the text string with the newly selected attributes, as shown in Listing 4.7.

FIGURE 4.5 Dynamically modifying a text string in a `<canvas>` slement.

The code and the logic for changing the text color and the input text string is very similar to the preceding code, so it will not be presented here. Figure 4.5 displays an HTML5 `<canvas>` element with a text string that you can dynamically modify by selecting different values in the various drop-down lists.

COPYING CANVAS WITH THE `toDataURL()` METHOD

HTML5 `Canvas` allows you to copy an HTML5 `<canvas>` element to an HTML `<img>` element or to another HTML5 `<canvas>` element. Listing 4.8 displays the contents of `CopyCanvas1.html`, which illustrates how to use the `toDataURL()` method in order to copy the contents of an HTML5 `<canvas>` element to an HTML `<img>` element.

Listing 4.8 `CopyCanvas1.html`

```
<!DOCTYPE html>
<html lang="en">
```

```
<head>
 <script type="text/javascript">
  var canvas, canvas1, ctx, myImage, imageElement;
  var maxW=0, maxH=0, deltaX=40, deltaY=40;
  var canvasW=0, canvasH=0;

  function init() {
    canvas = document.getElementById("myCanvas");

    if(canvas.getContext) {
        ctx = canvas.getContext("2d");
        canvasW = canvas.width;
        canvasH = canvas.height;
        maxW    = canvas.width + 200;
        maxH    = canvas.height + 200;

        drawCanvas();
    }
  }

  function shrinkCanvas() {
    canvasW -= deltaX;
    canvasH -= deltaY;

    if(canvasW < deltaX) {
        canvasW = deltaX;
    }

    if(canvasH < deltaY) {
        canvasH = deltaY;
    }
```

```
    canvas.width  = canvasW;

    canvas.height = canvasH;

  //canvas.style = "width:"+canvasW+"px;
height:"+canvasH+"px";

    drawCanvas();

}


function expandCanvas() {

  canvasW += deltaX;

  canvasH += deltaY;

  if(canvasW > maxW) {

    canvasW = maxW;

  }


  if(canvasH > maxH) {

    canvasH = maxH;

  }


    canvas.width  = canvasW;

    canvas.height = canvasH;

    drawCanvas();

}


function drawCanvas() {

    // clear the canvas before drawing new set of
            rectangles

    ctx.clearRect(0, 0, canvas.width, canvas.height);
```

```
        // render yellow, red, and blue rectangles
        ctx.beginPath();
        ctx.fillStyle="yellow";
        ctx.rect(10,10,canvasW,canvasH);
        ctx.fill();

        ctx.beginPath();
        ctx.fillStyle="red";
        ctx.rect(50,50,100,100);
        ctx.fill();

        ctx.beginPath();
        ctx.fillStyle="blue";
        ctx.rect(160,50,100,100);
        ctx.fill();
    }

    function copyImage() {
        canvas1 = document.getElementById("myCanvas");

        if(canvas1.getContext) {
            ctx = canvas1.getContext("2d");
            myImage = canvas1.toDataURL("image/png");
        }

        imageElement = document.getElementById("myImage");
        imageElement.src = myImage;
    }
    </script>
</head>
```

```
<body onload="init()" bgcolor="#CCC" >
  <div>
    <button onclick="expandCanvas()">Expand Canvas</button>
    <button onclick="shrinkCanvas()">Shrink Canvas</button>
    <button onclick="copyImage()">Copy Image</button>
  </div>

  <div>
    <canvas id="myCanvas" width="300" height="300" ></canvas>
    <img id="myImage">
  </div>
</body>
</html>
```

Listing 4.8 contains a JavaScript `draw()` method that renders a white, red, and blue rectangle in an HTML5 `<canvas>` element when the HTML page is launched. This HTML5 `<canvas>` element is copied into the `<img>` element when users click on the button at the top of the screen. The key idea is to invoke the `toDataURL()` method in order to get a reference to the `<canvas>` element as a PNG file, and then set the `src` attribute of the `<img>` element equal to this reference, as shown here:

```
if(canvas1.getContext) {
  ctx = canvas1.getContext("2d");
  myImage = canvas1.toDataURL("image/png");
}

imageElement = document.getElementById("MyImage");
imageElement.src = myImage;
```

Figure 4.6 displays an HTML5 <canvas> element on the left that is copied to an <img> element on the right.

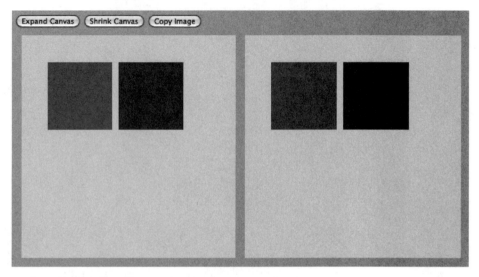

FIGURE 4.6 A copy of an HTML5 <canvas> element.

SUMMARY

This chapter gave you an introduction to HTML5 Canvas graphics, and you learned how to render some basic shapes using colors and gradients. You learned about some new APIs and also how to render new 2D shapes. Specifically, you learned how to:

- use the fillRect() method
- use startPath() and closePath() methods
- use moveTo(), lineTo(), and drawText() methods
- draw rectangles with basic color patterns
- use line segments to create rectangles with gradient-line effects

- render a `Canvas` element with a CSS3-based background
- dynamically update the attributes of a text string on a Canvas element
- copy a `Canvas` element programmatically

Now that you understand how to create basic 2D shapes, you're ready to learn how to create HTML5 `Canvas`-based linear and radial gradients and how to apply them to 2D shapes, all of which is covered in Chapter 5.

2D SHAPES WITH LINEAR AND RADIAL GRADIENTS

H TML5 Canvas supports linear gradients and radial gradients that enable you to create rich and appealing visual effects when you apply them to 2D shapes. Compared to the custom gradient effects (using a JavaScript array containing colors) that are created programmatically in Chapter 1, "Introduction to CSS3," you will find that it's much easier to use the built-in support for gradients in HTML5 Canvas. The code samples in this chapter involve basic 2D shapes so that you can focus on understanding the details of linear and radial gradients in HTML5 Canvas.

Many code samples in this chapter contain a mixture of CSS3-based gradients and HTML5 Canvas-based gradients because this combination of gradients can create a more attractive visual experience. In addition, the HTML pages often contain a clickable Redraw button that renders a new image, superimposed on the previous image, when users click on the Redraw button. Because each newly generated image is rendered with a small offset from the previous image, users can easily create a rich composite effect. If you prefer, you can also modify the HTML pages so that the <canvas> element is refreshed every time a new image is rendered, simply uncomment one line of code. Please note that the code for some of the CSS3 stylesheets in this chapter are not presented when they are similar to other stylesheets, but the source code is available on the DVD for this book. Furthermore, the Canvas-based chapters contain additional CSS3 stylesheets also on the DVD that you can use as alternatives to the CSS3 stylesheets that are referenced in the code samples in this chapter.

The first part of this chapter contains examples of rendering 2D shapes with linear gradients and radial gradients in HTML5 Canvas. You can immediately use those gradients samples to enhance the code samples from Chapter 4, "Rendering Basic 2D Shapes in HTML5 Canvas," and observe the much-improved visual effects. The second part of this chapter shows you how to render JPG files on HTML5 <canvas> elements, and also how to apply CSS3-based animation effects to those JPG files. The last part of this chapter shows you how to manipulate the pixel values of JPG files programmatically to create inverted visual effects. You will also learn techniques for making more subtle modifications to pixel values, which will give you a better programmatic understanding of the techniques that are used in image manipulation tools.

This chapter introduces two HTML5 Canvas Application Programming Interfaces (APIs): createLinearGradient() and the createRadialGradient() methods for creating linear and radial gradients, respectively. These two APIs are simple to use and as you will see, they can create very compelling visual effects when you apply them to 2D shapes.

HTML5 CANVAS LINEAR GRADIENTS

HTML5 Canvas provides two primary types of color gradients: linear gradients and radial gradients. Linear color gradients can be further subdivided into three types: horizontal linear gradients, vertical linear gradients, and diagonal linear gradients. A linear gradient is defined in terms of addColorStop elements, each of which contains a decimal (between 0 and 1) and a hexadecimal value that represents a color. For example, if you define a linear gradient with an initial color of #FF0000 (the hexadecimal value for red) and a final color of #000000 (the hexadecimal value for black), then the resultant color gradient will range (in a linear fashion) from red to black. Note that the terms *linear gradient* and *linear color gradient* are used interchangeably in this book.

Horizontal, Vertical, and Diagonal Linear Gradients

As you learned in the introduction of this chapter, HTML5 Canvas supports the method createLinearGradient(), which you can use to programmatically create linear gradients. The HTML5 page LGradRectangles1.html in Listing 5.1 demonstrates how to render a set of rectangles with horizontal, vertical, and diagonal linear gradients.

Listing 5.1 references the CSS3 stylesheet `HoverAnimation1.css`, which applies CSS3 keyframe-based 2D animation to the first HTML5 `<canvas>` element when users hover over this element with their mouse. Listing 5.1 also references the CSS3 stylesheet `HoverAnimation2.css`, which acts in a similar fashion; however, this stylesheet applies CSS3 3D animation effects to the second HTML5 `<canvas>` element in Listing 5.1. Because the animation techniques in these stylesheets are discussed in Chapter 2, "CSS3 2D/3D Animation and CSS Frameworks," we will omit them from this chapter, but the entire source code is available on the DVD.

Listing 5.1 `LGradRectangles1.html`

```html
<!DOCTYPE html>
<html lang="en">
   <head>
       <meta charset="utf-8">
       <title>Canvas Linear Gradient Rectangles</title>
       <link href="HoverAnimation1.css" rel="stylesheet"
             type="text/css">
       <link href="HoverAnimation2.css" rel="stylesheet"
             type="text/css">

   <style>
     input {
       width:350px;
       font-size:24px;
       background-color:#f00;

     }
   </style>

   <script type="text/javascript"><!--
     window.addEventListener('load', function () {
```

```
var elem = document.getElementById('myCanvas');
if (!elem || !elem.getContext) {
  return;
}

var context = elem.getContext('2d');
if (!context) {
  return;
}

var elem2 = document.getElementById('myCanvas2');
if (!elem2 || !elem2.getContext) {
  return;
}

var context2 = elem2.getContext('2d');
if (!context2) {
  return;
}

var basePointX = 0;
var basePointY = 0;
var currentX   = 0;
var currentY   = 0;
var rectWidth  = 200;
var rectHeight = 200;
var clickCount = 0;
var gradient1;
```

```
redrawCanvas = function() {
    // clear the canvas before drawing new set of
        rectangles
    //context.clearRect(0, 0, elem.width, elem.
        height);
    //context2.clearRect(0, 0, elem.width, elem.
        height);

    // upper left rectangle: horizontal linear
        gradient
    currentX = basePointX;
    currentY = basePointY;

    gradient1 = context.createLinearGradient
                (currentX, currentY,
                 currentX+rectWidth,
                 currentY+0*rectHeight);

    gradient1.addColorStop(0, '#f00');
    gradient1.addColorStop(1, '#00f');
    context.fillStyle = gradient1;
    context.fillRect(currentX, currentY,

                     rectWidth, rectHeight);

    // upper right rectangle: vertical linear
        gradient
    currentX = basePointX+rectWidth;
    currentY = basePointY;

    gradient1 = context.createLinearGradient
                (currentX, currentY,
                 current X+0*rectWidth,
                 currentY+rectHeight);
```

```
gradient1.addColorStop(0, '#ff0');

gradient1.addColorStop(1, '#00f');

context.fillStyle = gradient1;

context.fillRect(currentX, currentY,
              rectWidth, rectHeight);


// render the lower rectangles in the second
        <canvas> element
// lower left rectangle: diagonal linear
        gradient
currentX = basePointX;

currentY = basePointY;

//currentY = basePointY+rectHeight;


gradient1 = context2.createLinearGradient
           (currentX, currentY,
            currentX+rectWidth,
            currentY+rectHeight);


gradient1.addColorStop(0,   '#f00');

gradient1.addColorStop(0.5,'#0f0');

gradient1.addColorStop(1,   '#00f');

context2.fillStyle = gradient1;

context2.fillRect(currentX, currentY,
              rectWidth, rectHeight);


// lower right rectangle: diagonal linear
        gradient
currentX = basePointX+rectWidth;

currentY = basePointY;

//currentY = basePointY+rectHeight;
```

```
gradient1 = context2.createLinearGradient
          (currentX+rectWidth, currentY,
          currentX+0*rectWidth,
          currentY+rectHeight);


gradient1.addColorStop(0,  '#fff');

gradient1.addColorStop(0.3,'#000');

gradient1.addColorStop(0.6,'#ff0');

gradient1.addColorStop(1,  '#f00');

context2.fillStyle = gradient1;

context2.fillRect(currentX, currentY,
             rectWidth, rectHeight);


++clickCount;

basePointX += 4;

basePointY += 2;

}


// render linear gradient rectangles
redrawCanvas();
}, false);
// --></script>
</head>


<body>
  <div>
    <canvas id="myCanvas" width="600" height="250">
          No support for Canvas
```

```
            alt="Rendering linear gradient rectangles.">
    </canvas>
    </div>


    <div>
      <canvas id="myCanvas2" width="600" height="250">
            No support for Canvas

            alt="Rendering linear gradient rectangles.">
      </canvas>
    </div>


    <div>
      <input type="button" onclick="redrawCanvas();
            return false"

            value="Redraw the Rectangles" />
    </div>
  </body>
</html>
```

Listing 5.1 renders four rectangles with linear gradient shading. The linear gradients have two, three, or four invocations of the `addColor-Stop()` method, using various combinations of colors (expressed in hexadecimal form) so that you can see some of the gradient effects that are possible. Experiment with different values for the color stop definitions to see how their values change the appearance of the rendered rectangles.

Figure 5.1 renders a set of rectangles with three types of linear gradient shading.

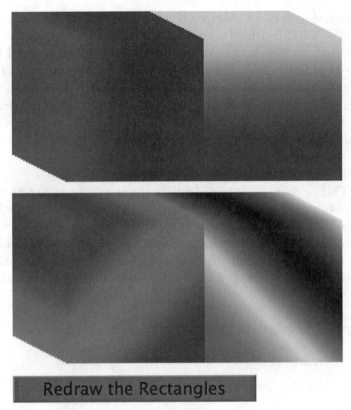

FIGURE 5.1 Rectangles with HTML5 Canvas linear gradients.

RADIAL COLOR GRADIENTS

A radial color gradient is the second type of HTML5 `Canvas`-based color gradient, and you can define a radial color gradient via the `creat-eRadialGradient()` method, using the `addColorStop()` method to add color values. A radial color gradient can be compared to the ripple effect that is created when you drop a stone in a pond, where each ripple has a color that changes in a gradient fashion. Each ripple corresponds to a color stop element. For example, if you define a radial gradient with a start color of #FF0000 (which is red) and an end color of #000000 (which is black), then the resultant color gradient will range—in a radial fashion—from red to black. Radial gradients can also contain multiple start-/stop-color combinations. The point to keep in mind is that radial gradients change colors in a *linear* fashion, but the rendered colors are drawn in an expanding *radial* fashion. Note that the terms *radial gradient* and *radial color gradient* are used interchangeably in this book.

Rendering 2D Shapes with Radial Gradients

HTML5 Canvas provides the createRadialGradient() method to programmatically create linear gradients. Listing 5.2 displays the contents of the HTML page RGradRectangles1.html, which demonstrates how to use radial gradients in order to render a rectangular grid of rectangles. Note that Listing 5.2 also references the CSS3 stylesheet HoverAnimation1.css, whose entire source code is available on the DVD.

Listing 5.2 RGradRectangles1.html

```
<!DOCTYPE html>
<html lang="en">
 <head>
  <meta charset="utf-8">
  <title>Canvas Radial Gradient Rectangles</title>
  <link href="HoverAnimation1.css" rel="stylesheet"
        type="text/css">

  <style>
    input {
      width:300px;
      font-size:24px;
      background-color:#f00;
    }
  </style>
```

```
<script type="text/javascript"><!--
  window.addEventListener('load', function () {
    var elem = document.getElementById('myCanvas');
    if (!elem || !elem.getContext) {
      return;
    }

    var context = elem.getContext('2d');
    if (!context) {
      return;
    }

    var basePointX = 10;
    var basePointY = 10;
    var currentX   = 0;
    var currentY   = 0;
    var rectWidth  = 200;
    var rectHeight = 200;
    var clickCount = 0;
    var gradient1;

    redrawCanvas = function() {
        // clear the canvas before drawing new set of
              rectangles
        //context.clearRect(0, 0, elem.width, elem.
              height);

        // upper left rectangle
        currentX = basePointX;
        currentY = basePointY;
```

```
gradient1 = context.createRadialGradient
          (currentX, currentY,
           0,currentX+rectWidth,
           currentY+rectHeight, rectWidth);

gradient1.addColorStop(0, '#f00');

gradient1.addColorStop(1, '#00f');

context.fillStyle = gradient1;

context.fillRect(currentX, currentY,
          rectWidth, rectHeight);

// upper right rectangle

currentX = basePointX+rectWidth;

currentY = basePointY;

gradient1 = context.createRadialGradient
          (currentX, currentY,
           0,currentX+rectWidth,
           currentY+rectHeight,rectWidth);

gradient1.addColorStop(0, '#ff0');

gradient1.addColorStop(1, '#00f');

context.fillStyle = gradient1;

context.fillRect(currentX, currentY,
          rectWidth, rectHeight);

// lower left rectangle

currentX = basePointX;

currentY = basePointY+rectHeight;

gradient1 = context.createRadialGradient
          (currentX,currentY,
           0,currentX+rectWidth,
           currentY+rectHeight,rectWidth);
```

2D Shapes with Linear and Radial Gradients • **193**

```
gradient1.addColorStop(0,  '#f00');

gradient1.addColorStop(0.5,'#0f0');


gradient1.addColorStop(1,  '#00f');

context.fillStyle = gradient1;

context.fillRect(currentX, currentY,
                 rectWidth, rectHeight);


// lower right rectangle

currentX = basePointX+rectWidth;

currentY = basePointY+rectHeight;


gradient1 = context.createRadialGradient
             (currentX,currentY,
              0,currentX+rectWidth,
              currentY+rectHeight,rectWidth);


gradient1.addColorStop(0,  '#fff');

gradient1.addColorStop(0.3,'#000');

gradient1.addColorStop(0.6,'#ff0');

gradient1.addColorStop(1,  '#f00');

context.fillStyle = gradient1;

context.fillRect(currentX, currentY,
                 rectWidth, rectHeight);


++clickCount;

basePointX += 2;

basePointY += 2;
}
```

```
        // render a set of rectangles
        redrawCanvas();
    }, false);
    // --></script>
</head>

<body>
  <div>
    <canvas id="myCanvas" width="600" height="500">
            No support for Canvas

            alt="Rendering radial gradient rectangles.">
    </canvas>
  </div>

  <div>
    <input type="button" onclick="redrawCanvas();
            return false"

            value="Redraw the Rectangles" />
  </div>
 </body>
</html>
```

Listing 5.2 is similar to Listing 5.1, except for the use of a radial gradient (instead of a linear gradient) that ranges in a radial fashion from blue to red. The method `addColorStop()` is invoked four times in order to add four stop values to the radial gradient. Figure 5.2 renders a set of nested rectangles with radial gradient shading. You can define a radial gradient with an `id` attribute that can then be referenced as the gradient definition for other HTML5 `Canvas` elements in the same HTML5 page. The next example shows you how to specify this color definition for a set of rectangles.

FIGURE 5.2 A nested set of rectangles with radial gradient shading.

RENDERING GRADIENT 2D SHAPES WITH SINE WAVES

So far you have seen how to render sets of rectangles using linear gradients and radial gradients, and you can use other functions as a "path" for the rectangles.

Listing 5.3 shows you how to create another interesting effect by moving a set of rectangles (rendered with linear gradients and radial gradients) along the path of a sine wave.

Listing 5.3 LRGradSineWaveRectangles1.html

```
<!DOCTYPE html>
<html lang="en">
 <head>
  <meta charset="utf-8">
  <title>Canvas Sine Wave Rectangles</title>
  <link href="HoverAnimation1.css" rel="stylesheet"
        type="text/css">

  <style>
    input {
      width:300px;
      font-size:24px;
      background-color:#f00;
    }
  </style>

  <script type="text/javascript"><!--
    window.addEventListener('load', function () {
      var elem = document.getElementById('myCanvas');
      if (!elem || !elem.getContext) {
        return;
      }

      var context = elem.getContext('2d');
      if (!context) {
        return;
      }
```

```
var basePointX  = 20;
var basePointY  = 200;
var currentX    = 0;
var currentY    = 0;
var clickCount  = 0;
var amplitude   = 180;
var phaseOffset = 180;
var offsetX     = 0;
var offsetY     = 0;
var rectCount   = 380;
var rectWidth   = 50;
var rectHeight  = 80;
var gradient1;


redrawCanvas = function() {
    // clear the canvas before drawing new set of
            rectangles
    //context.clearRect(0, 0, elem.width, elem.
            height);


    // first sine wave...
    for(var r=0; r<rectCount; r++) {
        offsetX  = r;
        offsetY  = amplitude*Math.sin(r*Math.
            PI/180);
        currentX = basePointX+offsetX;
        currentY = basePointY+offsetY;
```

```
        context.beginPath();

        gradient1 = context.createLinearGradient(
                currentX,currentY,
                currentX+rectWidth,
                currentY+rectHeight);

        gradient1.addColorStop(0, '#f00');

        gradient1.addColorStop(1, '#00f');

        context.fillStyle = gradient1;

        context.fillRect(currentX, currentY,
                    rectWidth, rectHeight);

        context.stroke();
    }


    // second sine wave...
    for(var r=0; r<rectCount; r++) {
        offsetX  = r;
        offsetY  = amplitude*Math.
                sin((r+phaseOffset)*Math.PI/180);
        currentX = basePointX+offsetX;
        currentY = basePointY+offsetY;


        context.beginPath();

        gradient1 = context.createRadialGradient(
                currentX,currentY,
                0,currentX+rectWidth,
                currentY+rectHeight,rectWidth);

        gradient1.addColorStop(0,  '#fff');

        gradient1.addColorStop(0.3,'#000');

        gradient1.addColorStop(0.7,'#ff0');

        gradient1.addColorStop(1,  '#f00');
```

```
        context.fillStyle = gradient1;

        context.fillRect(currentX, currentY,
                       rectWidth, rectHeight);
        context.stroke();

      }

      ++clickCount;
      basePointX += 4;
      basePointY += 2;
    }

    // render rectangles
    redrawCanvas();
  }, false);
  // --></script>
</head>

<body>
  <div>
    <canvas id="myCanvas" width="700" height="520">
            No support for Canvas

        alt="Rendering gradient rectangles on a
            sine wave.">
    </canvas>
  </div>

  <div>
    <input type="button" onclick="redrawCanvas();
            return false"

        value="Redraw the Rectangles" />
```

```
   </div>
  </body>
</html>
```

The code in Listing 5.3 is straightforward, and the linear gradients and radial gradients are the same as Listing 5.2. The key difference is that the rectangles follow the path of a sine curve instead of being translated along the path of a diagonal line. Figure 5.3 renders a set of translated rectangles with linear and radial gradient shading.

Redraw the Rectangles

FIGURE 5.3 A set of gradient rectangles following a sine wave.

RENDERING IMAGES ON CANVAS WITH CSS3 SELECTORS

HTML5 Canvas supports the rendering of JPG files, and you can also apply CSS selectors to the HTML5 <canvas> element. Listing 5.4 displays the contents of Image1.html and Listing 5.5 displays the contents of Image1.css whose selectors are applied to the HTML5 <canvas> element in Listing 5.4.

Listing 5.4 `Image1.html`

```html
<!DOCTYPE html>
<html lang="en">
<head>
  <meta charset="utf-8" />
  <title>Rendering JPG Files in HTML5 Canvas</title>
  <link href="Image1.css" rel="stylesheet" type="text/css">
  <link href="HoverAnimation1.css" rel="stylesheet"
        type="text/css">

<script type="text/javascript">
  function renderJPG() {
      // Get the canvas element
      var elem = document.getElementById('myCanvas');
      if (!elem || !elem.getContext) {
        return;
      }

      // Get the canvas 2d context
      var context = elem.getContext('2d');
      if (!context) {
        return;
      }

      var basePointX  = 30;
      var basePointY  = 30;
      var rectWidth   = 150;
      var rectHeight  = 200;
      var borderX     = rectWidth/2;
```

```
var borderY     = rectHeight/2;

var offsetX     = 20;

var offsetY     = 20;

var gradientR   = 60;


// Create a radial gradient:

var rGradient = context.createRadialGradient(
                basePointX+rectWidth/2,
                basePointY+rectWidth/2,
                gradientR,
                basePointX+rectWidth/2,
                basePointY+rectWidth/2,
                3*gradientR);


rGradient.addColorStop(0,    '#FF0000');

rGradient.addColorStop(0.5, '#FFFF00');

rGradient.addColorStop(1,    '#000044');


// rectangular background with radial gradient:
context.fillStyle = rGradient;
context.fillRect(basePointX-offsetX,
                basePointY-offsetY,
                rectWidth+borderX+2*offsetX,
                rectHeight+borderY+2*offsetY);


// Load the JPG

var myImage = new Image();

myImage.onload = function() {

   context.drawImage(myImage,
                     basePointX,
                     basePointY,
                     rectWidth,
                     rectHeight);

}
```

```
        myImage.src = "Lauriel.jpeg";
    }
  </script>

  <style type="text/css">
    canvas {
      border: 0px solid #888;
      background: #FFF;
    }
  </style>
</head>

<body onload="renderJPG();">
  <header>
    <h1>Hover Over the Image</h1>
  </header>

  <div>
   <canvas id="myCanvas" width="500" height="300">
        No support for Canvas
   </canvas>
  </div>
</body>
</html>
```

Listing 5.4 contains JavaScript code that creates a radial gradient rGradient with three color stops. Next, a rectangle is rendered by using the radial gradient that is referenced by the variable rGradient, followed by a section of code that renders the JPG file Lauriel.jpeg. The inline CSS code in the <style> element renders a white background with a zero-width border (so it's invisible), but you can modify this CSS code to produce additional effects. The <body> element contains the onload attribute whose value is `renderJPG()`, which is a JavaScript function that renders the JPG file inside the HTML5 `<canvas>` element.

Listing 5.5 `Image1.css`

```
#myCanvas:hover {

width:  500px;

height: 300px;

position: relative; top: 0px; left: 0px;


background-color:white;

background-image:
  -webkit-radial-gradient(red 4px, transparent 24px),
  -webkit-repeating-radial-gradient (red 1px, green 4px,
        yellow 8px, blue 12px, transparent 16px,
        red 20px, blue 24px, transparent 28px,
        transparent 32px);

background-size: 30px 30px, 40px 40px;

background-position: 0 0;

}


#myCanvas {

width:  500px;

height: 300px;

position: relative; top: 0px; left: 0px;


background-color:white;

background-image:
  -webkit-radial-gradient(black 4px, transparent 20px),
  -webkit-repeating-radial-gradient(blue 1px,
        yellow 4px, blue 8px, red 12px,
```

```
           transparent 16px, red 20px, blue 24px,
           transparent 28px, transparent 32px);
background-size: 30px 30px, 40px 40px;
background-position: 0 0;
}
```

The first selector in Listing 5.5 displays another pattern, based on a different radial gradient, when users hover with their mouse over the HTML5 <canvas> element. The second selector in Listing 5.5 renders a colorful pattern, also based on a radial gradient, as a background rectangle for the HTML5 <canvas> element.

Incidentally, HTML5 Canvas also supports a clip() method that enables you to "clip" JPG files in various ways. Moreover, you can perform compositing effects, and you can even manipulate the individual pixels of a JPG file. Search the Internet for articles that describe the technical details of these effects. Figure 5.4 displays a JPG file with two radial gradient background effects.

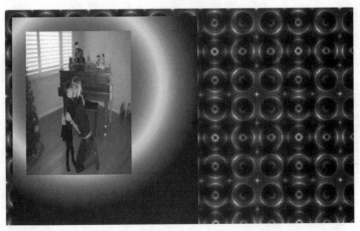

FIGURE 5.4 A JPG file in HTML5 Canvas.

RENDERING A CUBE IN HTML5 CANVAS
WITH CSS3 ANIMATION

In the previous chapter you saw an example of applying CSS3-based linear and radial gradients to an HTML5 <canvas> element. The code sample in this section illustrates how to use CSS3 selectors to create 2D animation effects with HTML5 Canvas. Note that in Chapter 7, "Applying Canvas Transforms to 2D Shapes," you will learn how to create HTML5 Canvas-based 2D animation effects (i.e., animation effects without CSS3). Listing 5.6 displays the contents of LRGradCube1CSS3.css, which illustrates how to rotate a cube using CSS3 selectors.

Listing 5.6 LRGradCube1CSS3.css

```
@-webkit-keyframes rotate2D {
    0% {
        -webkit-transform: translate(0px,0px) rotate
                           (-60deg) skew(-15deg,0);
    }
    50% {
        -webkit-transform: translate(50px,50px) rotate
                           (-120deg) skew(-25deg,0);
    }
    75% {
        -webkit-transform: translate(100px,100px) rotate
                           (-180deg) skew(-15deg,0);
    }
    100% {
        -webkit-transform: translate(0px,0px) rotate(0)
                           skew(0,0);
    }
}
```

```
#myCanvas:hover {

  -webkit-animation-name: rotate2D;

  -webkit-animation-duration: 6s;

}
```

The #rotate2D selector in Listing 5.6 creates an animation effect using the CSS3 functions translate(), rotate(), and skew(). When users hover over the HTML5 <canvas> element, the #myCanvas:hover selector in Listing 5.6 creates a CSS3-based 2D animation effect that rotates the HTML5 Canvas-based cube.

The HTML5 page LRGRadCube1CSS3.html contains JavaScript code for rendering a rectangle (the front face) and two parallelograms (the top face and right face), and applying linear gradients to these three shapes. Because this code is very simple and no new concepts are introduced, the code is omitted from this chapter; see the DVD for the entire code listing. Figure 5.5 displays a cube that is rotated using the CSS3 selectors in the CSS3 stylesheet LRGradCube1CSS3.css.

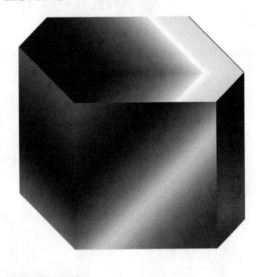

Hover Over the Cube

Redraw the Cube

FIGURE 5.5 Rotating an HTML5 Canvas cube using CSS3 selectors.

ACCESSING AND UPDATING CANVAS PIXELS

HTML5 Canvas provides read/write access to the pixels in an HTML5 <canvas> element, which are represented from left to right and from top to bottom. Each pixel has a four-tuple (R, G, B, A) that represents the red, green, blue, and alpha values of the pixel. Listing 5.7 displays the contents of UpdatePixels1.html, which illustrates how to modify the (R, G, B) value of each pixel using randomly generated numbers between 0 and 255.

Listing 5.7 UpdatePixels1.html

```
<!DOCTYPE html>
<html lang="en">
  <head>
   <meta charset="utf-8">
   <title>Modifying pixels via ImageData</title>

   <script type="text/javascript"><!--
     var basePointX = 0, basePointY = 0;
     var rVal = 255, gVal = 0, bVal = 0, aVal = 255;
     var imageData, width = 500, height = 350, xPos = 0,
        yPos = 0;

    updatePixels = function() {
      // Get the canvas element
      var elem = document.getElementById('myCanvas');
      if (!elem || !elem.getContext) {
        return;
      }

      // Get the canvas 2d context
      var context = elem.getContext('2d');
```

```
if (!context || !context.putImageData) {
  return;
}


// Browser support for createImageData varies
if (context.createImageData) {
  imageData = context.createImageData
            (width, height);
} else if (context.getImageData) {
  imageData = context.getImageData(basePointX,
            basePointX, width, height);
} else {
  imageData = {'width' : width, 'height' : height,
            'data' : new Array(width*height*4)};
}


rVal = Math.floor(255*Math.random());
gVal = Math.floor(255*Math.random());
bVal = Math.floor(255*Math.random());


// Loop through the pixels
var pixels = imageData.data;
for(var i=0, n=pixels.length; i<n; i+=4) {
  pixels[i+0] = rVal; // red channel
  pixels[i+1] = gVal; // green channel
  pixels[i+2] = bVal; // blue channel
  pixels[i+3] = aVal; // alpha channel
}
```

```
        // Render the ImageData object
        context.putImageData(imageData, xPos, yPos);

    }


  window.addEventListener('load', updatePixels, false);
    // --></script>
  </head>

<body>
  <div><canvas id="myCanvas" width="800"
        height="400">Your browser does not have
  support for Canvas.
  </div>

  <div>
    <input type="button" onclick="updatePixels();
        return false" value="Update My Color" />
  </div>
  </body>
</html>
```

Listing 5.7 contains the usual initialization of variables, followed by conditional logic that initializes a rectangular image area called image-Data, as shown here:

```
  if (context.createImageData) {
    imageData = context.createImageData(width,
            height);
  } else if (context.getImageData) {
    imageData = context.getImageData(basePointX,
            basePointX, width, height);
```

```
   } else {
      imageData = {'width' : width, 'height' : height,
                   'data' : new Array(width*height*4)};

   }
```

Next, the variable `pixels` is a reference to the pixel values of the image area, as shown here:

```
   var pixels = imageData.data;
```

The randomly generated values for red, green, and blue for the pixels in the image area are calculated here:

```
rVal = Math.floor(255*Math.random());

gVal = Math.floor(255*Math.random());

bVal = Math.floor(255*Math.random());
```

The key point to remember is that four bytes are required for each pixel in order to store the red, green, blue, and opacity values for that pixel. Consequently, the loop variable must be incremented by four in order to access the (R,G,B,A) values for the next pixel, as shown here:

```
   for(var i=0, n=pixels.length; i<n; i+=4) {
      pixels[i+0] = rVal; // red channel
      pixels[i+1] = gVal; // green channel
      pixels[i+2] = bVal; // blue channel
      pixels[i+3] = aVal; // alpha channel

   }
```

Figure 5.6 displays an image whose pixel values are updated with randomly generated values (between 0 and 255).

Update My Color

FIGURE 5.6 A randomly updated set of pixels of an image region.

CREATING PIXEL-BASED LINEAR GRADIENT EFFECTS

Now that you know how to modify `canvas` pixels, we can do something more interesting with the pixel values. As an example, Listing 5.8 displays the contents of the HTML page `UpdatePixels2.html`, which illustrates how to modify the (R, G, B) value of each pixel in order to create linear gradients.

Listing 5.8 `UpdatePixels2.html`

```
<!DOCTYPE html>

<html lang="en">

<head>

    <meta charset="utf-8">

    <title>Modifying pixels via ImageData</title>
```

```
<script type="text/javascript"><!--
  var basePointX = 0, basePointY = 0, clickCount = 0;
  var rVal = 255, gVal = 0, bVal = 0, aVal = 255, i = 0;
  var imageData = false,width = 400,height = 400,
      xPos = 0,yPos = 0;


updatePixels = function() {
 // Get the canvas element
 var elem = document.getElementById('myCanvas');
 if (!elem || !elem.getContext) {
   return;
 }


 // Get the canvas 2d context
 var context = elem.getContext('2d');
 if (!context || !context.putImageData) {
   return;
 }


 // Browser support for createImageData varies
 if (context.createImageData) {
   imageData = context.createImageData
               (width, height);
 } else if (context.getImageData) {
   imageData = context.getImageData (basePointX,
               basePointX, width, height);
 } else {
```

```
    imageData = { 'width' : width, 'height' : height,
                  'data' : new Array(width*height*4) };
}

// Loop over each row and each column (times 4)
var pixels = imageData.data;
for(var row=0; row<height; row++) {
  for(var col=0; col<4*width; col+=4) {
    rVal = 0; gVal = 0; bVal = 0;

    if(col >= 4*row) {
        if(clickCount % 3 == 0) {
            rVal = col*255/(4*width);
        } else if(clickCount % 3 == 1) {
            rVal = col*255/(4*width);
            gVal = col*255/(4*width);
        } else {
            bVal = col*255/(4*width);
        }
    } else {
      rVal = 255-col*255/(4*width);
    }

    i = row*4*width+col;
    pixels[i+0] = rVal; // red channel
    pixels[i+1] = gVal; // green channel
    pixels[i+2] = bVal; // blue channel
    pixels[i+3] = aVal; // alpha channel
  }
}
```

```
    // Render the ImageData object
    context.putImageData(imageData, xPos, yPos);
    ++clickCount;
}


window.addEventListener('load', updatePixels, false);
// --></script>
</head>


<body>
    <div><canvas id="myCanvas" width="800"
         height="400">Your browser does not have
    support for Canvas.
    </div>


    <div>
      <input type="button" onclick="updatePixels();
             return false" value="Update the Gradient" />
    </div>
 </body>
</html>
```

Listing 5.8 contains the same initialization code as Listing 5.6, but this time the pixels in the image area are processed as a set of rows and columns in a nested loop, as shown here:

```
    // Loop over each row and each column (times 4)
    var pixels = imageData.data;
    for(var row=0; row<height; row++) {
       for(var col=0; col<4*width; col+=4) {
         rVal = 0; gVal = 0; bVal = 0;
```

The next part of Listing 5.8 generates a linear gradient for the upper triangular portion of the image area, where the gradient is calculated as a shade of red, yellow, or blue based on some conditional logic. The linear gradient for the lower triangular portion of the image area is a shade of red. The code that performs these calculations is shown here:

```
if(col >= 4*row) {
    if(clickCount % 3 == 0) {
        rVal = col*255/(4*width);
    } else if(clickCount % 3 == 1) {
        rVal = col*255/(4*width);
        gVal = col*255/(4*width);
    } else {
        bVal = col*255/(4*width);
    }
} else {
    rVal = 255-col*255/(4*width);
}
```

Finally, the current pixel is updated with the computed values for red, green, blue, and opacity:

```
i = row*4*width+col;
pixels[i+0] = rVal; // red channel
pixels[i+1] = gVal; // green channel
pixels[i+2] = bVal; // blue channel
pixels[i+3] = aVal; // alpha channel
```

Although the logic is slightly more complicated, you can also programmatically create radial gradient effects, which is, perhaps, an interesting way for you to test your understanding of how to manipulate pixel values. Figure 5.7 displays an image whose pixel values are updated with randomly generated values (between 0 and 255).

Update the Gradient

FIGURE 5.7 Creating a linear gradient for an image area.

INVERTING JPG FILES ON CANVAS

A previous code sample showed you how to render JPG files, and the example in this section shows you how to manipulate the pixels of a JPG so that you can create an inverted image. In this example you will modify pixel values, so you need to launch the HTML page from a Web server (launching this page from Finder® operating system software or from Windows Explorer will generate a security violation). For example, you can launch Mongoose (a very lightweight file server) from the directory that contains the HTML page in Listing 5.9. You can download Mongoose (for Windows or for MacBook) from this Web site: *http://code.google.com/p/ mongoose/downloads/list*. Download the appropriate distribution for your machine. If you have a Windows machine, open a command shell and launch the Mongoose binary file. If you have a MacBook, navigate to the directory where you downloaded the Mongoose distribution and perform these steps:

1. uncompress the distribution

2. run the `make` command

3. type `mongoose` from the command line

Then, open a browser session and navigate to *http://localhost:8080* and you will see a file listing for the directory where you launched Mongoose. Click on the HTML page `InvertedImage1.html` and you will see three images. Listing 5.9 displays the contents of `InvertedImage1.html`, which shows you how to render the inversion ("negative") of a JPG file.

Listing 5.9 `InvertedImage1.html`

```
<!DOCTYPE html>
<html lang="en">
<head>
   <meta charset="utf-8">
   <title>Canvas Image Inversion Example</title>
      var rVal=0, gVal=0, bVal=0, clickCount=0, factor=3;

   // FIRST IMAGE (ORIGINAL)
   function regularImage() {
     // Get the canvas element(for the original image)
     var elemOri = document.getElementById ('myCanvasOri');
     if (!elemOri || !elemOri.getContext) {
       return;
     }
```

```
    // Get the canvas 2d context
    var ctx = elemOri.getContext('2d');
    if(!ctx||!ctx.getImageData||!ctx.
      putImageData||!ctx.drawImage) {

      return;

    }


    // create a new image (original)
    var imageOri = new Image();


    imageOri.addEventListener('load', function () {
      var xPos = 0, yPos = 0;
      // render the image on the canvas
      ctx.drawImage(imageOri, xPos, yPos);
    }, false);


    imageOri.src = 'Laurie1.jpeg';
}


// SECOND IMAGE (INVERTED)
function invertedImage() {
    // Get the canvas element (for the inverted image)
    var elemInv = document.getElementById
                ('myCanvasInv');
    if (!elemInv || !elemInv.getContext) {

      return;

    }
```

```
// Get the canvas 2d context
var ctx2 = elemInv.getContext('2d');
if(!ctx2||!ctx2.getImageData||!ctx2.
   putImageData||!ctx2.drawImage) {
   return;
}

// create a new image (inverted)
var imageInv = new Image();

// Render the image and invert its colors
imageInv.addEventListener('load', function () {
   var xPos = 0, yPos = 0;

   // render the image on the canvas
   ctx2.drawImage(this, xPos, yPos);

   // get the pixels
   var imageData = ctx2.getImageData(xPos, yPos,
                    this.width, this.height);
   var pixels = imageData.data;

   // Invert the color of the pixels
   for(var i = 0, n = pixels.length; i < n; i += 4) {
      pixels[i+0] = 255-pixels[i+0]; // red
      pixels[i+1] = 255-pixels[i+1]; // green
      pixels[i+2] = 255-pixels[i+2]; // blue
   }
```

```
    // render the inverted object
    ctx2.putImageData(imageData, xPos, yPos);
  }, false);

  imageInv.src = 'Laurie1.jpeg';
}


// THIRD IMAGE (MODIFIABLE)
function modifyImage() {
  // Get the canvas element (for the inverted image)
  var elemMod = document.getElementById
                ('myCanvasMod');
  if (!elemMod || !elemMod.getContext) {
    return;
  }

  // Get the canvas 2d context
  var ctx3 = elemMod.getContext('2d');
  if(!ctx3||!ctx3.getImageData||!ctx3.putImageData||!
    ctx3.drawImage) {
    return;
  }

  // create a new image (inverted)
  var imageMod = new Image();

  // Render the image and update its colors
  imageMod.addEventListener('load', function () {
    var xPos = 0, yPos = 0, weighted = 0;
```

```
            // render the image on the canvas
            ctx3.drawImage(this, xPos, yPos);

            // get the pixels
            var imageData = ctx3.getImageData(xPos, yPos,
                             this.width, this.height);
            var pixels = imageData.data;

        // update pixel colors
        if(clickCount++ == 0) {
        for(var i = 0, n = pixels.length; i < n; i += 4) {
                weighted = pixels[i]*.3 + pixels[i+1]*.59 +
                             pixels[i+2]*.11;
                pixels[i+0] = weighted;
                pixels[i+1] = weighted;
                pixels[i+2] = weighted;
            }
        }
        else {
           for(var i = 0, n = pixels.length; i < n; i += 4) {
                rVal = (pixels[i+0]+factor*clickCount)%255;
                gVal = (pixels[i+1]+factor*clickCount)%255;
                bVal = (pixels[i+2]+factor*clickCount)%255;

                pixels[i+0] = rVal;
                pixels[i+1] = gVal;
                pixels[i+2] = bVal;
            }
        }
```

```
        // render the updated object
        ctx3.putImageData(imageData, xPos, yPos);
      }, false);

      imageMod.src = 'Laurie1.jpeg';
    }

    displayImages = function () {
      regularImage();
      invertedImage();
      modifyImage();
    }

    window.addEventListener('load', displayImages);

    displayImages();
  // --></script>
</head>

<body>
 <div>
   <canvas id="myCanvasOri" width="250" height="250">
          No support for Canvas.
     <img src="Laurie1.jpeg" alt="Image inversion">
   </canvas>

   <canvas id="myCanvasInv" width="250" height="250">
          No support for Canvas.
     <img src="Laurie1.jpeg" alt="Image inversion">
   </canvas>
```

```
<canvas id="myCanvasMod" width="250" height="250">
        No support for Canvas.
    <img src="Laurie1.jpeg" alt="Image inversion">
</canvas>
</div>

<input type="button" onclick="modifyImage();
        return false"
    value="Update Right-Most Image" />
</body>
</html>
```

Listing 5.9 contains the usual initialization code, and also three adjacent image areas. The key difference lies in the manner in which the new values are calculated for red, green, and blue for each pixel.

The first image is not modified, so no processing is performed on its pixels. The second image is inverted, so the value of each byte is replaced by performing a subtraction from 255, as shown here:

```
for(var i = 0, n = pixels.length; i < n; i += 4) {
    pixels[i+0] = 255-pixels[i+0]; // red
    pixels[i+1] = 255-pixels[i+1]; // green
    pixels[i+2] = 255-pixels[i+2]; // blue
}
```

The pixels in the third image are updated each time that users click on the Redraw button, and the new values for red, green, and blue for each pixel are calculated by incrementing the current values by the value factor*clickCount and then applying the modulus function (the % symbol) to ensure that the new values do not exceed a maximum value of 255, as shown here:

```
for(var i = 0, n = pixels.length; i < n; i += 4) {
    rVal = (pixels[i+0]+factor*clickCount)%255;
    gVal = (pixels[i+1]+factor*clickCount)%255;
    bVal = (pixels[i+2]+factor*clickCount)%255;
```

```
pixels[i+0] = rVal;

pixels[i+1] = gVal;

pixels[i+2] = bVal;
}
```

You can use the code that modifies the third image in Listing 5.9 as a starting point for writing code that creates a "smoothing" effect on JPG files. The key idea involves setting the (R,G,B) values of every fourth pixel equal to the average of the 3 × 3 "matrix" of pixels that surround each pixel. You need to take into account the fact that the pixels on the four borders do not have a 3 × 3 matrix around them, so your algorithm must handle those pixels accordingly.

After you finish writing the code that uses a 3 × 3 matrix around each pixel, you can also enhance this technique by working with a 5 × 5 matrix of pixels that "surrounds" each pixel. Experiment with these techniques, and apply them to a JPG file as well as its inverted image, which you learned how to create in this section.

There are other interesting effects that you can create with HTML5 Canvas. For example, you can create zoom and panning effects with images, and also embed audio files and video files in HTML5 Canvas. Due to space constraints, these topics are not covered in this text, but an Internet search can lead you to online articles that show you how to implement such functionality. Figure 5.8 displays an image whose pixel values are updated with randomly generated values (between 0 and 255) each time that users click on the Redraw button.

Update Right-Most Image

FIGURE 5.8 Creating inverted and dynamically updatable images.

SUMMARY

This chapter gave you an introduction to HTML5 `Canvas` linear gradients and radial gradients, and you learned how to render various 2D shapes using gradients. You saw code samples that illustrated how to use various HTML5 `Canvas` APIs, and learned to:

- use the `createLinearGradient()` method
- use the `createRadialGradient()` method
- draw 2D shapes with linear gradients and radial gradients
- render cubes with linear gradients and radial gradients
- render gradient rectangles that follow the path of a sine wave
- update the contents of bitmaps to create inverted images

The next chapter shows you how to render oval shapes, as well as quadratic and cubic Bezier curves, with linear and radial gradients.

CHAPTER 6

CIRCLES, ARCS, AND BEZIER CURVES

Now that you understand how to render basic 2D shapes with linear gradients and radial gradients, you can render other types of 2D shapes, such as Bezier curves, in HTML5 `Canvas` using some of the techniques that you saw in previous chapters. This chapter starts with code samples for rendering circles and circular arcs using linear and radial gradients, followed by examples of rendering quadratic and cubic Bezier curves. You will also learn how to specify radial color gradients in order to create basic 3D effects, which are based on the manner in which you specify the stop-color/offset combinations. In particular, you will see radial color gradients combined with circles in order to create pseudospheres.

As you will see, this chapter also contains many code samples that provide a Redraw button that, when it's clicked, renders a new graphics image with a slight offset to overlay the previously rendered graphics image, thereby creating a richer visual effect. In addition, when users hover over the HTML5 `<canvas>` element, it triggers a CSS3-based 2D or 3D animation effect (using a selector that is defined in a separate CSS3 stylesheet).

In previous chapters of this book, you saw how to create linear and radial gradient effects based on CSS3 selectors as well as HTML5 `Canvas` Application Programming Interfaces (APIs). Fortunately, you can use both types of gradient effects in the same HTML5 page, and in this chapter you will see code samples that use both techniques. When you finish reading this chapter, you will have learned how to use the following HTML5 `Canvas` APIs for rendering circles and Bezier curves: `arc()`, `arcTo()`, `quadraticCurveTo()`, and `bezierCurveTo()` methods.

RENDERING CIRCLES WITH LINEAR GRADIENTS

As you already know, HTML5 `Canvas` supports the `createLinearGradient()` method for linear gradients, along with the `addColorStop()` method for adding one or more color stops to your linear gradient. The example in this section shows you how to render circles using the HTML5 `Canvas` `arc()` method, and its syntax looks like this:

```
arc(centerX,centerY,radius,startAngle,endAngle,
    counterClockwise);
```

The start angle and end angle are measured in radians; `PI` radians equals `180` degrees. Fortunately, JavaScript provides the constant `Math.PI` whose value equals `PI` radians. Thus, you can render a circle at the point (`150,150`) with a radius `100` with the following code snippet (you can use either `true` or `false` for the final parameter):

```
arc(150, 150, 100, 0, 2*Math.PI, true);
```

The HTML5 page `LGradCircles1.html` in Listing 6.1 renders a rectangular grid of circles and circular arcs with linear gradient shading.

Listing 6.1 `LGradCircles1.html`

```
<!DOCTYPE html>

<html lang="en">

 <head>

  <meta charset="utf-8">

  <title>Canvas Drawing Gradient Arcs</title>

  <link href="CSS3Background2.css" rel="stylesheet"
        type="text/css">

  <link href="HoverAnimation1.css" rel="stylesheet"
        type="text/css">
```

```
<style>
  input {
    width:300px;
    font-size:24px;
    background-color:#f00;
  }
</style>

<script type="text/javascript"><!--
  window.addEventListener('load', function () {
    var elem = document.getElementById('myCanvas');
    if (!elem || !elem.getContext) {
      return;
    }

    var context = elem.getContext('2d');
    if (!context) {
      return;
    }

    var radius      = 100;
    var basePointX = radius/2;
    var basePointY = radius/2;
    var currentX    = 0;
    var currentY    = 0;
    var rowCount     = 4;
    var colCount     = 4;
    var colorIndex = 0;
```

```
var clickCount = 0;

var arcAngle   = 0;

var gradient1;


redrawCanvas = function() {

  // clear the canvas before drawing
         new set of arcs

  //context.clearRect(0, 0, elem.width, elem.
         height);


  for(var row=0; row<rowCount; row++) {

    for(var col=0; col<colCount; col++) {

      currentX = basePointX+col*radius;

      currentY = basePointY+row*radius;


      context.beginPath();

      gradient1 = context.createLinearGradient(
               currentX,currentY,
               currentX+radius,
               currentY+radius);


      if((row+col) % 2 == 0) {

        gradient1.addColorStop(0,  '#f00');

        gradient1.addColorStop(0.5,'#0f0');

        gradient1.addColorStop(1,  '#00f');

      }


      else {

        gradient1.addColorStop(0,  '#880');

        gradient1.addColorStop(0.5,'#0f0');

        gradient1.addColorStop(1,  '#00f');

      }
```

```
            context.fillStyle = gradient1;
            colorIndex = (row+col)%4;
            arcAngle   = Math.PI*2*(1+colorIndex)/4;

            context.arc(currentX, currentY,
                       radius/2, 0, arcAngle, true);
            context.fill();
         }
      }

      ++clickCount;
      basePointX += 8;
      basePointY += 3;
   }

   // render a cube
   redrawCanvas();
   }, false);
   // --></script>
</head>

<body>
  <div>
   <canvas id="myCanvas" width="800" height="450">
         No support for Canvas
         alt="Rendering gradient circles.">
   </canvas>
  </div>
```

```
<div>
  <input type="button" onclick="redrawCanvas();
         return false"
         value="Redraw the Circles" />
  </div>
 </body>
</html>
```

Listing 6.1 uses 0 as the start angle and `Math.PI*2*(1+color Index)/4` as the end angle for each circular arc, along with a linear gradient that is based on the current position of the circular arc, as shown here:

```
gradient1 = context.createLinearGradient(
            currentX,currentY,
            currentX+radius,currentY+radius);
```

Listing 6.1 also uses some conditional logic to determine which set of color stops to add to each linear gradient, along with a calculation of the start angle and end angle (as you saw in previous chapters). Figure 6.1 depicts a rectangular grid of circles and circular arcs that are rendered with linear gradient shading.

FIGURE 6.1 A set of circular arcs with linear gradients.

RENDERING CIRCLES WITH RADIAL GRADIENTS

HTML5 `Canvas` provides the method `createRadialGradient()` in order to create a radial gradient, after which you can invoke the `addColorStop()` method to add one or more color stops to your radial gradient. Listing 6.2 displays the contents of the HTML5 page `RGradCircles1.html`, which illustrates how to render a rectangular grid of circles with radial gradient shading.

Listing 6.2 `RGradCircles1.html`

```
<!DOCTYPE html>
<html lang="en">
 <head>
  <meta charset="utf-8">
  <title>Canvas Drawing Circles </title>
  <link href="CSS3Background11.css" rel="stylesheet"
        type="text/css">
  <link href="HoverAnimation2.css" rel="stylesheet"
        type="text/css">

  <style>
    input {
      width:300px;
      font-size:24px;
      background-color:#f00;
    }
  </style>

  <script type="text/javascript"><!--
    window.addEventListener('load', function () {
      var elem = document.getElementById('myCanvas');
      if (!elem || !elem.getContext) {
        return;
      }
```

```
var context = elem.getContext('2d');
if (!context) {
  return;
}

var radius     = 100;
var basePointX = 0;
var basePointY = 0;
var currentX   = 0;
var currentY   = 0;
var rowCount   = 4;
var colCount   = 4;
var clickCount = 0;
var gradient1;

redrawCanvas = function() {
  // clear the canvas before drawing
        new set of rectangles
  //context.clearRect(0, 0, elem.width, elem.
        height);

  for(var row=0; row<rowCount; row++) {
    for(var col=0; col<colCount; col++) {
      currentX = basePointX+col*radius;
      currentY = basePointY+row*radius;

      context.beginPath();
      gradient1 = context.createRadialGradient(
            currentX,currentY,0,
            currentX+radius,currentY+
            radius,radius);
```

```
       if((row+col) % 2 == 0) {
         gradient1.addColorStop(0,   '#f00');
         gradient1.addColorStop(0.9,'#0f0');
         gradient1.addColorStop(1,   '#f40');
       }

       else {
         gradient1.addColorStop(0,   '#880');
         gradient1.addColorStop(0.9,'#00f');
         gradient1.addColorStop(1,   '#af0');
       }

       context.fillStyle = gradient1;

       context.arc(currentX,currentY,radius, 0,
                  Math.PI*2, true);
                  //radius/2, 0, Math.PI*2, true);
       context.fill();
      }
    }

   ++clickCount;
   basePointX += 8;
   basePointY += 2;
  }

 // render a cube
 redrawCanvas();
}, false);
// --></script>
</head>
```

```
<body>

  <div>

    <canvas id="myCanvas" width="800" height="450">
          No support for Canvas

          alt="Rendering radial gradient circles.">

    </canvas>

  </div>


  <div>

    <input type="button" onclick="redrawCanvas();
          return false"

          value="Redraw the Circles" />

  </div>

 </body>

</html>
```

Listing 6.2 contains a nested loop for rendering a rectangular array of circles that are rendered with radial gradient shading by means of the `createRadialGradient()` method. The `addStopColor()` is invoked three times, and based on some conditional logic, different color values are specified. Unlike linear gradients, the intermediate colors are calculated by means of a radial gradient in order to achieve the effect that you see in Figure 6.2.

In order to understand how the intermediate colors are determined, imagine the effect dropping a stone into a pond and "capturing" the set of concentric circles. The colors of these circles are based on the set of colors that you obtain by a color gradient that starts from yellow (#FFFF00) and ends with black (#000000). Here's an interesting point about radial color gradients: if you drew a line segment with one end point coinciding with the center of all the concentric circles, that line segment would be colored with a *linear* gradient. Experiment with the values for the parameters in the `createRadialGradient()` method (and also the stop colors) to create different shapes and patterns. Figure 6.2 depicts a rectangular grid of ovals with radial gradient shading.

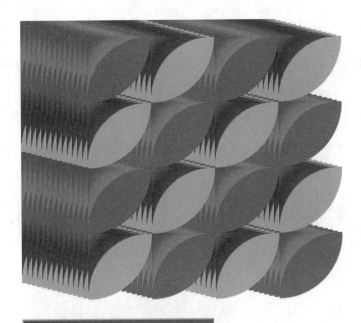

Redraw the Circles

FIGURE 6.2 Circles with a radial gradient.

VARIABLE ARCS AND LINEAR GRADIENTS

The previous code samples are straightforward examples of rendering circles and circular arcs. HTML5 Canvas also provides the arc() method, which enables you to create nice visual effects. Listing 6.3 displays the contents of ShiftArcs1.html, which illustrates how to render a set of circular arcs with linear gradients, producing the well-known Moiret effect.

Listing 6.3 ShiftArcs1.html

```
<!DOCTYPE html>
<html lang="en">
 <head>
  <meta charset="utf-8">
  <title>Canvas Drawing Line Segments</title>
```

```
<link href="CSS3Background1.css" rel="stylesheet"
    type="text/css">

<link href="HoverAnimation1.css" rel="stylesheet"
    type="text/css">

<style>
  input {
    width:300px;
    font-size:24px;
    background-color:#f00;
  }
</style>

<script type="text/javascript"><!--
  window.addEventListener('load', function () {
    var elem = document.getElementById('myCanvas');
    if (!elem || !elem.getContext) {
      return;
    }

    var context = elem.getContext('2d');
    if (!context) {
      return;
    }

    var basePointX  = 20;
    var basePointY  = 60;
    var currentX    = 0;
    var currentY    = 0;
    var startAngle  = 0;
```

```
var endAngle    = 0;
var arcCount    = 200;
var clickCount  = 0;
var radius      = 200;
var lineWidth   = 1;

redrawCanvas = function() {
    // clear the canvas before drawing new set of
            rectangles
    //context.clearRect(0, 0, elem.width, elem.
            height);

    for(var r=0; r<arcCount; r+=2) {
      context.strokeStyle = "#000";
      context.lineWidth   = lineWidth;

      gradient1 = context.createLinearGradient(
              currentX,currentY,
              currentX+radius,
              currentY+radius);

      gradient1.addColorStop(0, '#f00');
      gradient1.addColorStop(1, '#00f');
      context.fillStyle = gradient1;

      currentX = basePointX+r;
      currentY = basePointY+r;
      startAngle = (360-r/2)*Math.PI/180;
      endAngle   = (360+r/2)*Math.PI/180;

      context.beginPath();
      context.moveTo(currentX, currentY);
```

```
                    context.arc(currentX, currentY, radius,
                               startAngle, endAngle, false);

                    context.closePath();
                    context.stroke();
                    context.fill();
                }

                ++clickCount;
                basePointX += 4;
                basePointY += 2;
            }

            // render a cube
            redrawCanvas();
        }, false);
        // --></script>
    </head>

    <body>
      <div>
        <canvas id="myCanvas" width="800" height="520">
               No support for Canvas
               alt="Rendering gradient arcs.">
        </canvas>
      </div>

      <div>
        <input type="button" onclick="redrawCanvas();
               return false"
               value="Redraw the Arcs" />
      </div>
    </body>
</html>
```

The code for linear gradients in Listing 6.3 is similar to previous examples in this chapter. The key idea for creating the visual effect in this example is actually based on the following four lines of code:

```
currentX = basePointX+r;

currentY = basePointY+r;

startAngle = (360-r/2)*Math.PI/180;

endAngle   = (360+r/2)*Math.PI/180;
```

The preceding code block is inside a loop, and each arc has a start angle that is calculated by subtracting the value r/2 from 360, whereas the end angle is calculated by adding the value r/2 to 360, where r is the loop variable. Figure 6.3 displays a set of arcs with gradient shading that create a Moiret effect.

Redraw the Arcs

FIGURE 6.3 Circular arcs with linear gradient shading.

ROUNDED RECTANGLES WITH LINEAR GRADIENTS

The previous example used the `arc()` method to create rounded rectangles. The example in this section uses the `arcTo()` method and linear gradients to render a set of rectangles with rounded corners with an interesting visual effect. The syntax of the `arcTo()` API looks like this:

```
arcTo(startX, startY, endX, endY, radius);
```

The `arcTo()` method enables you to create a rounded corner (whose radius equals the value of `radius`) for a rectangle. You can use a combination of the `Canvas` methods `moveTo()`, `lineTo()`, and `arcTo()` in order to render a rectangle with rounded corners having different radii. Listing 6.4 displays the contents of `LGradRRectangles1.html`, which illustrates how to render a set of rounded rectangles with linear gradient shading.

Listing 6.4 `LGradRRectangles1.html`

```html
<!DOCTYPE html>
<html lang="en">
 <head>
  <meta charset="utf-8">
  <title>Canvas Drawing Rounded Rectangles</title>

  <link href="CSS3Background5.css" rel="stylesheet"
        type="text/css">
  <link href="HoverAnimation2.css" rel="stylesheet"
        type="text/css">

  <style>
    input {
      width:300px;
      font-size:24px;
      background-color:#f00;
    }
  </style>
```

```
<script type="text/javascript"><!--
  window.addEventListener('load', function () {
    var elem = document.getElementById('myCanvas');
    if (!elem || !elem.getContext) {
      return;
    }

    var context = elem.getContext('2d');
    if (!context) {
      return;
    }

    var basePointX = 80;
    var basePointY = 10;
    var currentX   = 0;
    var currentY   = 0;
    var radiusX    = 80;
    var radiusY    = 80;
    var rectCount  = 180;
    var rectWidth  = 280;
    var rectHeight = 280;
    var clickCount = 0;

    redrawCanvas = function() {
      // clear the canvas before drawing new set of
            rectangles
      //context.clearRect(0, 0, elem.width, elem.
            height);
```

```
for(var r=0; r<rectCount; r++) {

  currentX = basePointX+2*r;

  currentY = basePointY+1*r;


  gradient1 = context.createLinearGradient(
              currentX,currentY,
              currentX+rectWidth,
              currentY+rectHeight);


  if(r % 2 == 0) {

    gradient1.addColorStop(0, '#f00');

    gradient1.addColorStop(1, '#00f');

  } else {

    gradient1.addColorStop(0,  '#0f0');

    gradient1.addColorStop(0.5,'#f00');

    gradient1.addColorStop(1,  '#00f');

  }


  context.fillStyle = gradient1;


  context.beginPath();

  context.moveTo(currentX, currentY);

  context.arcTo(currentX+1*radiusX,
              currentY+0*radiusY,
              currentX+1*radiusX,
              currentY+2*radiusY,r);


  context.arcTo(currentX+1*radiusX,
  currentY+2*radiusY,
  currentX-1*radiusX,
  currentY+2*radiusY,r);


  context.arcTo(currentX-1*radiusX,
              currentY+2*radiusY,
              currentX-1*radiusX,
              currentY+0*radiusY,r);
```

```
            context.arcTo(currentX-1*radiusX,
                    currentY+0*radiusY,
                    currentX+1*radiusX,
                    currentY+0*radiusY,r);

            context.closePath();

            context.fill();
        }

        ++clickCount;

        basePointX += 4;

        basePointY += 2;

    }

    // render a set of rectangles
    redrawCanvas();

}, false);
// --></script>
</head>

<body>
  <div>
    <canvas id="myCanvas" width="900" height="550">
            No support for Canvas

            alt="Rendering Gradient Rounded Rectangles.">
  </canvas>
  </div>

  <div>
  <input type="button" onclick="redrawCanvas(); return false"
            value="Redraw the Rectangles" />
  </div>
</body>
</html>
```

Listing 6.4 contains a loop that constructs rectangles with four rounded corners using code such as the following:

```
context.arcTo(currentX+1*radiusX,
             currentY+0*radiusY,
             currentX+1*radiusX,
             currentY+2*radiusY,r);
```

The preceding code fragment renders an arc in the upper-right corner of each rectangle. Notice that the value of the loop variable r specifies the radius of the rendered arc. Because the value of r varies from 0 to rect-Count, the initial rectangle is transformed into a circle. This example uses a linear gradient and also conditional logic to determine the specific values in the addColorStop() invocations. Figure 6.4 depicts a set of rounded rectangles with linear gradient shading.

Redraw the Rectangles

FIGURE 6.4 Rounded rectangles with gradient shading.

CREATING 3D EFFECTS WITH CIRCLES

The radial gradient method `createRadialGradient()` enables you to specify the center of the radial pattern, which is convenient when you want to render circles with 3D-like visual effects. Listing 6.5 displays the contents of the HTML5 page `RGrad3DCircles1.html`, which illustrates how to render circles with radial gradients in order to create a three-dimensional effect. The complete source code for the two CSS3 stylesheets `CSS3Background8.css` and `HoverAnimation2.css` that are referenced in Listing 6.5 are available on the DVD for this book.

Listing 6.5 `RGrad3DCircles1.html`

```
<!DOCTYPE html>
<html lang="en">
 <head>
  <meta charset="utf-8">
  <title>Canvas Radial Gradient 3D Circles</title>

  <link href="CSS3Background8.css" rel="stylesheet"
      type="text/css">
  <link href="HoverAnimation2.css" rel="stylesheet"
      type="text/css">

  <style>
    input {
      width:300px;
      font-size:24px;
      background-color:#f00;
    }
  </style>
```

```
<script type="text/javascript"><!--
  window.addEventListener('load', function () {
    var elem = document.getElementById('myCanvas');
    if (!elem || !elem.getContext) {
      return;
    }

    var context = elem.getContext('2d');
    if (!context) {
      return;
    }

    var currentX    = 120;
    var currentY    = 120;
    var currentX2   = currentX;
    var currentY2   = currentY;
    var lineWidth   = 8;
    var factorX     = 0.3;
    var factorY     = 0.3;
    var radius      = 100;
    var clickCount  = 0;
    var gradient1;

    redrawCanvas = function() {
        // clear the canvas before drawing new set of
                rectangles
        //context.clearRect(0, 0, elem.width, elem.
                height);

        currentX = currentX2;
        currentY = currentY2;
```

```
// upper-left 3D circle
gradient1 = context.createRadialGradient(
          currentX,currentY,0,
          currentX-factorX*radius,
          currentY-factorY*radius, radius);

gradient1.addColorStop(0,  '#FFF');

gradient1.addColorStop(0.4,'#00A');

gradient1.addColorStop(1,  '#006');

context.beginPath();

context.lineWidth = lineWidth;

context.fillStyle = "#F00";

context.fillStyle = gradient1;

context.arc(currentX,currentY,
       radius, 0, Math.PI*2, true);

context.fill();

// upper-right 3D circle
currentX = currentX2 + 2*radius;

gradient1 = context.createRadialGradient(
          currentX,currentY,0,
          currentX+factorX*radius,
          currentY+factorY*radius,radius);

gradient1.addColorStop(0,  '#FFF');

gradient1.addColorStop(0.4,'#0A0');

gradient1.addColorStop(1,  '#060');

context.beginPath();

context.lineWidth = lineWidth;

context.fillStyle = gradient1;
```

```
context.arc(currentX,currentY,
         radius, 0, Math.PI*2, true);

context.fill();

// lower-right 3D circle

currentY = currentY2 + 2*radius;

gradient1 = context.createRadialGradient(
            currentX,currentY,0,
            currentX+factorX*radius,
            currentY+factorY*radius,radius);

gradient1.addColorStop(0,  '#FFF');

gradient1.addColorStop(0.4,'#AA0');

gradient1.addColorStop(1,  '#660');

context.beginPath();

context.lineWidth = lineWidth;

context.fillStyle = gradient1;

context.arc(currentX,currentY,
         radius, 0, Math.PI*2, true);

context.fill();

// lower-left 3D circle

currentX = currentX - 2*radius;

gradient1 = context.createRadialGradient(
            currentX,currentY,0,
            currentX+factorX*radius,
            currentY+factorY*radius,radius);

gradient1.addColorStop(0,  '#FFF');

gradient1.addColorStop(0.4,'#A00');

gradient1.addColorStop(1,  '#600');
```

```
            context.beginPath();

            context.lineWidth = lineWidth;

            context.fillStyle = gradient1;

            context.arc(currentX,currentY,
                    radius, 0, Math.PI*2, true);

            context.fill();

            ++clickCount;

            ++currentX2;

            ++currentY2;

        }

        // render 3D circles
        redrawCanvas();
    }, false);
    // --></script>
</head>

<body>
  <div>
    <canvas id="myCanvas" width="800" height="500">
            No support for Canvas

            alt="Rendering gradient circles.">
    </canvas>
  </div>

  <div>
    <input type="button" onclick="redrawCanvas();
            return false"

            value="Redraw the Circles" />
```

```
    </div>
  </body>
</html>
```

Listing 6.5 contains the definitions of four circles using red, green, yellow, and blue as the base colors for rendering those circles with a three-dimensional effect. The key idea is to create a radial gradient and then add three color stops with the addColorStop() method. For example, the upper-left circle is created with a bluish 3D effect by adding white, medium blue, and dark blue stop colors, as shown here:

```
gradient1.addColorStop(0,  '#FFF');
gradient1.addColorStop(0.4,'#00A');
gradient1.addColorStop(1,  '#006');
```

The other three circles use a similar technique to create 3D effects using green, yellow, and blue. Figure 6.5 renders four circles using radial gradient shading to create a 3D effect.

Redraw the Circles

FIGURE 6.5 Four circles with a 3D effect.

BEZIER CURVES

HTML5 `Canvas` provides support for both quadratic Bezier curves and cubic Bezier curves. The code samples in this section show you how to generate interesting combinations of Bezier curves using various types of gradient shading.

Bezier curves are named after Pierre Bezier (1910–1999), who promoted (but did not invent) them during the 1970s. Bezier curves can represent many nonlinear shapes, and they can be found in interesting applications, including Adobe PostScript® language for the representation of fonts. An Internet search will yield many Web pages with interesting demonstrations, some of which also require additional plug-ins. You'll find computer programs written in C and Java, some of which are interactive, that demonstrate Bezier curves.

Cubic Bezier curves have two end points and two control points, whereas quadratic Bezier curves have two end points and a single control point. The x-coordinate and y-coordinate of a cubic Bezier curve can be represented as a parameterized cubic equation whose coefficients are derived from the control points and the end points. The beauty of HTML5 `Canvas` is that it allows you to define both quadratic and cubic Bezier curves via the Path element without having to delve into the mathematical underpinnings of Bezier curves. If you are interested in learning the specific details, you can browse the Web, where you'll find books and plenty of articles that cover this interesting topic.

BEZIER CURVES WITH LINEAR AND RADIAL GRADIENTS

HTML5 `Canvas` provides the `quadraticCurveTo()` method for creating quadratic Bezier curves, which requires one control point and an end point. HTML5 `Canvas` also provides the `bezierCurveTo()` method for creating cubic Bezier curves, which requires you to specify two control points and an end point. The context point (which is the location of the most recently rendered point) is used as the start point for quadratic Bezier curves and cubic Bezier curves.

The syntax for the HTML5 `CanvasquadraticCurveTo()` method looks like this:

```
quadraticCurveTo(controlX,controlY, endX, endY);
```

The syntax for the HTML5 `Canvas bezierCurveTo()` method looks like this:

```
bezierCurveTo(controlX1,controlY1,controlX2,controlY2,
            endX,endY);
```

The HTML5 page `LRGradQCBezier1.html` in Listing 6.6 demonstrates how to render a quadratic Bezier curve with linear gradient shading and a cubic Bezier curve with radial gradient shading. The source code for `CSS3Background4.css` and `HoverAnimation1.css` that are referenced in Listing 6.6 are available on the DVD.

Listing 6.6 LRGradQCBezier1.html

```
<!DOCTYPE html>

<html lang="en">
 <head>
  <meta charset="utf-8">
  <title>Canvas Quadratic and Cubic Bezier Curves</
        title>
  <link href="CSS3Background4.css" rel="stylesheet"
        type="text/css">
  <link href="HoverAnimation1.css" rel="stylesheet"
        type="text/css">

  <style>
    input {
      width:300px;
      font-size:24px;
      background-color:#f00;
    }
  </style>
```

```
<script type="text/javascript"><!--
  window.addEventListener('load', function () {
    var elem = document.getElementById('myCanvas');
    if (!elem || !elem.getContext) {
      return;
    }

    var context = elem.getContext('2d');
    if (!context) {
      return;
    }

    var basePointX  = 0;
    var basePointY  = 250;
    var currentX    = basePointX;
    var currentY    = basePointY;
    var currentX2   = currentX;
    var currentY2   = currentY;
    var lineWidth   = 8;
    var rectWidth   = 50;
    var rectHeight  = 40;
    var clickCount  = 0;
    var multiplier  = 5;
    var gradient1;

    redrawCanvas = function() {
        // clear the canvas before drawing new set of
              rectangles
        //context.clearRect(0, 0, elem.width, elem.
              height);
```

```
// DRAW THE CUBIC BEZIER CURVE
currentX = currentX2/2;
currentY = currentY2/2;

gradient1 = context.createRadialGradient(
            currentX,currentY,0, currentX+
            multiplier*rectWidth, currentY+
            multiplier*rectHeight, 3*rectWidth);

gradient1.addColorStop(0,  '#f00');
gradient1.addColorStop(0.2,'#ff0');
gradient1.addColorStop(0.4,'#fff');
gradient1.addColorStop(0.6,'#f00');
gradient1.addColorStop(0.8,'#00f');
gradient1.addColorStop(1,  '#f00');

context.fillStyle = gradient1;
context.fill();

context.beginPath();
context.lineWidth = lineWidth;
context.moveTo(currentX, currentY);

context.bezierCurveTo(
currentX+3*multiplier*rectWidth,
currentY+2*multiplier*rectHeight,
currentX+2*multiplier*rectWidth,
currentY-multiplier*rectHeight,
currentX+100, currentY+300);
context.fill();
```

```
// DRAW THE QUADRATIC BEZIER CURVE
currentX = currentX2/2;
currentY = currentY2/2;

gradient1 = context.createLinearGradient(
          currentX,currentY,
          currentX+multiplier/2*rectWidth,
          currentY+multiplier/2*rectHeight);

gradient1.addColorStop(0,  '#f00');
gradient1.addColorStop(0.3,'#ff0');
gradient1.addColorStop(0.6,'#00f');
gradient1.addColorStop(0.9,'#0f0');
gradient1.addColorStop(1,  '#f00');

context.fillStyle = gradient1;

context.beginPath();
context.lineWidth = lineWidth;
context.moveTo(currentX, currentY);
context.quadraticCurveTo(
currentX+3*multiplier*rectWidth,
currentY+1*multiplier*rectHeight,
currentX+2*multiplier*rectWidth,
currentY-multiplier*rectHeight);

context.fill();

++clickCount;
currentX2 += 10;
++currentY2;
}
```

```
    // render bezier curves
    redrawCanvas();
  }, false);
  // --></script>
</head>

<body>
  <div>
    <canvas id="myCanvas" width="800" height="500">
          No support for Canvas

          alt="Rendering Bezier Curves.">
    </canvas>
  </div>

  <div>
    <input type="button" onclick="redrawCanvas();
          return false"
          value="Redraw Bezier Curves" />
  </div>
</body>
</html>
```

Listing 6.6 initializes some JavaScript variables and then defines the JavaScript function `redrawCanvas()`, which contains code for creating linear gradients that you have seen in previous code samples, so we will omit their details. Notice that the HTML5 Canvas `moveTo()` method is invoked before rendering both quadratic Bezier curves, and that point serves as the initial or "context" point for both curves.

The cubic Bezier curve in Listing 6.6 is rendered with a radial gradient using six color stops, based on several calculated points, as shown here:

```
context.bezierCurveTo(
currentX+3*multiplier*rectWidth,
```

```
currentY+2*multiplier*rectHeight,

currentX+2*multiplier*rectWidth,

currentY-multiplier*rectHeight,

currentX+100, currentY+300);
```

There is nothing special about the manner in which the coordinates of the two control points and the end point are calculated, so feel free to experiment with your own values to create other pleasing visual effects. The next portion of Listing 6.6 renders a quadratic Bezier curve using a linear gradient with five color stops.

Note that when users click on the Redraw button, another cubic and quadratic Bezier curve are drawn, based on the value of the variable clickCount that is incremented each time that users click on the Redraw button. The new curves are superimposed on the previous curves, thereby creating a nice visual effect. If you want to refresh the <canvas> element prior to rendering another pair of Bezier curves, simply uncomment the following line of code:

```
// clear the canvas before drawing new set of
        rectangles
//context.clearRect(0, 0, elem.width, elem.height);
```

Figure 6.6 renders the quadratic and cubic Bezier curves that are defined in Listing 6.6.

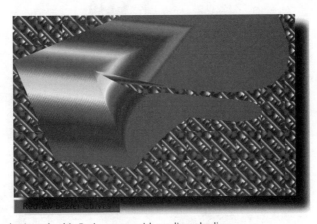

FIGURE 6.6 Quadratic and cubic Bezier curves with gradient shading.

SUMMARY

This chapter showed you how to render circles with 3D effects and different types of Bezier curves using linear and radial gradients. This chapter introduced some new HTML5 `Canvas` APIs and showed you how to render new 2D shapes. You learned how to:

- use the `arc()` and `arcTo()` methods
- use the `quadraticCurveTo()` and `bezierCurveTo()` methods
- draw circles with opacity linear gradients and radial gradients
- render circular arcs with gradients
- render quadratic Bezier curves and cubic Bezier curves
- render 2D shapes that also create the well-known Moiret effect
- apply CSS3-based 3D animation effects to HTML5 `<canvas>` elements

The next chapter shows you how to use the HTML5 `Canvas` transforms `translate()`, `rotate()`, `scale()`, `strokeText()`, and `fillText()`, which (in conjunction with CSS3) enable you to create some very nice visual effects.

CHAPTER 7

APPLYING CANVAS TRANSFORMS TO 2D SHAPES

HTML5 Canvas supports four transforms: translate, scale, rotate, and shear (also called skew) effects. Although you have already seen some examples of Canvas transforms in previous chapters, this chapter consolidates the description of these transforms. You will see how to use them in conjunction with 2D shapes, text strings, and JPG files to create some interesting visual effects.

Recall that Chapters 4, 5, and 6 showed you how to apply CSS3-based linear and radial gradients, 2D animation, and 3D animation effects to HTML5 <canvas> elements. When you've finished this chapter, you will have an understanding of the myriad ways of easily creating HTML5 Canvas transforms and combining them not only with each other, but also with CSS3-based 2D/3D animation effects. They can also be easily combined with color gradients in order to create graphics images that are impossible to achieve with a comparable amount of effort in traditional programming languages. Many of the code samples contain a Redraw button, and each time that users click on this button, a new graphics image is rendered with a slight offset to overlay the previously rendered graphics image, thereby creating a richer visual effect. In addition, when users hover over the HTML5 <canvas> element, it triggers a CSS3-based 2D or 3D animation effect (using a selector that is defined in a separate CSS3 stylesheet).

This chapter introduces the HTML5 `Canvas` Application Programming Interfaces (APIs) `translate()`, `rotate()`, `scale()`, `strokeText()`, and `fillText()`. Although these transforms are simple, you can apply multiple transforms to 2D shapes, which can greatly enhance the visual appeal of your graphics images, especially when you use transforms in conjunction with animation effects.

The `translate()` method is probably the simplest of the HTML5 `Canvas` transforms, which you can use to shift (translate) the contents of an HTML5 `Canvas` shape anywhere in the plane. This method makes for simpler code because you can avoid using hard-coded values to specify location of individual objects. For example, you can define a rectangle whose upper-left vertex is the origin (0,0), and then use the `translate()` method in order to render multiple copies of that rectangle on the screen. This approach is useful when you need to render 2D shapes that can be decomposed into many logical components.

Scaling effects simplify the resizing of 2D shapes that are rendered inside an HTML5 `<canvas>` element. While this functionality is much more difficult to achieve in imperative programming languages, HTML5 `Canvas` provides a `scale()` API that is straightforward and involves simple code. If you combine the `translate()` and `scale()` methods, it's quite easy to render many scaled copies of a graphics image. Rotations and skew effects can also be applied to 2D shapes with simple code fragments.

TRANSLATING 2D SHAPES

HTML5 `Canvas` provides a `translate()` method that enables you to translate (shift) 2D shapes by specifying the (x,y) coordinates of the upper-left corner of the drawing region, and the API looks like this:

```
context.translate(offsetX, offsetY);
```

The `translate()` method is the simplest of the HTML5 `Canvas` transforms, and you can easily create the same effect by using a loop. The HTML5 page `Rect1Translate1.html` in Listing 7.1 demonstrates how to use the `translate()` function in order to translate or shift a set of rectangles.

Listing 7.1 Rect1Translate1.html

```html
<!DOCTYPE html>
<html lang="en">
<head>
  <meta charset="utf-8">
  <title>Canvas Translate Transformation</title>

<link href="CSS32Background3.css" rel="stylesheet"
      type="text/css">
<link href="HoverAnimation2.css" rel="stylesheet"
      type="text/css">

<style>
  input {
    width:300px;
    font-size:24px;
    background-color:#f00;
  }
</style>

<script type="text/javascript"><!--
  window.addEventListener('load', function () {
    var basePointX = 120;
    var basePointY = 120;
    var currentX   = 0;
    var currentY   = 0;
    var offsetX    = 0;
    var offsetY    = 0;
    var rectCount  = 360;
```

```
var rectWidth  = 100;

var rectHeight = 50;

var clickCount = 0;

var radius     = rectWidth;

var gradient1;


var elem = document.getElementById('myCanvas');

if (!elem || !elem.getContext) {

  return;

}


var context = elem.getContext('2d');

if (!context) {

  return;

}


// Load the JPG

var myImage = new Image();

myImage.onload = function() {

 context.drawImage(myImage, basePointX, basePointY,
                3*rectWidth,3*rectHeight);

}


myImage.src = "Laurie1.jpeg";


redrawCanvas = function() {

   // clear the canvas before drawing new set of
          rectangles

   //context.clearRect(0, 0, elem.width, elem.
          height);
```

```
//context.translate(basePointX/2, basePointY/2);
  context.translate(clickCount, clickCount);

  for(var a=0; a<rectCount; a++) {
    context.beginPath();

    offsetX = radius*Math.cos(a*Math.PI/180);
    offsetY = radius*Math.sin(a*Math.PI/180);

    currentX = basePointX+0*offsetX;
    currentY = basePointY+0*offsetY;
  //currentX = basePointX+1*offsetX;
  //currentY = basePointY+1*offsetY;

    gradient1 = context.createLinearGradient(
              currentX,currentY,currentX+
              rectWidth,currentY+rectHeight);

    gradient1.addColorStop(0,   '#f00');
    gradient1.addColorStop(0.5,'#ff0');
    gradient1.addColorStop(1,   '#00f');
    context.fillStyle = gradient1;

    context.translate(offsetX, offsetY);
    context.fillRect(basePointX, basePointY,
    rectWidth, rectHeight);

  //context.fillRect(basePointX+offsetX,
  //                  basePointY+offsetY,
  //                  rectWidth, rectHeight);
```

```
            context.stroke();
            context.translate(-offsetX, -offsetY);
        }

        ++clickCount;
        basePointX += 3;
        ++basePointY;
    }

    // render rectangles
    redrawCanvas();
}, false);
// --></script>
</head>

<body>
  <div>
    <canvas id="myCanvas" width="800" height="500">
              No support for Canvas
          alt="Rendering Gradient Rectangles.">
    </canvas>
  </div>

  <div>
    <input type="button" onclick="redrawCanvas();
              return false"
          value="Redraw the Rectangles" />
  </div>
</body>
</html>
```

Listing 7.1 contains a loop that creates a linear gradient and invokes the `translate()` method before rendering each rectangle with a linear gradient. The key point is that because this method moves the underlying `<canvas>` element, you must return the `<canvas>` element to its previous position after a rectangle is rendered. Therefore the code will look like this:

```
context.translate(offsetX, offsetY);

// draw something here

context.translate(-offsetX, -offsetY);
```

As an alternative, if you remove the `translate` code, and use the commented out code instead of the current code, you can achieve a similar visual effect. Figure 7.1 displays translated rectangles rendered with linear gradient shading.

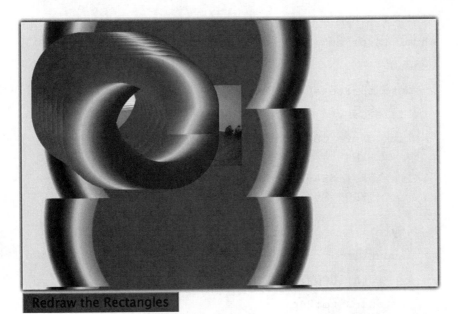

Redraw the Rectangles

FIGURE 7.1 Gradient rectangles with a translate transform.

ROTATING TEXT STRINGS

HTML5 `Canvas` provides a `rotate()` method for rotating 2D shapes that involves specifying an angle (in radians) of rotation, and the API looks like this:

```
context.rotate(angle);
```

Keep in mind that a positive angle involves a clockwise rotation and a negative angle involves a counterclockwise rotation, which is the opposite of other programming languages, such as Java™.

The HTML5 page `TextRotate1.html` in Listing 7.2 demonstrates how to render a set of text strings with a shadow background and a rotate effect. The complete source code for the stylesheets `CSS3Background10.css` and `HoverAnimation2.css` that are referenced in Listing 7.2 are available on the DVD for this book.

Listing 7.2 `TextRotate1.html`

```
<!DOCTYPE html>

<html lang="en">

 <head>

  <meta charset="utf-8">

  <title>Canvas Rotate Text</title>

  <link href="CSS32Background10.css" rel="stylesheet"
        type="text/css">

  <link href="HoverAnimation2.css" rel="stylesheet"
        type="text/css">

  <style>

    input {

      width:300px;

      font-size:24px;

      background-color:#f00;

    }

  </style>
```

```
<script type="text/javascript"><!--
  window.addEventListener('load', function () {
    var lineCount  = 180;
    var lineLength = 400;
    var lineWidth  = 5;
    var basePointX = lineLength/2;
    var basePointY = lineLength/2+20;
    var radius     = lineLength/2;
    var clickCount = 0;
    var lineColor  = "";
    var fillColors = new Array('#f00', '#ff0', '#00f');
    var hexArray   = new Array('0','1','2','3','4',
                               '5','6','7','8','9','a','b','c',
                               'd','e','f');

    var elem = document.getElementById('myCanvas');
    if (!elem || !elem.getContext) {
      return;
    }

    var context = elem.getContext('2d');
    if (!context) {
      return;
    }

    // Load the JPG
    var myImage = new Image();
    myImage.onload = function() {
      context.drawImage(myImage, 10, 10, 200, 200);
    }
```

```
myImage.src = "Laurie1.jpeg";


redrawCanvas = function() {

context.fillStyle = fillColors[clickCount%fillColors.
                    length];

    context.shadowColor   = "rgba(0,0,255,0.3)";

    context.shadowOffsetX = 3;

    context.shadowOffsetY = 3;

    context.shadowBlur    = 2;

    context.lineWidth     = 1;

    context.font          = "Bold 50pt Helvetica";


    // clear the canvas before drawing new set of
           rectangles
    //context.clearRect(0, 0, elem.width, elem.
           height);


    for(var y=0; y<lineCount; y++) {

       lineColor = '#' + hexArray[y%16] + '00';

       context.strokeStyle = lineColor;

       context.lineWidth   = lineWidth;


       offsetX = radius*Math.cos(y*Math.PI/180);

       offsetY = radius*Math.sin(y*Math.PI/180);


       context.rotate(y/10*Math.PI/180);

       context.fillText("Hello World",
                    basePointX+offsetX,
                    basePointY+offsetY);

    }
```

```
        ++clickCount;
        ++basePointX;
        ++basePointY;
    }

    context.drawImage(myImage, 10, 10, 200, 200);

    // render the rotated text
    redrawCanvas();
}, false);
// --></script>
</head>

<body>
    <div>
      <canvas id="myCanvas" width="800" height="450">
              No support for Canvas

           alt="Rendering rotated text.">
      </canvas>
    </div>

    <div>
      <input type="button" onclick="redrawCanvas();
              return false"

           value="Redraw the Rotated Text" />
    </div>
  </body>
</html>
```

Listing 7.2 contains code that you have seen in previous examples in order to create a background shadow effect, followed by a loop that that calculates a new location for the text string "Hello World." The rotating effect uses the loop variable y to calculate a radian value for the rotation angle in this line of code:

```
context.rotate(y/10*Math.PI/180);
```

Figure 7.2 displays text strings with a rotate effect.

FIGURE 7.2 Rotated text strings.

SCALED TEXT

HTML5 Canvas supports the scale() method that enables you to scale text strings and 2D shapes along the horizontal axis, the vertical axis, or both axes, and the API looks like this:

```
context.scale(scaleX, scaleY);
```

The value of scaleX affects the horizontal scaling of a 2D shape. If you set scaleX to a value less than 1, the rendered shape will be compressed (scaled down), whereas setting scaleX to a value greater than

1 will be expanded to create a larger image; if you set scaleX equal to 1, there will be no scaling effect. Similar comments apply to scaleY, which affects the vertical scaling of a 2D shape.

The HTML5 page TextScale1.html in Listing 7.3 demonstrates how to use the HTML5 Canvas scale() method in order to render a set of text strings with a shadow background and a scaling effect. The complete source code for the CSS3 stylesheets CSS3Background11.css and HoverAnimation2.css that are referenced in Listing 7.3 are available on the DVD.

Listing 7.3 TextScale1.html

```
<!DOCTYPE html>
<html lang="en">
 <head>
  <meta charset="utf-8">
  <title>Canvas Scale Text</title>
  <link href="CSS32Background11.css" rel="stylesheet"
        type="text/css">
  <link href="HoverAnimation1.css" rel="stylesheet"
        type="text/css">

  <style>
    input {
      width:300px;
      font-size:24px;
      background-color:#f00;
    }
  </style>

  <script type="text/javascript"><!--
    window.addEventListener('load', function () {
      var lineCount  = 159;
```

```
var lineLength = 400;

var lineWidth  = 5;

var sign       = 1;

var factor     = 3;

var basePointX = 250;

var basePointY = 200;

var radius     = lineLength/2;

var clickCount = 0;

var lineColor  = "";

var hexArray   = new Array('0','1','2','3','4',
                           '5','6','7','8','9','a','b','c',
                           'd','e','f');


var elem = document.getElementById('myCanvas');

if (!elem || !elem.getContext) {

  return;

}


var context = elem.getContext('2d');

if (!context) {

  return;

}


// Load the JPG

var myImage = new Image();

myImage.onload = function() {

  context.drawImage(myImage, 10, 10, 300, 200);

}


myImage.src = "Laurie1.jpeg";
```

```
context.shadowColor   = "rgba(0,0,128,0.5)";

context.shadowOffsetX = 5;

context.shadowOffsetY = 5;

context.shadowBlur    = 10;

context.lineWidth     = 2;

context.font          = "Bold 80pt Helvetica";


redrawCanvas = function() {
   // clear the canvas before drawing new
           set of rectangles
   //context.clearRect(0, 0, elem.width,
           elem.height);

   context.scale(0.8, 0.8);
   for(var y=0; y<lineCount; y++) {
      // gradient red
    //lineColor = '#' + hexArray[y%16] + '00';


      // gradient yellow
      lineColor = '#'+hexArray[y%16]+hexArray
                  [y%16]+'0';


      context.fillStyle   = lineColor;
      context.strokeStyle = lineColor;
      context.lineWidth   = lineWidth;


      offsetX = radius*Math.cos(y*Math.PI/180);
      offsetY = radius*Math.sin(y*Math.PI/180);


      sign *= -1;
      context.scale(1+sign*0.01, 1-sign*0.01);
```

```
            context.fillText("Hello World",
                                basePointX+offsetX,
                                basePointY+offsetY);
        }

        ++clickCount;
        basePointX += 80;
        basePointY += 80;
    }

    context.drawImage(myImage, 10, 10, 300, 200);

    // render scaled text strings
    redrawCanvas();
  }, false);
  // --></script>
</head>

<body>
  <div>
    <canvas id="myCanvas" width="800" height="450">
            No support for Canvas

          alt="Rendering scaled text">
    </canvas>
  </div>

  <div>
    <input type="button" onclick="redrawCanvas();
            return false"
          value="Redraw the Text" />
  </div>
</body>
</html>
```

Listing 7.3 contains code to specify various attributes for creating a background shadow effect (which you learned in Chapter 4, "Rendering Basic 2D Shapes in HTML5 Canvas"), followed by a loop that uses `Math.sin()`, `Math.cos()`, and the loop variable `r` to calculate a new location for the text string "Hello World." The scaling effect is applied to the text strings using this line of code:

```
context.scale(1.01, 0.99);
```

Figure 7.3 displays a set of scaled text strings that follow the path of a semicircle.

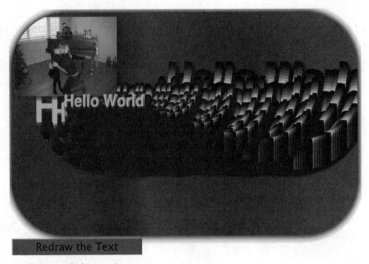

FIGURE 7.3 Rendering scaled text strings.

SHEAR TRANSFORM ON 2D SHAPES

The HTML5 Canvas `transform()` method can be applied to 2D shapes to create a sheared effect, and the API looks like this:

```
transform(1, shearX, shearY, 1, 0, 0);
```

The value of `shearX` specifies the horizontal shear, and the value of `shearY` specifies the vertical shear. The HTML5 page `Rect1Shear1.html` in Listing 7.4 demonstrates how to render a set of sheared rectangles.

The complete source code for the two CSS3 stylesheets `CSS3Background2.css` and `HoverAnimation1.css` that are referenced in Listing 7.4 are available on the DVD.

Listing 7.4 `Rect1Shear1.html`

```
<!DOCTYPE html>
<html lang="en">
 <head>
  <meta charset="utf-8">
  <title>Canvas Shear Transform</title>

  <link href="CSS32Background2.css" rel="stylesheet"
        type="text/css">
  <link href="HoverAnimation1.css" rel="stylesheet"
        type="text/css">

  <style>
    input {
      width:300px;
      font-size:24px;
      background-color:#f00;
    }
  </style>

  <script type="text/javascript"><!--
    window.addEventListener('load', function () {
      var basePointX = 5;
      var basePointY = 5;
      var rectCount  = 50;
```

```
var rectWidth  = 100;

var rectHeight = 100;

var clickCount = 0;

var context, gradient1;


var elem = document.getElementById('myCanvas');

if (!elem || !elem.getContext) {

  return;

}


var context = elem.getContext('2d');

if (!context) {

  return;

}


// Load the JPG

var myImage = new Image();

myImage.onload = function() {

  context.drawImage(myImage, basePointX, basePointY,
                    3*rectWidth,3*rectHeight);

}


myImage.src = "Lauriel.jpeg";


redrawCanvas = function() {

    // clear the canvas before drawing new set of
           rectangles

    //context.clearRect(0, 0, elem.width, elem.
           height);
```

```
context.save();

for(var a=0; a<rectCount; a++) {

    context.beginPath();

    gradient1 = context.createLinearGradient(
                basePointX, basePointY,
                basePointX+rectWidth,
                basePointY+rectHeight);

    gradient1.addColorStop(0,   '#f00');
    gradient1.addColorStop(0.5,'#00f');
    gradient1.addColorStop(1,   '#ff0');

    context.fillStyle = gradient1;

    context.transform(1,2*a*Math.PI/180,
                      a*Math.PI/180,1,0,0);

    if(a % 2 == 0) {

    context.fillRect(basePointX, basePointY,
                rectWidth, rectHeight);

    } else {

    context.fillRect(basePointX, basePointY,
                rectHeight, rectWidth);

    }

    context.fill();
}

context.restore();
```

```
            ++clickCount;

            basePointX += 50;

            basePointY += 20;

        }


        // render the rectangles

        redrawCanvas();

    }, false);

    // --></script>

</head>


<body>

  <div>

    <canvas id="myCanvas" width="800" height="500">
            No support for Canvas

          alt="Rendering Sheared Gradient
            Rectangles.">

    </canvas>

  </div>


  <div>

    <input type="button" onclick="redrawCanvas();
          return false"

          value="Redraw the Rectangles" />

  </div>

</body>

</html>
```

Listing 7.4 contains a loop for shearing a set of rectangles and then rendering them with linear gradient shading. Conditional logic uses the loop variable a to alternate the width and the height of the rendered rectangle, as shown here:

```
if(a % 2 == 0) {
    context.fillRect(basePointX, basePointY,
                     rectWidth, rectHeight);
} else {
    context.fillRect(basePointX, basePointY,
                     rectHeight, rectWidth);
}
```

Figure 7.4 displays a set of sheared rectangles with linear gradient shading.

FIGURE 7.4 A set of sheared rectangles.

RENDERING TEXT WITH SHADOW EFFECTS ON CURVES

As you can probably surmise, it is very straightforward to render text with a shadow effect in HTML5 Canvas. The HTML5 page Text1. html in Listing 7.5 demonstrates how to render a set of text strings with a shadow background effect. The complete source code for the two CSS3 stylesheets CSS3Background9.css and HoverAnimation2.css that are referenced in Listing 7.5 are available on the DVD.

Listing 7.5 Text1.html

```
<!DOCTYPE html>
<html lang="en">
 <head>
  <meta charset="utf-8">
  <title>Canvas Drawing Text</title>
  <link href="CSS32Background9.css" rel="stylesheet"
        type="text/css">
  <link href="HoverAnimation2.css" rel="stylesheet"
        type="text/css">

  <style>
    input {
      width:300px;
      font-size:24px;
      background-color:#f00;
    }
  </style>

  <script type="text/javascript"><!--
    window.addEventListener('load', function () {
      var lineCount  = 180;
      var lineLength = 400;
```

```
var lineWidth  = 5;

var basePointX = lineLength/2;

var basePointY = lineLength/2+20;

var radius     = lineLength/2;

var clickCount = 0;

var lineColor  = "";

var hexArray   = new Array('0','1','2','3','4','5',
                           '6','7','8','9','a','b','c','d',
                           'e','f');

var elem = document.getElementById('myCanvas');
if (!elem || !elem.getContext) {
   return;
}

var context = elem.getContext('2d');
if (!context) {
   return;
}

// Load the JPG
var myImage = new Image();
myImage.onload = function() {
   context.drawImage(myImage, 10, 10, 200, 200);
}

myImage.src = "Laurie1.jpeg";

redrawCanvas = function() {
   // clear the canvas before drawing new set of
          rectangles
   //context.clearRect(0, 0, elem.width, elem.
          height);
```

```
// Define some drawing attributes
context.font = "bold 40pt New Times Roman";
context.lineWidth  = 2;        // Narrow lines
context.strokeStyle = "#000"; // Black lines

// Outline a text string
context.strokeText("Hello World", 10, 80);

// Fill a text string
context.fillStyle   = "#F00";
context.fillText("Goodbye World", 380, 80);

// Define a shadow effect
context.shadowColor    = "rgba(0,0,255,0.3)";
context.shadowOffsetX = 3;
context.shadowOffsetY = 3;
context.shadowBlur    = 2;
context.lineWidth     = 1;
context.font          = "Bold 40pt Helvetica";

for(var y=0; y<lineCount; y+=3) {
   lineColor = '#' + hexArray[y%16] + '00';
   context.strokeStyle = lineColor;
   context.lineWidth   = lineWidth;

   offsetX = radius*Math.cos(y*Math.PI/180);
   offsetY = radius*Math.sin(y*Math.PI/180);

   context.fillText("Hello World",
           basePointX+offsetX,
           basePointY+offsetY);
}
```

```
        ++clickCount;

        ++basePointX;

        ++basePointY;

    }

    // render text strings

    redrawCanvas();

  }, false);

  // --></script>

</head>

<body>

  <div>

    <canvas id="myCanvas" width="800" height="450">
          No support for Canvas

          alt="Rendering Text.">

  </canvas>

  </div>

  <div>

    <input type="button" onclick="redrawCanvas();
          return false"

          value="Redraw the Text" />

  </div>

</body>

</html>
```

Listing 7.5 contains a section of code that specifies various attributes for creating a background shadow effect, as shown here:

```
// Define a shadow effect

context.shadowColor = "rgba(0,0,255,0.3)";
```

```
context.shadowOffsetX = 3;

context.shadowOffsetY = 3;

context.shadowBlur    = 2;
```

The next portion of Listing 7.5 contains a loop that uses `Math.sin()`, `Math.cos()`, and the loop variable `r` to calculate a new location for the text string "Hello World."

Figure 7.5 displays a set of text strings with a shadow effect that follow the path of a semicircle.

FIGURE 7.5 Rendering text strings with shadow effects.

APPLYING TRANSFORMS TO IMAGES ON CANVAS

HTML5 `Canvas` enables you to apply transformations to JPG files as well as 2D shapes. The HTML5 page `TransformedImage1.html` in Listing 7.6 demonstrates how to render a JPG file with multiple transformations, including translate, rotate, scale, and shear effects. The complete source code for the stylesheets `CSS3Background13.css` and `HoverAnimation2.css` that are referenced in Listing 7.6 are available on the DVD.

Listing 7.6 `TransformedImage1.html`

```
<!DOCTYPE html>
<html lang="en">
<head>
  <meta charset="utf-8" />
  <title>HTML5 Canvas JPG File Transformations</title>
  <link href="CSS32Background13.css" rel="stylesheet"
        type="text/css">
  <link href="HoverAnimation2.css" rel="stylesheet"
        type="text/css">

  <script type="text/javascript">
    function drawGraph() {
       var basePointX  = 30;
       var basePointY  = 30;
       var rectWidth   = 200;
       var rectHeight  = 200;
       var offsetX     = 20;
       var offsetY     = 20;

       var elem = document.getElementById('myCanvas');
       if (!elem || !elem.getContext) {
         return;
       }

       var context = elem.getContext('2d');
       if (!context) {
         return;
       }
```

```
    // Load the JPG

    var myImage = new Image();

    myImage.onload = function() {

    context.drawImage (myImage, basePointX, basePointY,
                       rectWidth,rectHeight);


    context.translate(200, 100);

    context.rotate(-30*Math.PI/180);


    context.drawImage(myImage,basePointX, basePointY,
                      rectWidth,rectHeight);


    context.rotate(30*Math.PI/180);

    context.translate(100, 200);

    context.scale(0.8, 0.4);


    context.drawImage(myImage, basePointX, basePointY,
                      rectWidth,rectHeight);


    context.translate(-350, -150);

    context.transform(1, 0, 25*Math.PI/180, 2, 0, 0);

    context.drawImage(myImage, basePointX, basePointY,
                      rectWidth,rectHeight);

    }


    myImage.src = "Laurie1.jpeg";

  }
</script>

<style type="text/css">
  canvas {
    border: 5px solid #888;
```

```
        background: #CCC;
    }
  </style>
</head>

<body onload="drawGraph();">
  <header>
    <h2>Hover Over the Rounded Rectangle: </h2>
  </header>

  <div>
    <canvas id="myCanvas" width="800" height="450">
            No support for Canvas
    </canvas>
  </div>
</body>
</html>
```

Listing 7.6 applies various combinations of the HTML5 Canvas methods translate(), rotate(), and scale() to the JPG file Laurie1.jpeg.

Figure 7.6 displays a JPG file with various transforms.

FIGURE 7.6 A JPG file with various transforms.

SUMMARY

This chapter showed you how to apply various transformations to 2D shapes and text strings using the following HTML5 Canvas APIs:

- `translate()`
- `rotate()`
- `scale()`
- `strokeText()`
- `fillText()`

The next chapter contains code samples that explore mouse-related events, and also how to write HTML5 Canvas code that provides mouse-based interactivity.

CHAPTER 8

HTML5 CANVAS AND MOUSE EVENTS

HTML5 Canvas provides methods for handling different types of mouse events and as you can surmise, this type of functionality is useful for HTML5-based interactive applications or games. This chapter contains code samples handling mouse-over events as well mouseclick events. The mouse-over event handling is used in the HTML5 Canvas sketching code sample, and the mouseclick functionality is used in the tic-tac-toe code sample.

The second part of the chapter discusses animation effects, and you will see an example of rendering a checkerboard pattern using animation. After that you will learn how to render a moving rectangle that simulates a bouncing effect inside a stationary rectangle. The final example in this chapter extends the bouncing rectangle code sample and shows you how to create animation effects involving multiple objects and also how to incorporate mouse-related events. The mouse-related concepts in this chapter and the animation-related concepts in the next chapter give you a rudimentary understanding of game mechanics, and perhaps you will be inspired to learn about game programming in HTML5.

Recall that HTML5 Canvas uses immediate mode instead of retained mode, so there is no Document Object Model (DOM) that you can manipulate to make objects visible or invisible. You can, however, redraw shapes on the screen to create such an effect.

Note that this chapter does not introduce any new HTML5 `Canvas` Application Programming Interfaces (APIs); the graphics effects are based on APIs that you have learned in previous chapters, and you will learn how to write code that combines those APIs with mouse-related events.

MOUSECLICK EVENTS AND OBJECT CREATION

The HTML5 `Canvas` element supports the `onclick` attribute for handling mouseclick events, and you can specify a JavaScript handler that is invoked to process such an event. Listing 8.1 displays the contents of `MouseDynamicRectangles2.html`, which illustrates how to handle mouseclick events. The complete source code for the CSS3 stylesheet `CSS32Background1.css` that is referenced in Listing 8.1 is available on the DVD for this book.

Listing 8.1 `MouseDynamicRectangles2.html`

```
<!DOCTYPE html>

<html lang="en">
 <head>

  <meta charset="utf-8">

  <title>Dynamic Rectangle Creation via Mouse Click
       Events</title>


  <link href="CSS32Background1.css" rel="stylesheet"
       type="text/css">


  <script type="text/javascript"><!--
      var basePointX = 10;

      var basePointY = 10;

      var rectWidth  = 100;

      var rectHeight = 100;

      var clickCount = 0;

      var fillStyles = ['#f00', '#ff0', '#0f0', '#00f'];
```

```
window.addEventListener('load', function () {

  var elem = document.getElementById('myCanvas');

  if (!elem || !elem.getContext) {

    return;

  }


  // Get the canvas 2d context.

  var context = elem.getContext('2d');

  if (!context) {

    return;

  }


  // upper left rectangle

  context.fillStyle = fillStyles[0];

  context.fillRect(basePointX, basePointY,
              rectWidth, rectHeight);


  // upper right rectangle

  context.fillStyle = fillStyles[1];

  context.fillRect(basePointX+rectWidth, basePointY,
              rectWidth, rectHeight);


  // lower left rectangle

  context.fillStyle = fillStyles[2];

  context.fillRect(basePointX, basePointY+rectHeight,
              rectWidth, rectHeight);


  // lower right rectangle

  context.fillStyle = fillStyles[3];

  context.fillRect(basePointX+rectWidth, basePointY+
              rectHeight, rectWidth, rectHeight);

}, false);
```

```
    function addRectangle(e) {
      var mycanvas  = document.getElementById
                        ("myCanvas");

      var mycontext = mycanvas.getContext('2d');

      var event = window.event || e;
      var xPos  = event.clientX-10;
      var yPos  = event.clientY-10;

      // create new rectangle
      mycontext.fillStyle = fillStyles[clickCount%4];
      mycontext.fillRect(xPos, yPos, rectWidth,
                        rectHeight);
      mycontext.fill();

      ++clickCount;
    }
    // --></script>
  </head>

  <body>
    <div style="margin-left:0px;">
      <canvas id="myCanvas" width="600" height="400"
              style="border: 5px blue solid"
              onclick="addRectangle()">
      </canvas>
    </div>

    <footer>
      <h1>Click Randomly Inside the Large Rectangle</h1>
    </footer>
  </body>
</html>
```

The `onmouseover` attribute in the HTML5 `<canvas>` element specifies the JavaScript function `setWhite()`, which is executed when users move their mouse inside the `canvas` region, which is a 600 x 500 rectangle. Notice that the rectangle with a blue border is displayed so that you know when your mouse is inside or outside the `canvas` region. The `setWhite()` function redraws the upper-left rectangle with the color white, which creates the impression that it has become invisible.

Listing 8.1 contains a block of code that renders four colored rectangles in a checkerboard pattern after the HTML5 page is loaded into a browser. The `onclick` attribute in the HTML5 `<canvas>` element specifies the JavaScript `addRectangle()`, which is executed when users click on their mouse. The `addRectangle()` method determines the location of the mouseclick with this code block:

```
var event = window.event || e;

var xPos  = event.clientX-10;

var yPos  = event.clientY-10;
```

The remaining code in this JavaScript function renders a rectangle whose upper-left corner is the location of the mouseclick. Figure 8.1 displays a sample output after users have clicked random locations on the screen.

Click Randomly Inside the Large Rectangle

FIGURE 8.1 Dynamically adding new rectangles.

MOUSE EVENTS AND ROTATING LINE SEGMENTS

Let's look at how to combine mouse events with simple rotation effects involving line segments. Listing 8.2 displays the contents of `MouseRo-tateLines1.html`, which illustrates how to rotate a set of line segments each time that users click their mouse. The complete source code for the CSS3 stylesheet `CSS32Background1.css` that is referenced in Listing 8.2 is available on the DVD.

Listing 8.2 `MouseRotateLines1.html`

```
<!DOCTYPE html>

<html lang="en">
 <head>
  <meta charset="utf-8">

  <title>Canvas Line Segments Mouse Events</title>

  <link href="CSS32Background1.css" rel="stylesheet"
       type="text/css">

  <script type="text/javascript"><!--
      var basePointX    = 250;

      var basePointY    = 200;

      var offsetX       = 0;

      var offsetY       = 0;

      var segmentXPts   = [40, 70, 110, 140];

      var segmentYPts   = [40, 70, 110, 140];


      var lineColor     = "";

      var lineWidth     = 0;

      var angleIndex    = 0;

      var styleIndex    = 0;

      var baseAngle     = 0;
```

```
    var baseDelta    = 7;
    var currAngle    = 0;
    var clickCount   = 0;
    var angleCount   = 10;
    var deltaAngle   = 360/angleCount;

    var rotateAngles = new Array(angleCount);
    var fillStyles   = ['#f00', '#ff0', '#0f0',
                        '#00f', '#000', '#f0f'];
    var lineWidths   = [2, 4, 6, 3, 5, 7];

window.addEventListener('load', function () {
  var elem = document.getElementById('myCanvas');
  if (!elem || !elem.getContext) {
    return;
  }

  // Get the canvas 2d context.
  var context = elem.getContext('2d');
  if (!context) {
    return;
  }

  for(var v=0; v<angleCount; v++) {
    rotateAngles[v] = v*deltaAngle;
  }

  renderSegments();
}, false);
```

```
function renderSegments() {
   var mycanvas = document.getElementById
                   ("myCanvas");

   var context  = mycanvas.getContext('2d');


   for(var i=0; i<segmentXPts.length; i++) {
      context.beginPath();
      angleIndex = ((clickCount+i) % rotateAngles.
                    length);
      currAngle  = (baseAngle+rotateAngles[angleIndex])
                    *Math.PI/180;


      offsetX  = segmentXPts[i]*Math.cos(currAngle);
      offsetY  = segmentYPts[i]*Math.sin(currAngle);


      // render the current line segment
      styleIndex = i % fillStyles.length;
      lineColor = fillStyles[styleIndex];
      lineWidth = lineWidths[styleIndex];


      context.strokeStyle = lineColor;
      context.lineWidth = lineWidth;


      context.lineTo(basePointX+offsetX, basePointY+
                     offsetY);
      context.lineTo(basePointX-offsetX, basePointY-
                     offsetY);
      context.stroke();
   }
```

```
        ++clickCount;

        baseAngle += baseDelta;

    }

    // --></script>

</head>


<body>

  <div style="margin-left:30px;">

    <canvas id="myCanvas" width="600" height="400"

            style="border: 5px blue solid"

            onclick="renderSegments()">

    </canvas>

  </div>


  <footer>

   <h1>Click Inside the Large Rectangle</h1>

  </footer>

 </body>

</html>
```

Listing 8.2 contains a block of code that renders a line segment after the HTML5 page is loaded into a browser. The `onclick` attribute in the HTML5 `<canvas>` element specifies the JavaScript `renderSegments()`, which is executed whenever users click their mouse. The `renderSegments()` method calculates the new positions for the set of rotated line segments and then renders the line segments in their new positions. Figure 8.2 displays a sample output after users have clicked on the screen.

FIGURE 8.2 Dynamically adding new rectangles.

MOUSE EVENTS AND ELLIPTIC ROTATION

We can use mouse events to control the rendering of rotated rectangles whose vertices are determined by the coordinates of an ellipse. Listing 8.3 displays the contents of `MouseEllipseRectRotation1.html`, which illustrates how to render a rotated rectangle each time that users click their mouse. The complete source code for the CSS3 stylesheet `CSS32Background1.css` that is referenced in Listing 8.3 is available on the DVD.

Listing 8.3 MouseEllipseRectRotation1.html

```
<!DOCTYPE html>
<html lang="en">
 <head>
  <meta charset="utf-8">
  <title>Canvas Rectangles and Mouse Events</title>
  <link href="CSS32Background1.css" rel="stylesheet"
        type="text/css">
```

```
<script type="text/javascript"><!--
    var basePointX    = 250;
    var basePointY    = 100;
    var offsetX       = 0;
    var offsetY       = 0;
    var majorAxis     = 150;
    var minorAxis     = 30;
    var maxAngle      = 360;
    var rectHeight    = 200;
    var ellipseXPts   = new Array(maxAngle);
    var ellipseYPts   = new Array(maxAngle);

    var lineColor     = "";
    var lineWidth     = 0;
    var styleIndex    = 0;
    var clickCount    = 0;
    var fillStyles    = ['#f00', '#ff0', '#0f0',
                         '#00f', '#000', '#f0f'];
    var lineWidths    = [2, 4, 6, 1, 3, 5];

  window.addEventListener('load', function () {
    var elem = document.getElementById('myCanvas');
    if (!elem || !elem.getContext) {
      return;
    }

    // Get the canvas 2d context.
    var context = elem.getContext('2d');
    if (!context) {
      return;
    }
```

```
    initializeEllipsePoints();

    renderRotatedRectangles();

}, false);


function initializeEllipsePoints() {

    for(var i=0; i<maxAngle; i++) {

        ellipseXPts[i] = majorAxis*Math.cos
                        (i*Math.PI/180);

        ellipseYPts[i] = minorAxis*Math.sin
                        (i*Math.PI/180);

    }

}


function renderRotatedRectangles() {

    var mycanvas = document.getElementById
                    ("myCanvas");

    var context  = mycanvas.getContext('2d');


    ++clickCount;


    offsetX = ellipseXPts[clickCount%maxAngle];

    offsetY = ellipseYPts[clickCount%maxAngle];


    // render the current rotated rectangle

    styleIndex = clickCount % fillStyles.length;

    lineColor = fillStyles[styleIndex];

    lineWidth = lineWidths[styleIndex];


    context.beginPath();

    context.strokeStyle = lineColor;

    context.lineWidth = lineWidth;
```

```
        context.moveTo(basePointX+offsetX, basePointY+
                offsetY);

        context.lineTo(basePointX-offsetX, basePointY-
                offsetY);

        context.lineTo(basePointX-offsetX, basePointY-
                offsetY+rectHeight);

        context.lineTo(basePointX+offsetX, basePointY+
                offsetY+rectHeight);

        context.lineTo(basePointX+offsetX, basePointY+
                offsetY);

        context.stroke();

    }
    // --></script>
</head>


<body>
 <header>
  <h1>Click/Move Inside the Large Rectangle</h1>
 </header>


 <div style="margin-left:30px;">
    <canvas id="myCanvas" width="600" height="400"
            style="border: 5px blue solid"
            onmousemove="renderRotatedRectangles()"
            onclick="renderRotatedRectangles()">
    </canvas>
 </div>
 </body>
</html>
```

Listing 8.3 contains a block of code that renders a rectangle after the HTML5 page is loaded into a browser. The `onclick` attribute in the HTML5 `<canvas>` element specifies the JavaScript `renderRotate-dRectangles()`, which is executed when users move or click their mouse. Figure 8.3 displays a sample output after users have clicked random locations on the screen.

Click/Move Inside the Large Rectangle

FIGURE 8.3 Dynamically rotating rectangles along an elliptic path.

A SIMPLE SKETCHING EXAMPLE

We can easily modify the code in Listing 8.3 in order to create a sketching program that renders a colored line segment when users move their mouse. Listing 8.4 displays the contents of the HTML5 page `Sketching1.html`, which illustrates how to perform freestyle sketching in an HTML5 `<canvas>` element. The complete source code for the CSS3 stylesheet `CSS32Background1.css` that is referenced in Listing 8.4 is available on the DVD.

Listing 8.4 `Sketching1.html`

```
<!DOCTYPE html>
<html lang="en">
 <head>
```

```
<meta charset="utf-8">

<title>Sketching and Canvas Mouse Events</title>

<link href="CSS32Background1.css" rel="stylesheet"
      type="text/css">

<script type="text/javascript"><!--
    var basePointX = 10;

    var basePointY = 10;

    var rectWidth  = 100;

    var rectHeight = 100;

    var clickCount = 0;

    var previousX  = 0;

    var previousY  = 0;

    var currentX   = 0;

    var currentY   = 0;

    var lineWidth  = 2;

    var lineColor  = "";

    var fillStyles = ['#f00', '#ff0', '#0f0', '#00f'];

  window.addEventListener('load', function () {
    var elem = document.getElementById('myCanvas');
    if (!elem || !elem.getContext) {
      return;
    }

    var context = elem.getContext('2d');
    if (!context) {
      return;
    }
  }, false);
```

```
function drawLineSegment(e) {
  var mycanvas  = document.getElementById
                       ("myCanvas");
  var mycontext = mycanvas.getContext('2d');

  previousX = currentX;
  previousY = currentY;

  var event = window.event || e;
  currentX  = event.clientX-10;
  currentY  = event.clientY-10;

  // render a new line segment
  mycontext.beginPath();

  lineColor = fillStyles[clickCount%4];
  mycontext.strokeStyle = lineColor;
  mycontext.lineWidth = lineWidth;

  mycontext.moveTo(previousX, previousY);
  mycontext.lineTo(currentX,  currentY);
  mycontext.stroke();

  ++clickCount;
 }
// --></script>
</head>

<body>
 <div style="margin-left:0px;">
   <canvas id="myCanvas" width="600" height="500"
```

```
          style="border: 5px blue solid"
          onmousemove="drawLineSegment()">
   </canvas>
  </div>

  <footer>
   <h1>Mouse Move Inside the Large Rectangle</h1>
  </footer>
 </body>
</html>
```

The HTML5 <canvas> element in Listing 8.4 contains an onmouse-move attribute that specifies the JavaScript drawLineSegment() that is executed when users move their mouse. The drawLineSegment() determines the current location of the mouse and assigns the values of the x-coordinate and the y-coordinate to the variables currentX and currentY, respectively.

This function then draws a line segment from (currentX, currentY) to the point (previousX, previousY), which is the location of the previous mouse move. Initially these points are the same, and the previous move location is set to the current move location each time users move their mouse. The preceding explanation corresponds to this code (with some code details omitted):

```
previousX = currentX;
previousY = currentY;
currentX  = event.clientX-10;
currentY  = event.clientY-10;
mycontext.moveTo(previousX, previousY);
mycontext.lineTo(currentX,  currentY);
```

This function also uses the variable clickCount to keep track of the number of times that users move their mouse. This variable is used as an index into an array of colors in order to determine the color of the rendered line segment, as shown here:

```
lineColor = fillStyles[clickCount%4];
```

Figure 8.4 displays a sample output after users have moved their mouse on the screen.

Mouse Move Inside the Large Rectangle

FIGURE 8.4 Freestyle sketching example.

A TIC-TAC-TOE EXAMPLE

You now possess the knowledge for simulating a tic-tac-toe board, which involves rendering a 3 x 3 game board, detecting user mouseclicks, updating the board appropriately, and determining whether a player has won the current game. Listing 8.5 displays the contents of the HTML5 page TicTacToe1.html, which illustrates how to play a game of tic-tac-toe. The complete source code for the CSS3 stylesheet CSS32Background1.css that is referenced in Listing 8.5 is available on the DVD.

Listing 8.5 `TicTacToe1.html`

```
<!DOCTYPE html>
<html lang="en">
 <head>
  <meta charset="utf-8" />
  <title>HTML5 Canvas Tic Tac Toe</title>
  <link href="CSS32Background1.css" rel="stylesheet"
        type="text/css">

  <script type="text/javascript">
    var basePointX   = 20;
    var basePointY   = 20;
    var currentX     = 0;
    var currentY     = 0;
    var rowCount     = 3;
    var colCount     = 3;
    var cellWidth    = 100;
    var cellHeight   = 100;
    var clickedRow   = 0;
    var clickedCol   = 0;
    var currPlayer   = 0;
    var cellIndex    = 0;
    var lineWidth    = 2;
    var cellColor    = "";
    var lineColor    = '#fff';
    var fillColors   = new Array("#F00", "#FF0", "#0F0",
                        "#00F");
```

```
var clickedCells = new Array(-1,-1,-1,-1,-1,
                    -1,-1,-1,-1);
var fillColors   = new Array("#F00", "#FF0", "#00F");
var canvas, context;

function initializeGame() {
   canvas = document.getElementById('myCanvas');

   if(canvas.getContext) {
      context = canvas.getContext('2d');
      initializeBoard();
   }
}

function initializeBoard() {
   for(var row=0; row<rowCount; row++) {
      for(var col=0; col<colCount; col++) {
         currentX  = basePointX+col*cellWidth;
         currentY  = basePointY+row*cellHeight;
         cellColor = fillColors[(row+col)%fillColors.
                     length];
         drawCell(cellColor);
      }
   }
}

function drawCell(color) {
    context.fillStyle = color;
    context.fillRect(currentX, currentY,
                 cellWidth, cellHeight);
} // drawCell
```

```
function initializeCells() {
    for(var row=0; row<rowCount; row++) {
        for(var col=0; col<colCount; col++) {
            cellIndex = row*rowCount+col;
            clickedCells[cellIndex] = -1;
        }
    }
}

function updateBoard(e) {
        var event = window.event || e;
        currentX  = event.clientX-10;
        currentY  = event.clientY-10;

        row = Math.floor((currentY-basePointY)/cellHeight);
        col = Math.floor((currentX-basePointX)/cellWidth);

        if((row>=0) && (row<rowCount) && (col>=0) &&
                (col<colCount)) {
            cellIndex = row*rowCount+col;

            if(clickedCells[cellIndex] == -1) {
                clickedCells[cellIndex] = currPlayer;
                // update the current blot:
                drawSymbol(row, col);

                // did the current player win?
                if(gameOver() == 'true') {
    alert("Winner is player "+ currPlayer);
```

```
                       // start new game
                       initializeBoard();
                       initializeCells();
                    } else {
                       // toggle the current player
                       currPlayer = 1-currPlayer;
        //alert("currPlayer is now: "+ currPlayer);
                    }
                } else {
        alert("Occupied by player "+ clickedCells[cellIndex]);
                }
            } else {
    //alert("out of bounds for row ="+row+" col="+col);
            }
        } // updateBoard

function gameOver() {
        var gameOver = false;
        // current player wins if a row, column,
        // or diagonal contains the same symbol
        return(gameOver);
    }

    function drawSymbol(row, col) {
        currentX = basePointX+col*cellWidth;
        currentY = basePointY+row*cellHeight;

        if(currPlayer == 0) {
            context.beginPath();
            context.strokeStyle = lineColor;
            context.lineWidth = lineWidth;
```

```
            context.arc(currentX+cellWidth/2,
                        currentY+cellHeight/2,
                        cellWidth/2, 0, Math.PI*2, true);

            context.stroke();

        } else {

            // render main diagonal

            context.beginPath();

            context.strokeStyle = lineColor;

            context.lineWidth   = lineWidth;


            context.moveTo(currentX, currentY);

            context.lineTo(currentX+cellWidth, currentY+
                    cellHeight);

            context.stroke();


            // render off diagonal

            context.beginPath();

            context.strokeStyle = lineColor;

            context.lineWidth   = lineWidth;


            context.moveTo(currentX+cellWidth, currentY);

            context.lineTo(currentX, currentY+cellHeight);

            context.stroke();

        }

    } // drawSymbol

    </script>

</head>
```

```
<body onload="initializeGame();">
  <div style="margin-left:0px;">
    <canvas id="myCanvas" width="600" height="400"
            onclick="updateBoard()">
    </canvas>
  </div>

  <footer>
    <h1>Click the Colored Squares to Play</h1>
  </footer>
</body>
</html>
```

The `onload` attribute in Listing 8.5 specifies the JavaScript function `initializeGame()`, which contains code for rendering a 3 x 3 tic-tac-toe board.

The HTML5 `<canvas>` element in Listing 8.5 contains an `onclick` attribute that specifies the JavaScript `updateBoard()` that is executed when users move their mouse. When users click inside the tic-tac-toe board, this function will ensure that the current cell is empty and then updates the board with either an "X" or with an "O", depending on the identity of the current player. Next, this function checks if the current player has won the game, in which case an alert message is displayed; if not, then this function toggles the current player so that the other player can make a selection.

Currently the function `gameOver()` returns a hard-coded value of `false`, and as an exercise you can add the section of code to determine whether the current player has won the game. Keep in mind that you also need to handle the situation where the board is full but neither player has won the game. Figure 8.5 displays a sample output of the tic-tac-toe board in Listing 8.5.

Click the Colored Squares to Play

FIGURE 8.5 Tic-tac-toe example.

COMBINING CSS3, SVG, AND HTML5 CANVAS

The example in this section is an instance of "forward referencing" because it contains code for bar charts and pie charts, which is covered in chapter ten. Chapter ten, however, focuses on rendering charts and graphs using only HTML5 Canvas, whereas this example combines CSS3, SVG (Scalable Vector Graphics), and HTML5 Canvas effects in an HTML page. Specifically, these examples show you how to perform the following:

- render text in multiple columns using CSS3

- render a bar chart from a static SVG document

- render a pie chart from an HTML Canvas element

- render a pie chart from an SVG/JavaScript Document

- the Update button dynamically updates the data in both pie charts

- CSS3-based hover effects for both pie charts

- CSS3-based gradient shading for the Canvas-based pie chart

The code for this example consists of the following four files:

- `MouseCSS3EllipticPieChart1.svg`

- `MouseCSS3SVGCanvas1.css`

- `MouseCSS3SVGCanvas1.html`

- `MouseCSS3SVGCanvas1.svg`

Listing 8.6 displays the JavaScript code that communicates from the HTML page to the SVG document, and Listing 8.7 displays the JavaScript code that is executed in the SVG document. The complete code for these two files, as well as the other two files (the CSS stylesheet and the SVG document with a static pie chart) are available on the DVD.

Listing 8.6 `MouseCSS3SVGCanvas1.html` (One Section)

```
//-----------------------------------------------
// call JS function in MouseCSS3EllipticPieChart1.svg
    var svgDoc = null, svgWin = null;

    function renderSVGPieChartInit() {
       var embed = document.getElementById('embed1');
       svgDoc = embed.getSVGDocument();

       if (svgDoc) {
         svgWin = svgDoc.defaultView;
       } else {
         alert("The embedded SVG document is null");
       }
    }

    function renderSVGPieChartMain() {
      svgWin.renderSVGEllipticPieChart();
    }
```

```
// pass the pieAngles array
function renderSVGPieChartAngles() {
  svgWin.renderSVGEllipticPieChartAngles(pieAngles);
}
//-----------------------------------------------
```

```
// bottom of code listing
<div id="ellipticPieChart1">
<embed id="embed1" src="MouseCSS3EllipticPieChart1.svg"
       width="550" height="300" type="image/svg+xml">
</embed>
</div>

<input type="button"
       onclick="drawPieChart();renderSVGPieChartMain();
            return false"
       value="Update Chart Values and Colors" />

<input type="button"
       onclick="drawPieChart();renderSVGPieChartAngles();
            return false"
       value="Send Chart Values to SVG" />
```

The JavaScript function `renderSVGPieChartInit()` in Listing 8.6 first obtains a reference to an <embed> object (shown in the code listing above) that references `MouseCSS3SVGEllipticPieChar.svg` (a section of this document is displayed in Listing 8.7) to generate an elliptic pie chart in the upper-right corner of the screen.

When users click on the first button, the function `renderSVG-PieChartMain()` is executed, which first renders the pie chart on the lower portion of the screen and then it executes `renderSVGElliptic-PieChart()` that is defined in `MouseCSS3EllipticPieChart.svg`, and this latter function simply changes the colors of the existing pie chart.

When users click on the second button, the function `renderSVG-PieChartAngles()` is executed, which first renders the pie chart in the lower part of the screen (as does the other button) and then invokes the `renderSVGEllipticPieChartAngles()` function that is defined in `MouseCSS3EllipticPieChart.svg`. In addition, this function uses the original array of pie chart values to update the pie chart in the SVG document, so both pie charts have the same number of slices or wedges.

Listing 8.7 `MouseCSS3EllipticPieChart1.svg` (One Section)

```
//-----------------------------------------------
// JS function called from MouseCSS3SVGCanvas1.html
    function renderSVGEllipticPieChart(evt) {
        // reset to original vertex count (to be safe)
        vertexCount = vertexCountOri;
        angles = new Array(vertexCount);

        initializeChart();
        drawChart();
    }


    function renderSVGEllipticPieChartAngles(pieAngles) {
        newPieAngles = pieAngles;

        updateLocalPieAngles();
        drawChart();
    }


    function updateLocalPieAngles() {
        var localCount = newPieAngles.length;
```

```
    if(localCount > angles.length) {

        localCount = angles.length;

    }

    // vertexCount of the shorter array
    vertexCount = localCount;

    angles = new Array(vertexCount);

    for(var v=0; v<vertexCount; v++) {

      angles[v] = newPieAngles[v];

    }

  }

  function initializeChart() {

    for(var v=0; v<vertexCount; v++) {

        angles[v] = initialValues[v];

    }

  } // initializeChart
//-----------------------------------------------
```

As you know, the function `renderSVGEllipticPieChart()` in Listing 8.7 is invoked from Listing 8.6, and notice that `vertexCount` is reset to its initial value. This is done because the two pie charts might have a different number of slices; if so, after users click the second button in Listing 8.6, `vertexCount` could be changed from its original value of 8 to the value 6, which is the number of pie slices in the pie chart that is displayed in the lower half of the screen.

There is one caveat to this code sample: this code was tested on Safari and Chrome browsers on a Macbook, and although the graphics renders correctly in both cases, the dynamically generated elliptic pie chart does not refresh correctly on Chrome. This behavior might be due to a bug in Chrome, or perhaps a different code block is required for Chrome in order to communicate correctly between the SVG/JavaScript code and the HTML page. Figure 8.6 displays the graphics image that is rendered by the code in this section.

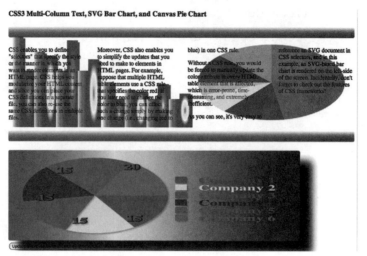

FIGURE 8.6 CSS3, static and dynamic SVG, and HTML5 `Canvas`.

SUMMARY

This chapter focused on showing you how to process mouse-related events in HTML5 pages. You saw code samples that showed how to bind JavaScript functions to mouse events, followed by examples of mouse-based interactivity. In summary, you learned how to write code to do the following:

- handle mouse-related events
- create interactive graphics code
- create a sketching program
- create a tic-tac-toe game

The next chapter contains some examples of HTML5 `Canvas` animation, and you will learn basic techniques for creating animation effects. If you plan to become a game developer, some of these techniques might serve you well in the initial stages of your game development career.

CHAPTER 9

HTML5 CANVAS AND ANIMATION EFFECTS

HTML5 Canvas provides methods for handling different types of mouse events as well as animation effects. This type of functionality is useful for HTML5-based interactive applications or games. The first part of this chapter introduces you to simple animation effects, with a code sample that shows how to render a rotating polygon, followed by an example of rendering a checkerboard pattern using animation. After that you will learn how to render a moving rectangle that simulates a bouncing effect inside a stationary rectangle. The final example in this chapter extends the bouncing rectangle code sample and shows you how to create animation effects involving multiple objects and also how to incorporate mouse-related events. One point that was mentioned in Chapter 8 merits repetition: although this book does not delve into developing HTML5-based games, this chapter provides you with a rudimentary understanding of game mechanics, and perhaps you will be inspired to learn about game programming in HTML5.

There is one more important point that you need to keep in mind about the animation code samples in this chapter. The traditional way to set a JavaScript timer is to invoke the setTimeout() function; however, HTML5 supports the more efficient method requestAnimation-Frame(). Information about the details of this function can be found here: *http://paulirish.com/2011/requestanimationframe-for-smart-animating/*.

If you intend to intend to use HTML5 animation effects, you need to seriously consider using the requestAnimationFrame() method instead of the setTimeout() method. Because the code samples in this chapter are intended for illustrative purposes (and not production environments), they use the old style of setting timers.

ANIMATION WITH ROTATING 2D SHAPES

Let's look at how to combine mouse events with simple rotation effects applied to polygons instead of line segments. Listing 9.1 displays the contents of RotatingPolygons1.html that illustrates how to rotate a set of polygons each time that users click their mouse. The complete source code for the CSS3 stylesheet CSS32Background2.css that is referenced in Listing 9.1 is available on the DVD for this book.

Listing 9.1 RotatingPolygons1.html

```
<!DOCTYPE html>
<html lang="en">
 <head>
  <meta charset="utf-8" />
  <title>HTML5 Canvas Rotating Polygons</title>
  <link href="CSS32Background2.css" rel="stylesheet"
        type="text/css">

  <style type="text/css">
    canvas {
       border: 5px solid #ccc;
       background: #ccc;
    }
  </style>

  <script type="text/javascript">
     var basePointX       = 250;
     var basePointY       = 200;
```

```
var maxCount           = 50;
var offsetX            = 0;
var offsetY            = 0;

var borderWidth        = 400;
var borderHeight       = 200;
var maxRadius          = 150;
var minRadius          = 20;
var radius             = maxRadius;
var deltaRadius        = 10;
var radDirection       = 1;

var outerFillColor     = "White";
var outerStrokeColor   = "Blue";
var outerStrokeWidth   = 4;
var rectFillColor      = "Red";
var rectStrokeColor    = "Yellow";
var rectStrokeWidth    = 1;
var rectWidth          = 20;
var rectHeight         = 20;
var deltaY             = 0;
var fillColors         = new Array("#F00", "#FF0",
                           "#0F0", "#00F");

var lineColor          = "";
var fillColor          = "";
var lineWidth          = 0;
var styleIndex         = 0;
var baseAngle          = 0;
```

```
var baseDelta          = 7;

var currAngle          = 0;

var clickCount         = 0;

var vertexCount        = 10;

var vertexAngle        = 360/vertexCount;


var vertexXPts         = new Array(vertexCount);

var vertexYPts         = new Array(vertexCount);

var rotateAngles       = new Array(vertexCount);

var fillStyles         = ['#f00', '#ff0', '#0f0',
                          '#00f', '#000', '#f0f'];

var lineWidths         = [1, 3, 5, 2, 4, 6];

var currentTick        = 0;

var shortPause         = 50;

var theTimeout         = null;


var canvas;

var context;


function initialize() {
   canvas = document.getElementById('myCanvas');

   if(canvas.getContext) {
      context = canvas.getContext('2d');
      updateVertices();
      renderLineSegments();
   }
}
```

```
function updateVertices() {
 for(var v=0; v<vertexCount; v++) {
  rotateAngles[v] = baseAngle+v*vertexAngle;
  vertexXPts[v] = radius*Math.cos(rotateAngles
                [v]*Math.PI/180);
  vertexYPts[v] = radius*Math.sin(rotateAngles
                [v]*Math.PI/180);

  }

  baseAngle += baseDelta;
  updateRadius();
}

function updateRadius() {
  radius += deltaRadius*radDirection;

  if(radius >= maxRadius) {
    radius = maxRadius;
    radDirection *= -1;
  }

  if(radius <= minRadius) {
    radius = minRadius;
    radDirection *= -1;
  }
}

function renderLineSegments() {
var canvas  = document.getElementById("myCanvas");
var context = canvas.getContext('2d');
```

```
context.beginPath();

styleIndex = clickCount++ % fillStyles.length;
lineColor = fillStyles[styleIndex];
fillColor = fillStyles[styleIndex];
lineWidth = lineWidths[styleIndex];

// render the current polygon
for(var i=0; i<vertexXPts.length; i++) {
    context.strokeStyle = lineColor;
    context.lineWidth = lineWidth;

if(i == 0) {
    context.moveTo(basePointX+vertexXPts[i],
            basePointY+vertexYPts[i]);
    }
    else {
    context.lineTo(basePointX+vertexXPts[i],
            basePointY+vertexYPts[i]);
    }
}

context.lineTo(basePointX+vertexXPts[0],
        basePointY+vertexYPts[0]);

    context.stroke();
    if(radDirection == -1) {
        context.fillStyle = fillColor;
        context.fill();
    }

    updateVertices();
```

```
// redraw the line segments?
if(++currentTick < maxCount) {
  theTimeout = setTimeout("renderLineSegments()",
              shortPause);
    }
  }

  function stopAnimation(event) {
    clearTimeout(theTimeout);
  }
</script>
</head>

<body onload="initialize();">
 <header>
  <h1>Canvas Rotating Polygons</h1>
 </header>

 <div>
  <canvas id="myCanvas" width="500" height="400">
      No support for Canvas
  </canvas>
 </div>
</body>
</html>
```

After performing some typical variable initialization, Listing 9.1 contains the function `initialize()`, which in turn invokes the function `updateVertices()`, which calculates the coordinates of the vertices of a polygon, followed by an invocation of the function `renderLineSegments()`, which renders the outline of the current polygon.

Note that `updateVertices()` also calls the function `updateRadius()`, which updates the variable radius (used in the calculation of the vertices) in a linear fashion and in such a way that its value is always between a maximum value `maxRadius` and a minimum value `minRadius`.

The function `renderLineSegments()` determines whether to redraw another rotated polygon with this conditional logic:

```
// redraw the line segments?
if(++currentTick < maxCount) {
theTimeout = setTimeout("renderLineSegments()",
            shortPause);

}
```

Each time that the `renderLineSegments()` function is invoked, the current polygon is rotated, thereby creating an animation effect. Figure 9.1 displays the result of the animation effect that is created by executing the code in Listing 9.1, which involves rotating polygons.

Canvas Rotating Polygons

FIGURE 9.1 Animation effect with rotating polygons.

CHECKERBOARD ANIMATION EFFECT

In the previous example you learned how to use mouseclicks to create animation effects. In this section you will learn about animation effects that occur independently of user-initiated events such as mouseclicks. Listing 9.2 displays the contents of the HTML page `AnimCheckerboard1.html`, which illustrates how to animate the creation of a checkerboard. The complete source code for the CSS3 stylesheet `CSS32Background2.css` that is referenced in Listing 9.2 is available on the DVD.

Listing 9.2 `AnimCheckerboard1.html`

```
<!DOCTYPE html>
<html lang="en">
 <head>
  <meta charset="utf-8" />
  <title>HTML5 Canvas Checkerboard</title>
  <link href="CSS32Background2.css" rel="stylesheet"
        type="text/css">

  <script type="text/javascript">
    var basePointX   = 20;
    var basePointY   = 20;
    var currentX     = basePointX;
    var currentY     = basePointY;
    var rowCount     = 10;
    var colCount     = 10;
    var currentRow   = 0;
    var currentCol   = 0;
    var rectWidth    = 40;
    var rectHeight   = 40;
```

```
var shortPause   = 50;
var fillColors   = new Array("#F00", "#FF0", "#0F0",
                   "#00F");
var theTimeout   = null;

var canvas;
var context;

function initialize() {
  canvas = document.getElementById('myCanvas');

  if(canvas.getContext) {
    context = canvas.getContext('2d');
    drawRectangle();
  }
}

function updateRectangleCoordinates() {

  if( ++currentCol >= colCount) {
    currentCol = 0;
    ++currentRow;
  }

  currentX = basePointX+currentRow*rectHeight;
  currentY = basePointY+currentCol*rectWidth;

} // updateRectangleCoordinates
```

```
function drawRectangle() {
  if(currentRow < rowCount) {
  context.fillStyle = fillColors[(currentRow+currentCol)%4];
  context.fillRect(currentX, currentY, rectWidth, rectHeight);

  theTimeout = setTimeout("drawRectangle()",
            shortPause);
    }

    updateRectangleCoordinates();

  } // drawRectangle

  function stopAnimation(event) {
    clearTimeout(theTimeout);
  }
  </script>
</head>

 <body onload="initialize();">
  <header>
    <h1>HTML5 Canvas Checkerboard</h1>
  </header>

  <div>
   <canvas id="myCanvas" width="600" height="500">
        No support for Canvas
   </canvas>
  </div>
 </body>
</html>
```

The `onload` attribute in Listing 9.2 specifies the JavaScript function `initialize()` that is executed when the HTML5 page is loaded. This function does some simple initialization and then invokes the JavaScript function `drawRectangle()`, which renders a checkerboard pattern of colored rectangles. The function `drawRectangle()` renders the leftmost column of colored rectangles, starting from the top row and proceeding downward toward the bottom row. This process is repeated for every column until the rightmost column of rectangles is rendered.

Instead of using a nested loop for rendering the checkerboard (which would not produce an animation effect), the function `drawRectangle()` draws a new rectangle after a delay of 50 milliseconds (which is the value assigned to the variable `shortPause`) by means of this commonly used JavaScript idiom:

```
theTimeout = setTimeout("drawRectangle()", shortPause);
```

Figure 9.2 displays a snapshot of populating a checkerboard pattern with an animation effect.

HTML5 Canvas Checkerboard

FIGURE 9.2 Checkerboard animation.

BOUNCING 2D SHAPES ANIMATION

We can use the animation code in Listing 9.2 to create a bouncing rectangle animation effect, after we make some necessary changes to that code. Listing 9.3 displays the contents of the HTML page `BouncingRect1.html`, which illustrates how to render a bouncing rectangle. The complete source code for the CSS3 stylesheet `CSS32Background2.css` that is referenced in Listing 9.3 is available on the DVD.

Listing 9.3 `BouncingRect1.html`

```
<!DOCTYPE html>
<html lang="en">
 <head>
  <meta charset="utf-8" />
  <title>HTML5 Canvas Bouncing Rectangle</title>
  <link href="CSS32Background2.css" rel="stylesheet"
        type="text/css">

  <script type="text/javascript">
    var borderWidth      = 400;
    var borderHeight     = 200;
    var basePointX       = 20;
    var basePointY       = 50;
    var currentX         = basePointX;
    var currentY         = basePointY;
    var maximumX         = 480;
    var minimumX         = 10;
    var maximumY         = 280;
    var minimumY         = 10;
    var xDelta           = 10;
```

```
var xDirection       = 1;
var yDelta           = 8;
var yDirection       = 1;
var maxCount         = 200;

var outerFillColor   = "White";
var outerStrokeColor = "Blue";
var outerStrokeWidth = 4;
var rectFillColor    = "Red";
var rectStrokeColor  = "Yellow";
var rectStrokeWidth  = 1;
var rectWidth        = 20;
var rectHeight       = 20;
var deltaY           = 0;
var currentTick      = 0;
var shortPause       = 50;
var fillColors       = new Array("#F00", "#FF0",
                         "#0F0", "#00F");

var theTimeout       = null;

var canvas;
var context;

function initialize() {
  canvas = document.getElementById('myCanvas');

  if(canvas.getContext) {
    context = canvas.getContext('2d');
    drawRectangle();
  }

}
```

```
function updateRectangleCoordinates() {
   currentX += xDelta*xDirection;

   if( currentX >= maximumX-rectWidth ) {
      currentX = maximumX-rectHeight;
      xDirection *= -1;
   }

   if( currentX <= minimumX ) {
      currentX = minimumX;
      xDirection *= -1;
   }

   currentY += yDelta*yDirection;

   if( currentY >= maximumY-rectHeight ) {
      currentY = maximumY-rectHeight;
      yDirection *= -1;
   }

   if( currentY <= minimumY ) {
      currentY = minimumY;
      yDirection *= -1;
   }

} // updateRectangleCoordinates

function drawRectangle() {
   updateRectangleCoordinates();
```

```
            context.fillStyle = fillColors[currentTick%4];

            context.fillRect(currentX, currentY, rectWidth,
                            rectHeight);

            // redraw the rectangle?

            if(++currentTick < maxCount) {

                theTimeout = setTimeout("drawRectangle()",
                            shortPause);

            }


    } // drawRectangle


    function stopAnimation(event) {

        clearTimeout(theTimeout);

    }
    </script>
  </head>


  <body onload="initialize();">
    <header>

        <h1>HTML5 Canvas Bouncing Rectangle</h1>

    </header>


    <div>

        <canvas id="myCanvas" width="500" height="300">
                No support for Canvas

        </canvas>

    </div>

  </body>
</html>
```

Listing 9.3 introduces the concept of a time interval that is available in JavaScript, which enabled us to use an animation effect while rendering a checkerboard with colored rectangles. For this code sample we need make the following changes to Listing 9.2:

- render one colored rectangle (and not the entire checkerboard)
- move the colored rectangle in a diagonal-like manner (and not vertically)
- make sure that the colored rectangle remains inside the outer rectangle

The `onload` attribute in Listing 9.3 specifies the JavaScript function `initialize()` that is executed when the HTML5 page is loaded. This function does some simple initialization and then invokes the JavaScript function `drawRectangle()`, which renders a colored rectangle.

Notice that the JavaScript function `drawRectangle()` invokes the JavaScript function `updateRectangleCoordinates()`, which updates the location of the upper-left vertex of the colored rectangle with these two lines of code:

```
currentX += xDelta*xDirection;
currentY += yDelta*yDirection;
```

Whenever the colored rectangle moves beyond the left border or the right border, the variable `xDirection` is reversed with the following line of code:

```
xDirection *= -1;
```

Similarly, whenever the colored rectangle moves beyond the top border or the bottom border, the variable `yDirection` is reversed with the following line of code:

```
yDirection *= -1;
```

The function `drawRectangle()` draws a new rectangle after a delay of 50 milliseconds (which is the value assigned to the variable `shortPause`) by means of the following code, which is the same code that you saw in Listing 9.2:

```
theTimeout = setTimeout("drawRectangle()",shortPause);
```

Figure 9.3 displays a small rectangle that bounces around inside a stationary outer rectangle.

HTML5 Canvas Bouncing Rectangle

FIGURE 9.3 A bouncing rectangle with an animation effect.

MULTIPLE BOUNCING 2D SHAPES ANIMATION

Now that you understand how to render a bouncing rectangle, we are going to enhance the code in Listing 9.3 to render a set of colored rectangles that bounce up and down. Listing 9.4 displays the contents of the HTML page `VBouncingRectangles1.html`, which illustrates how to render a set of rectangles that appear to bounce up and down. The complete source code for the CSS3 stylesheet `CSS32Background2.css` that is referenced in Listing 9.4 is available on the DVD.

Listing 9.4 VBouncingRectangles1.html

```html
<!DOCTYPE html>
<html lang="en">
 <head>
  <meta charset="utf-8" />
  <title>HTML5 Canvas Bouncing Rectangles</title>
  <link href="CSS32Background2.css" rel="stylesheet"
        type="text/css">

  <script type="text/javascript">
      var rectWidth        = 20;
      var rectHeight       = 20;
      var widgetCount      = 40;
      var borderWidth      = widgetCount*rectWidth;
      var borderHeight     = 400;
      var basePointX       = 0;
      var basePointY       = 0;
      var currentX         = basePointX;
      var currentY         = basePointY;
      var maximumX         = basePointX+borderWidth;
      var minimumX         = basePointX;
      var maximumY         = basePointY+borderHeight;
      var minimumY         = basePointY;
      var currentXPts      = Array(widgetCount);
      var currentYPts      = Array(widgetCount);
      var xDeltaPts        = Array(widgetCount);
      var xDirectionPts    = Array(widgetCount);
      var yDeltaPts        = Array(widgetCount);
      var yDirectionPts    = Array(widgetCount);
```

```
var loopCount          = 0;

var maxCount           = 200;

var outerFillColor     = "White";

var outerStrokeColor   = "Blue";

var outerStrokeWidth   = 4;

var ellipseFillColor   = "Red";

var ellipseStrokeColor = "Yellow";

var ellipseStrokeWidth = 1;

var currentTick        = 0;

var shortPause         = 50;


var fillColors         = new Array("#F00","#FF0",
                         "#0F0","#00F");

var widgetColors       = ['Red','Green','Blue',
                         'Yellow'];

var colorCount         = widgetColors.length;

var theTimeout         = null;

var canvas;

var context;


function initialize() {
   initializeWidgets();

   canvas = document.getElementById('myCanvas');

   if(canvas.getContext) {
      context = canvas.getContext('2d');
      drawWidgets();
   }
}
```

```
function initializeWidgets() {
   for(var w=0; w<widgetCount; w++) {
      currentXPts[w]    = basePointX+w*rectWidth;
      currentYPts[w]    = basePointY;

      xDeltaPts[w]      = Math.floor(10*Math.
                          random())+2;
      yDeltaPts[w]      = Math.floor(10*Math.
                          random())+2;

    //xDirectionPts[w] = 1-2*Math.floor(Math.
                          random()+0.5);
      xDirectionPts[w] = 0;
      yDirectionPts[w] = 1-2*Math.floor(Math.
                          random()+0.5);

      fillColor = widgetColors[w%colorCount];
   }
}


function updateWidgetCoordinates() {
   for(var w=0; w<widgetCount; w++) {
      currentXPts[w]  += xDeltaPts[w]*
                         xDirectionPts[w];

      if( currentXPts[w] >= maximumX-rectWidth) {
         currentXPts[w] = maximumX-rectWidth;
         xDirectionPts[w] *= -1;
      }
```

```
        if( currentXPts[w] <= minimumX ) {
          currentXPts[w] = minimumX;
          xDirectionPts[w] *= -1;
        }


        currentYPts[w] += yDeltaPts[w]*
                          yDirectionPts[w];


        if( currentYPts[w] >= maximumY-rectHeight) {
          currentYPts[w] = maximumY-rectHeight;
          yDirectionPts[w] *= -1;
        }


        if( currentYPts[w] <= minimumY ) {
          currentYPts[w] = minimumY;
          yDirectionPts[w] *= -1;
        }

     }

  } // updateWidgetCoordinates

  function eraseWidgets()
  {
    for(var w=0; w<widgetCount; w++) {
      // note: use the style in the CSS selector
      context.fillStyle = "#ccc";
      context.fillRect(currentXPts[w], currentYPts[w],
                       rectWidth, rectHeight);
    }
  }
```

```
function drawWidgets() {
    eraseWidgets();

    updateWidgetCoordinates();

    for(var w=0; w<widgetCount; w++) {
     context.fillStyle = fillColors[w%4];
     context.fillRect(currentXPts[w], currentYPts[w],
                      rectWidth, rectHeight);

    }

    updateLoop();

  } // drawWidgets

function updateLoop() {
    if(++loopCount < maxCount) {
      theTimeout = setTimeout("drawWidgets()",
                   shortPause);
    }
  }

function stopAnimation(event) {
    clearTimeout(theTimeout);
  }
</script>
</head>
```

```
<body onload="initialize();">
 <header>
   <h1>HTML5 Canvas Bouncing Rectangles</h1>
 </header>

 <div>
   <canvas id="myCanvas" width="800" height="400">
           No support for Canvas
   </canvas>
 </div>
 </body>
</html>
```

As usual, the `onload` attribute in Listing 9.4 specifies the JavaScript function `initialize()` that is executed when the HTML5 page is loaded. This function does some simple initialization and then invokes the JavaScript function `initializeWidgets()`, which initializes a set of arrays for handling the set of bouncing colored rectangles.

In Listing 9.3 we used the variables `xDirection` and `yDirection` to keep track of the horizontal and vertical direction of the bouncing rectangle. In this code sample we use the arrays `xDirectionPts` and `yDirectionPts` to keep track of the horizontal and vertical direction of a set of bouncing rectangles.

The `initializeWidgets()` method contains a loop that sets the initial direction of motion for the bouncing rectangles with this code block:

```
//xDirectionPts[w] = 1-2*Math.floor(Math.random()+0.5);
xDirectionPts[w] = 0;
yDirectionPts[w] = 1-2*Math.floor(Math.random()+0.5);
```

Because the `xDirectionPts` array is initialized with the value 0, there will only be vertical motion and no side-to-side motion effect.

Next, the JavaScript function `initialize()` invokes the function `drawWidgets()` in order to render the colored rectangles. This function does four things:

- erases the current rectangles via `eraseWidgets()`
- updates the location of the rectangles via `updateWidgets()`
- renders the rectangles in their new positions using a loop
- uses the JavaScript idiom to redraw the board via `updateLoop()`

Whenever a colored rectangle moves beyond the top border or the bottom border, the function `updateWidgets()` updates the array `yDirectionPts` by reversing the appropriate location with the following line of code:

```
yDirectionPts[w] *= -1;
```

The function `updateLoop()` draws a new board after a delay of 50 milliseconds (which is the value assigned to the variable `shortPause`) by means of the following code, which is the same code that you saw in Listing 9.3:

```
theTimeout = setTimeout("drawRectangle()", shortPause);
```

Figure 9.4 displays a set of colored rectangles that are bouncing up and down inside a stationary outer rectangle.

HTML5 Canvas Bouncing Rectangles

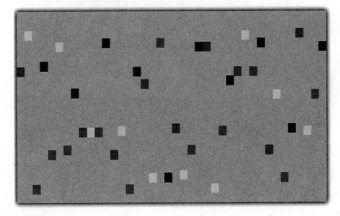

FIGURE 9.4 A set of bouncing rectangles.

THE POPTHEBALLS GAME

The final code sample in this chapter incorporates mouse-related events and animation techniques that you have seen in previous code samples. You can use this code as a starting point for an actual game and perhaps investigate how to run the code on a mobile device.

When users click on one of the bouncing circles, that circle stops moving and its color changes to red. You can enhance this code in several ways: keep track of the number of clicked blue circles and also the number of clicked yellow circles; update a scoreboard at the top (or the bottom) of the screen; reanimate the stopped circles after a two-second delay. The user who clicks the most circles wins the game. Listing 9.5 displays the contents of the HTML page `PopTheBalls.html`, which is a simple game that combines animation effects (multiple bouncing circles) and mouse events (mouseclicks).

Listing 9.5 `PopTheBalls.html`

```
<!DOCTYPE html>
<html lang="en">
 <head>
  <meta charset="utf-8" />
  <title>HTML5 Canvas Bouncing Circles</title>

<script type="text/javascript">
   var rectWidth        = 40;

   var rectHeight       = 40;

   var widgetCount      = 20;

   var borderWidth      = widgetCount*rectWidth;

   var borderHeight     = 400;

   var basePointX       = 0;

   var basePointY       = 0;

   var currentX         = basePointX;
```

```
var currentY           = basePointY;
var maximumX           = basePointX+borderWidth;
var minimumX           = basePointX;
var maximumY           = basePointY+borderHeight;
var minimumY           = basePointY;
var currentXPts        = Array(widgetCount);
var currentYPts        = Array(widgetCount);
var xDeltaPts          = Array(widgetCount);
var xDirectionPts      = Array(widgetCount);
var yDeltaPts          = Array(widgetCount);
var yDirectionPts      = Array(widgetCount);
var clickedBalls       = Array(widgetCount);

var loopCount          = 0;
var outerFillColor     = "White";
var outerStrokeColor   = "Blue";
var outerStrokeWidth   = 4;
var ellipseFillColor   = "Red";
var ellipseStrokeColor = "Yellow";
var ellipseStrokeWidth = 1;
var seconds            = 20;
var milliSeconds       = seconds*1000;
var shortPause         = 150;
var maxCount           = milliSeconds/shortPause;
var currentTick        = 0;

var fillColors         = new Array("#FF0",
                         "#00F", "#F00");

var widgetColors       = ['Red','Green','Blue',
                         'Yellow'];
```

```
    var colorCount           = widgetColors.length;

    var theTimeout           = null;

    var canvas;

    var context;


function initialize() {
  initializeWidgets();

    canvas = document.getElementById('mycanvas');

    if(canvas.getContext) {
      context = canvas.getContext('2d');
      drawWidgets();
    }
}


function initializeWidgets() {
    for(var w=0; w<widgetCount; w++) {
      currentXPts[w]     = basePointX+w*rectWidth;
      currentYPts[w]     = basePointY;

      xDeltaPts[w]       = Math.floor(10*Math.random())+2;
      yDeltaPts[w]       = Math.floor(10*Math.random())+2;

      xDirectionPts[w] = 1-2*Math.floor(Math.
                            random()+0.5);
    //xDirectionPts[w] = 0;
      yDirectionPts[w] = 1-2*Math.floor(Math.
                            random()+0.5);
```

```
        //fillColor = widgetColors[w%colorCount];
        fillColor = widgetColors[w%2];
        clickedBalls[w] = 0;
     }
  }

function updateWidgetCoordinates() {
   for(var w=0; w<widgetCount; w++) {
      if(clickedBalls[w] == 0) {
         currentXPts[w] += xDeltaPts[w]*
                        xDirectionPts[w];

         if(currentXPts[w] >= maximumX-rectWidth) {
            currentXPts[w] = maximumX-rectWidth;
            xDirectionPts[w] *= -1;
         }

         if(currentXPts[w] <= minimumX ) {
            currentXPts[w] = minimumX;
            xDirectionPts[w] *= -1;
         }

         currentYPts[w] += yDeltaPts[w]*
                        yDirectionPts[w];

         if(currentYPts[w] >= maximumY-rectHeight) {
            currentYPts[w] = maximumY-rectHeight;
            yDirectionPts[w] *= -1;
         }
```

```
            if(currentYPts[w] <= minimumY) {
                currentYPts[w] = minimumY;
                yDirectionPts[w] *= -1;
            }
        }
    }
} // updateWidgetCoordinates

function eraseWidgets()
{

    for(var w=0; w<widgetCount; w++) {
        // note: use the style in the CSS selector
        context.fillStyle = "#ccc";

        // render a rectangle:
       //context.fillRect(currentXPts[w], currentYPts[w],
       //                  rectWidth, rectHeight);

        // render a circle:
        context.beginPath();
        context.arc(currentXPts[w], currentYPts[w],
                    rectWidth/2, 0, Math.PI*2, true);
        context.fill();
    }
}

function drawWidgets() {
    eraseWidgets();

    updateWidgetCoordinates();
```

```
for(var w=0; w<widgetCount; w++) {

   if(clickedBalls[w] == 0) {

    //context.fillStyle = fillColors[w%4];

      context.fillStyle = fillColors[w%2];


      // render a rectangle:

    //context.fillRect(currentXPts[w], currentYPts[w],

    //               rectWidth, rectHeight);


      // render a circle:

      context.beginPath();

      context.arc(currentXPts[w], currentYPts[w],
              rectWidth/2, 0, Math.PI*2, true);

      context.fill();

   } else {

      context.fillStyle = fillColors[2];


      // render a rectangle:

    //context.fillRect(currentXPts[w], currentYPts[w],

    //               rectWidth, rectHeight);


      // render a circle:

      context.beginPath();

      context.arc(currentXPts[w], currentYPts[w],
              rectWidth/2, 0, Math.PI*2, true);

      context.fill();

   }

}


   updateLoop();

} // drawWidgets
```

```
function updateLoop() {
   if(++loopCount < maxCount) {
     theTimeout = setTimeout("drawWidgets()",
                shortPause);
   }
}

function checkForClickedBall(e) {
   var event = window.event || e;
   currentX  = event.clientX-10;
   currentY  = event.clientY-10;

   for(var w=0; w<widgetCount; w++) {
      if((currentX >= currentXPts[w]) &&
         (currentX <= currentXPts[w]+rectWidth) &&
         (currentY >= currentYPts[w]) &&
         (currentY <= currentYPts[w]+rectHeight)) {
            // alert("clicked on ball #"+w);
            clickedBalls[w] = 1;
            break;
      }
   }
}

function stopAnimation(event) {
   clearTimeout(theTimeout);
}
</script>

  <style type="text/css">
    canvas {
```

```
      border: 5px solid #ccc;

      background: #ccc;

   }

  </style>

</head>

<body onload="initialize();">

  <div>

   <canvas id="mycanvas" width="800" height="400"

        onclick="checkForClickedBall()">

   </canvas>

  </div>

  </body>

  <header>

    <h1>HTML5 Canvas Bouncing Circles</h1>

  </header>

</html>
```

The animation-related code in Listing 9.5 is very similar to the corresponding code in Listing 9.4, except that in this code sample we render circles instead of rectangles (but the code is retained so that you can switch between the two shapes).

The HTML5 <canvas> element in Listing 9.5 contains an onclick attribute that specifies the JavaScript function checkForClicked-Ball(), which is executed when users click their mouse. This function uses the coordinates of the mouseclick while looping through the list of circles to check if a circle has been clicked using this logic:

```
  if((currentX >= currentXPts[w]) &&

     (currentX <= currentXPts[w]+rectWidth) &&

     (currentY >= currentYPts[w]) &&

     (currentY <= currentYPts[w]+rectHeight)) {

       // alert("clicked on ball #"+w);

   }
```

Note that the preceding conditional logic tests for a mouseclick inside a rectangle, whereas the conditional logic testing for a mouseclick inside a circle involves calculating the distance between the clicked point and the center of each circle, but it's accurate enough for our purposes. Figure 9.5 displays a sample result of clicking on a set of balls that are bouncing around inside a stationary outer rectangle.

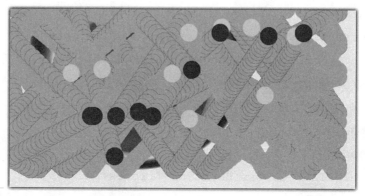

Click The Moving Balls

FIGURE 9.5 A set of bouncing balls.

SUMMARY

This chapter focused on how to apply transformations to elements in HTML5 pages. Although these effects require considerable effort in traditional programming languages, you may be surprised that these effects can be created with a few lines of simple code.

In particular you learned how to do the following:

- create animation effects by rotating shapes
- create an animation effect with a single bouncing ball
- create an animation effect with multiple bouncing balls

CHAPTER 10

CHARTS AND GRAPHS IN HTML5 CANVAS

H TML5 Canvas enables you to create charts and graphs using some of the Canvas Application Programming Interfaces (APIs) that you have seen in earlier chapters. The code samples use material that you have learned in earlier chapters, including Canvas-based linear and radial gradients and CSS3 stylesheets with gradient effects. The bar charts use the fillRect() method to render rectangles; the line graphs use the lineTo() method to render line segments; the area graph uses the lineTo() method to render a set of adjacent trapezoids; and the pie chart uses the arc() method to render each wedge of the pie chart.

This chapter starts with an example of a basic bar chart, followed by an example of mouse-enabled bar charts as well as bar charts with gradient shading. In the last part of this chapter you will learn how to render line graphs, followed by how to render a three-dimensional bar chart.

RENDERING GRADIENT BAR CHARTS

You can render a bar chart in HTML5 Canvas with a gradient effect by adding a linear gradient or a radial gradient, which can create a much richer visual effect than using standard colors for the bar chart.

The HTML page BarChart2LG1.html in Listing 10.1 illustrates how to render a bar chart with linear gradient shading. The complete source code for the CSS3 stylesheet CSS32Background2.css that is referenced in Listing 10.1 is available on the DVD for this book.

Listing 10.1 BarChart2LG1.html

```html
<!DOCTYPE html>
<html lang="en">
 <head>
  <meta charset="utf-8" />
  <title>HTML5 Canvas Bar Chart Linear Gradient</title>

  <link href="CSS32Background1.css" rel="stylesheet"
            type="text/css">
  <script type="text/javascript">
      var currentX      = 0;
      var currentY      = 0;
      var barCount      = 12;
      var barWidth      = 40;
      var barHeight     = 0;
      var maxHeight     = 280;
      var xAxisWidth    = (2*barCount+1)*barWidth/2;
      var yAxisHeight   = maxHeight;
      var labelY        = 0;
      var indentY       = 5;
      var shadowX       = 2;
      var shadowY       = 2;
      var axisFontSize  = 12;
      var fontSize      = 16;
      var leftBorder    = 30;
      var topBorder     = 15;
      var arrowWidth    = 10;
      var arrowHeight   = 6;
      var barHeights    = new Array(barCount);
      var elem, context, gradient1;
```

```
function drawGraph() {
  // Get the canvas element
  elem = document.getElementById('myCanvas');
  if (!elem || !elem.getContext) {
    return;
  }


  // Get the canvas 2d context
  context = elem.getContext('2d');
  if (!context) {
    return;
  }


  drawGraph2();
}


function drawAndLabelAxes() {
    // draw vertical axis...
    context.beginPath();
    context.fillStyle = "rgb(0,0,0)";
    context.lineWidth = 2;
    context.moveTo(leftBorder, topBorder);
    context.lineTo(leftBorder, yAxisHeight);
    context.stroke();

    // draw top arrow...
    context.beginPath();
   context.moveTo(leftBorder-arrowHeight/2, topBorder);
   context.lineTo(leftBorder+arrowHeight/2, topBorder);
```

```
context.lineTo(leftBorder, topBorder-arrowWidth);
context.lineTo(leftBorder-arrowHeight/2, topBorder);
context.fill();

// draw horizontal axis...
context.beginPath();
context.moveTo(leftBorder, yAxisHeight);
context.lineTo(xAxisWidth, yAxisHeight);
context.stroke();

// draw right arrow...
context.beginPath();
context.moveTo(xAxisWidth, yAxisHeight-arrowHeight/2);
context.lineTo(xAxisWidth+arrowWidth, yAxisHeight);
context.lineTo(xAxisWidth, yAxisHeight+arrowHeight/2);
context.lineTo(xAxisWidth, yAxisHeight);
context.fill();

// label the horizontal axis
context.font = "bold "+axisFontSize+"pt
                New Times Roman";
context.lineWidth   = 2;
context.strokeStyle = "#000";

for(var i=0; i<barCount; i++) {
  context.beginPath();
  currentX = leftBorder+i*barWidth;
  currentY = maxHeight+axisFontSize;
  //context.fillStyle = fillColors[i%4];
  context.fillStyle = "#000";
```

```
// Outline a text string
context.strokeText(""+currentX, currentX+shadowX,
                   currentY+shadowY);

// Fill a text string
context.fillStyle = "#FF0";
context.fillText(""+currentX, currentX,currentY);
}

// label the vertical axis
context.font = "bold "+axisFontSize+"pt
              New Times Roman";
context.lineWidth   = 2;
context.strokeStyle = "#000";

for(var i=0; i<barCount; i++) {
  context.beginPath();
  currentX = 0;
  currentY = Math.floor(maxHeight-i*maxHeight/
            barCount);
  labelY   = Math.floor(i*maxHeight/barCount);

  //context.fillStyle = fillColors[i%4];
  context.fillStyle = "#000";

  // Outline a text string
  context.strokeText(""+labelY, currentX+shadowX,
                     currentY+shadowY);

  // Fill a text string
  context.fillStyle = "#FF0";
  context.fillText(""+labelY, currentX, currentY);
  }

  }
```

```
function randomBarValues() {

  for(var i=0; i<barCount; i++) {

    barHeight = (maxHeight-indentY)*Math.random();

    barHeights[i] = barHeight;

  }

}


function drawGraph2() {

  // clear the canvas before drawing new set of
          rectangles
  context.clearRect(0, 0, elem.width, elem.height);

  drawAndLabelAxes();

  randomBarValues();

  drawElements();

}


function drawElements() {

  for(var i=0; i<barCount; i++) {

    currentX = leftBorder+i*barWidth;

    currentY = maxHeight-barHeights[i],


    gradient1 = context.createLinearGradient
                (currentX, currentY,
                 currentX+barWidth,
                 currentY+barHeights[i]);


    gradient1.addColorStop(0,   '#f00');

    gradient1.addColorStop(0.3,'#000');

    gradient1.addColorStop(0.6,'#ff0');

    gradient1.addColorStop(1,   '#00f');
```

```
        context.fillStyle = gradient1;


        context.shadowColor   = "rgba(100,100,100,.5)";
        context.shadowOffsetX = 3;
        context.shadowOffsetY = 3;
        context.shadowBlur    = 5;


        context.fillRect(leftBorder+i*barWidth, maxHeight-
                    barHeights[i], barWidth,
                    barHeights[i]);
    }


    drawBarText();
}


function drawBarText() {
    // Define some drawing attributes
    context.font = "bold "+fontSize+"pt
                New Times Roman";
    context.lineWidth   = 2;
    context.strokeStyle = "#000";


    for(var i=0; i<barCount; i++) {
        context.beginPath();
        currentX = leftBorder+i*barWidth;
        currentY = maxHeight-barHeights[i]+fontSize/4;
      //context.fillStyle = fillColors[i%4];
        context.fillStyle = "#000";


        barHeight = Math.floor(barHeights[i]);
```

```
        // Outline a text string
        context.strokeText(""+barHeight,current
                        X+shadowX, currentY+shadowY);


        // Fill a text string
        context.fillStyle = "#F00";
        context.fillText(""+barHeight, currentX,
                        currentY);

      }

    }

  </script>
</head>


<body onload="drawGraph();">
  <header>
    <h1>Linear Gradient Bar Chart</h1>
  </header>


  <div>
   <canvas id="myCanvas" width="500" height="300">
            No support for Canvas</canvas>
  </div>


  <input type="button" onclick="drawGraph();return
            false"

        value="Update Graph Values" />
</body>
</html>
```

Listing 10.1 contains one loop for initializing the randomly generated heights of the bar chart elements, followed by another loop that renders those bar chart elements with a linear gradient consisting of four color stops.

The variable `barHeight` is used for the height of each rectangle, and it is assigned an integer-based value of a randomly generated number. A simple conditional ensures that the bar height is always at least equal to a minimum value. The x-coordinate of the upper-left vertex for the current bar element is assigned to the variable `currentX` and the variable `currentY` is assigned a value that will be used in the computation of the y-coordinate of this same vertex.

The width and height of each rectangle are assigned the values of `barWidth` and `barHeight`, respectively, and each rectangle is rendered with a linear gradient. Because the bar heights are based on randomly generated numbers, the chart will change each time that you refresh the display. You can use the code in this example as a starting point from which you can add more detail, such as labels for the horizontal and vertical axes. Figure 10.1 renders a bar chart with linear gradient shading.

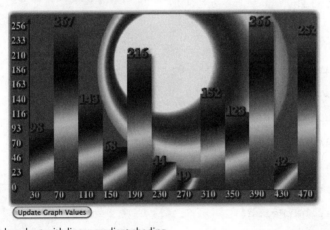

FIGURE 10.1 A bar chart with linear gradient shading.

MOUSE-ENABLED BAR CHARTS

HTML5 `Canvas` supports all the mouse-related events that have worked in earlier versions of HTML, and those mouse events can be processed in JavaScript functions. Listing 10.2 displays the contents of the HTML page `MouseBarChart2LG1.html`, which illustrates how to handle mouseclick events in an HTML5 `<canvas>` element.

Listing 10.2 `MouseBarChart2LG1.html`

```html
<!DOCTYPE html>
<html lang="en">
 <head>
  <meta charset="utf-8" />
  <title>HTML5 Canvas Bar Chart With Mouse Events</title>

  <style type="text/css">
    canvas {
       border: 5px solid #888;
       background: #CCC;
     }
  </style>

  <script type="text/javascript">
    var basePointX   = 20;
    var basePointY   = 0;
    var currentX       = basePointX;
    var currentY       = basePointY;
    var barCount      = 12;
    var barWidth       = 40;
    var barHeight      = 0;
    var shadowX        = 2;
    var shadowY        = 2;
    var axisFontSize = 12;
    var fontSize       = 16;
    var lineWidth     = 2;
    var currentBar    = 0;
```

```
var maxHeight     = 330;

var xAxisWidth    = (2*barCount+1)*barWidth/2;

var yAxisHeight   = maxHeight;

var labelY        = 0;

var indentY       = 5;

var leftBorder    = 30;

var topBorder     = 15;

var arrowWidth    = 10;

var arrowHeight   = 6;

var barHeights    = new Array(barCount);

var gradient1;

var elem, context, gradient1;

function drawGraph() {
    elem = document.getElementById('myCanvas');
    if (!elem || !elem.getContext) {
      return;
    }

    // Get the canvas 2d context.
    context = elem.getContext('2d');
    if (!context) {
      return;
    }
    drawGraph2();
}

function drawAndLabelAxes() {
    // code omitted for brevity
}
```

```
function randomBarValues() {
    for(var i=0; i<barCount; i++) {
        barHeight = (maxHeight-indentY)*Math.random();
        barHeights[i] = barHeight;
    }
}

function drawGraph2() {
    // clear the canvas...
    context.fillStyle = "#ccc";

    context.fillRect(0, 0, 600, 350);
    context.fill();

    drawAndLabelAxes();
    randomBarValues();
    drawElements();
}

function drawElements() {
    for(var i=0; i<barCount; i++) {
        currentX = leftBorder+i*barWidth;
        currentY = maxHeight-barHeights[i],

        gradient1 = context.createLinearGradient
                        (currentX, currentY, currentX+
                        barWidth, currentY+barHeights[i]);

        gradient1.addColorStop(0,  '#f00');
        gradient1.addColorStop(0.3,'#000');
        gradient1.addColorStop(0.6,'#ff0');
        gradient1.addColorStop(1,  '#00f');
        context.fillStyle = gradient1;
```

```
        context.shadowColor    = "rgba(100,100,100,.5)";

        context.shadowOffsetX = 3;

        context.shadowOffsetY = 3;

        context.shadowBlur     = 5;


        context.fillRect(leftBorder+i*barWidth,
                         maxHeight-barHeights[i],
                         barWidth, barHeights[i]);

    }

}


function drawBarText(e) {
  var event = window.event || e;
  var currX = event.clientX;


  currentBar = Math.floor((currX-basePointX)/
             barWidth);


  if((currentBar >= 0) && (currentBar < barCount)) {
     barHeight = Math.floor(barHeights[currentBar]);


     currentX  = leftBorder+currentBar*barWidth;

     currentY  = maxHeight-barHeight;


     // Define some drawing attributes
     context.font = "bold "+fontSize+"pt
                     New Times Roman";

     context.lineWidth   = 2;

     context.strokeStyle = "#000";


     // Outline a text string
     context.strokeText(""+barHeight, currentX+
                     shadowX, currentY+shadowY);
```

```
                // Fill a text string
                context.fillStyle = "#F00";
                context.fillText(""+barHeight, currentX,
                                 currentY);
            }
         }
      </script>
   </head>


   <body onload="drawGraph();">
      <header>
         <h1>HTML5 Canvas Bar Chart Linear Gradient</h1>
      </header>


      <div style="margin-left:0px;">
         <canvas id="myCanvas" width="600" height="350"
                 style="border: 5px blue solid"
                 onmousemove="drawBarText()"
                 onclick="drawBarChart()">
         </canvas>
      <div>


      <input type="button" onclick="drawGraph();return false"
             value="Update Graph Values" />
   </body>
   </html>
```

Listing 10.3 renders a bar chart with code that is familiar from earlier examples in this chapter. There are two key differences in this code sample.

The first difference is the additional attributes in the HTML5 <canvas> element, as shown here:

```
<canvas id="myCanvas" width="600" height="350"
        style="border: 5px blue solid"
        onmousemove="drawBarText()"
        onclick="drawBarChart()">
</canvas>
```

When users click inside the HTML5 <canvas> element, the JavaScript function `drawBarChart()` is invoked, which refreshes the bar chart. When users move their mouse, the `drawBarText()` method is invoked, which checks whether users have clicked inside the bar chart by means of the following code fragment:

```
var currX = event.clientX;
currentBar = Math.floor((currX-basePointX)/barWidth);
if((currentBar >= 0) && (currentBar < barCount)) {
    barHeight = Math.floor(barHeights[currentBar]);
    // the omitted code displays a text string that
    // contains the height of the current rectangle
}
```

Note that the preceding code only checks if the x-coordinate of a mouseclick is inside one of the bar elements of the bar chart; if you want ensure that the y-coordinate is also inside a bar chart, you need additional conditional logic in the code. Figure 10.2 displays a bar chart that displays bar-related information as users move their mouse around the screen.

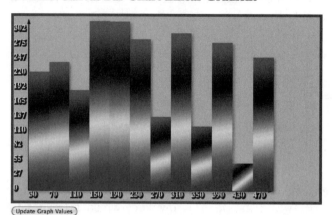

FIGURE 10.2 Mouse-enabled bar chart.

RENDERING 3D BAR CHARTS

In Chapter 4, "Rendering Basic 2D Shapes in HTML5 `Canvas`," you saw how to render a cube in HTML5 `Canvas` by rendering the top face (a parallelogram), the front face (a rectangle), and the right face (a parallelogram) of the cube. The same technique is used in this section in order to render each bar element in the bar chart. The HTML page `BarChart-13D1Mouse1.html` in Listing 10.3 illustrates how to render a mouse-enabled bar chart with a three-dimensional effect.

Listing 10.3 `BarChart13D1Mouse1.html`

```
<!DOCTYPE html>
<html lang="en">
 <head>
  <meta charset="utf-8" />
  <title>HTML5 Canvas 3D Bar Chart Linear Gradient</title>

  <script type="text/javascript">
   var currentX    = 0;
   var currentY    = 0;
```

```
var barCount    = 12;
var barWidth    = 40;
var barHeight   = 0;
var maxHeight   = 330;
var slantX      = barWidth/3;
var slantY      = barWidth/3;
var shadowX     = 2;
var shadowY     = 2;
var axisFontSize = 12;
var fontSize    = 16;
var labelY      = 0;
var indentY     = 10;
var leftBorder  = 30;
var topBorder   = 15;
var arrowWidth  = 10;
var arrowHeight = 6;
var topShading  = "#888";
var rightShading = "#444";
var xAxisWidth   = (barCount+1)*barWidth;
var yAxisHeight = maxHeight;
var barHeights  = new Array(barCount);
var elem, context, gradient1;

function drawGraph() {
    elem = document.getElementById('myCanvas');
    if (!elem || !elem.getContext) {
      return;
    }
}
```

```
    // Get the canvas 2d context.
    context = elem.getContext('2d');
    if (!context) {
      return;
    }

    drawBarChart();
}

function drawAndLabelAxes() {
    // code omitted for brevity
}

function randomBarValues() {
    for(var i=0; i<barCount; i++) {
        barHeight = (maxHeight-indentY)*Math.random();
        barHeights[i] = barHeight;
    }
}

function drawBarChart() {
    // clear the canvas before drawing new set of
            rectangles
    context.clearRect(0, 0, elem.width, elem.height);

    drawAndLabelAxes();
    randomBarValues();
    drawElements();
}
```

```
function drawElements() {
    for(var i=0; i<barCount; i++) {
        currentX = leftBorder+i*barWidth;
        currentY = maxHeight-barHeights[i];

        // front face (rectangle)
        gradient1 = context.createLinearGradient
                    (currentX, currentY, currentX+
                    barWidth, currentY+barHeights[i]);

        gradient1.addColorStop(0,  '#f00');
        gradient1.addColorStop(0.3,'#000');
        gradient1.addColorStop(0.6,'#ff0');
        gradient1.addColorStop(1,  '#00f');

        context.fillStyle = gradient1;

        context.shadowColor   = "rgba(100,100,
                                100,.5)";
        context.shadowOffsetX = 3;
        context.shadowOffsetY = 3;
        context.shadowBlur    = 5;

        context.fillRect(currentX, currentY, barWidth,
                    barHeights[i]);

        // top face (parallelogram)
        // CCW from lower-left vertex
        context.beginPath();
        context.fillStyle = topShading;
        context.shadowColor   = "rgba(100,100,100,.5)";
```

```
        context.shadowOffsetX = 3;

        context.shadowOffsetY = 3;

        context.shadowBlur    = 5;


        context.moveTo(currentX, currentY);

        context.lineTo(currentX+barWidth, currentY);

        context.lineTo(currentX+barWidth+slantX,
                     currentY-slantY);

        context.lineTo(currentX+slantX,
                     currentY-slantY);

        context.closePath();

        context.fill();


        // right face (parallelogram)

        // CW from upper-left vertex

        context.beginPath();

        context.fillStyle = rightShading;


        context.shadowColor   = "rgba(100,100,100,.5)";

        context.shadowOffsetX = 3;

        context.shadowOffsetY = 3;

        context.shadowBlur    = 5;


        context.moveTo(currentX+barWidth, currentY);

        context.lineTo(currentX+barWidth+slantX,
                     currentY-slantY);

        context.lineTo(currentX+barWidth+slantX,
                     currentY+barHeights[i]-slantY);

        context.lineTo(currentX+barWidth,
                     currentY+barHeights[i]);

        context.closePath();

        context.fill();

    }
```

```
        drawBarText();
    }


function drawBarText() {
    // Define some drawing attributes
    context.font = "bold "+fontSize+"pt
            New Times Roman";
    context.lineWidth   = 2;
    context.strokeStyle = "#000";


    for(var i=0; i<barCount; i++) {
        context.beginPath();
        currentX = leftBorder+i*barWidth;
        currentY = maxHeight-barHeights[i]+fontSize/4;
     //context.fillStyle = fillColors[i%4];
        context.fillStyle = "#000";


        barHeight = Math.floor(barHeights[i]);


        // Outline a text string
        context.strokeText(""+barHeight,
                        currentX+shadowX,
                        currentY+shadowY);


        // Fill a text string
        context.fillStyle = "#F00";
        context.fillText(""+barHeight, currentX,
                    currentY);

    }
}
</script>
```

```
<style type="text/css">
  canvas {
     border: 5px solid #888;
     background: #CCC;
  }
</style>
</head>

<body onload="drawGraph();">
  <header>
    <h1>HTML5 Canvas 3D Bar Chart</h1>
  </header>

  <figure>
   <canvas id="myCanvas" width="600" height="350">
         No support for Canvas</canvas>
  </figure>

  <input type="button" onclick="drawGraph();
                  return false"
        value="Update Graph Values" />
</body>
</html>
```

Listing 10.3 extends the functionality of the code in Listing 10.2 by adding a parallelogram above and to the right of each rectangle in the bar chart, thereby creating a three-dimensional effect. Listing 10.3 contains code for creating the front face of the bar elements and for rendering the horizontal and vertical axes, which is the same as the code in Listing 10.2.

The main loop in Listing 10.3 creates a linear gradient with four stop colors that is used for rendering the top, front, and right face of each bar element in the bar chart.

Figure 10.3 displays a three-dimensional bar chart in which the height of individual bar elements is highlighted when users move their mouse over the bar elements.

HTML5 Canvas 3D Bar Chart

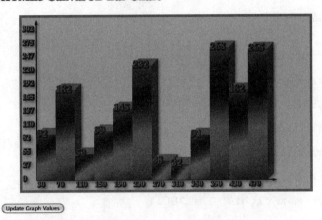

FIGURE 10.3 A mouse-enabled 3D bar chart.

RENDERING MULTIPLE LINE GRAPHS

In the previous section you learned how to render a simple line graph, and in this section you will see how to render multiple line graphs in the same HTML page. Listing 10.4 displays the contents of the HTML page `MultiLineGraphs2.html`, which illustrates how to render a set of line graphs.

Listing 10.4 `MultiLineGraphs2.html`

```
<!DOCTYPE html>
<html lang="en">
 <head>
  <meta charset="utf-8" />
  <title>HTML5 Canvas Line Graphs</title>
```

```
<style type="text/css">
  canvas {
      border: 5px solid #888;
      background: #CCC;
  }
</style>

<script type="text/javascript">
  var currentX      = 0;
  var currentY      = 0;
  var barCount      = 12;
  var barWidth      = 40;
  var barHeight     = 0;
  var maxHeight     = 280;
  var xAxisWidth    = barCount*barWidth;
  var yAxisHeight   = maxHeight;
  var shadowX       = 2;
  var shadowY       = 2;
  var axisFontSize  = 12;
  var fontSize      = 16;
  var labelY        = 0;
  var indentY       = 5;
  var leftBorder    = 30;
  var topBorder     = 15;
  var arrowWidth    = 10;
  var arrowHeight   = 6;
  var dotRadius     = 6;
  var lineCount     = 3;
```

```
var barHeights    = new Array(barCount);

var barHeights2   = new Array(barCount);

var barHeights3   = new Array(barCount);

var currHeights   = new Array(barCount);

var multiLines    = new Array(lineCount);

var fillColors    = new Array("#F00", "#FF0",
                              "#0F0", "#00F");

var elem, context, gradient1;

function drawGraph() {
    // Get the canvas element
    elem = document.getElementById('myCanvas');
    if (!elem || !elem.getContext) {
      return;
    }


    // Get the canvas 2d context
    context = elem.getContext('2d');
    if (!context) {
      return;
    }


    drawGraph2();
}

function drawAndLabelAxes() {
    // code omitted for brevity
}
```

```
function randomBarValues() {
    for(var i=0; i<barCount; i++) {
        barHeight = maxHeight*Math.random();
        barHeights[i] = barHeight;

        barHeight = maxHeight*Math.random();
        barHeights2[i] = barHeight;

        barHeight = maxHeight*Math.random();
        barHeights3[i] = barHeight;
    }

    multiLines[0] = barHeights;
    multiLines[1] = barHeights2;
    multiLines[2] = barHeights3;
}

function drawGraph2() {
    // clear the canvas before drawing new set of
            rectangles
    context.clearRect(0, 0, elem.width, elem.height);

    randomBarValues();
    drawAndLabelAxes();
    drawElements();
}

function drawElements() {
    for(var h=0; h<multiLines.length; h++) {
        currHeights = multiLines[h];
```

```
   currentX = leftBorder;
//currentY = maxHeight-barHeights[0];
   currentY = maxHeight-currHeights[0];

   // draw line segments...
   for(var i=0; i<barCount; i++) {
      context.beginPath();
      context.moveTo(currentX, currentY);
      currentX = leftBorder+i*barWidth;
    //currentY = maxHeight-barHeights[i];
      currentY = maxHeight-currHeights[i];

      context.shadowColor   = "rgba(100,100,
                               100,.5)";
      context.shadowOffsetX = 3;
      context.shadowOffsetY = 3;
      context.shadowBlur    = 5;

      context.lineWidth   = 4;
      context.strokeStyle = fillColors[i%4];
      context.lineCap     = "miter"; // "round";

      context.lineTo(currentX, currentY);
      context.stroke();
   }

   // draw the dots...
   for(var i=0; i<barCount; i++) {
      context.beginPath();
      currentX = leftBorder+i*barWidth;
```

```
        //currentY = maxHeight-barHeights[i];
          currentY = maxHeight-currHeights[i];
          context.fillStyle = fillColors[i%4];

          context.arc(currentX, currentY, dotRadius, 0,
                    Math.PI*2, 0);
          context.fill();
      }
  }

  drawBarText();
}

function drawBarText() {
  // Define some drawing attributes
  context.font = "bold "+fontSize+"pt
              New Times Roman";
  context.lineWidth   = 2;
  context.strokeStyle = "#000";

  for(var h=0; h<multiLines.length; h++) {
    currHeights = multiLines[h];

    for(var i=0; i<barCount; i++) {
      context.beginPath();
      currentX = leftBorder+i*barWidth;
     //currentY = maxHeight-barHeights
                  [i]+fontSize/4;
      currentY = maxHeight-currHeights
                  [i]+fontSize/4;
    //context.fillStyle = fillColors[i%4];
      context.fillStyle = "#000";
```

```
            //barHeight = Math.floor(barHeights[i]);
            barHeight = Math.floor(currHeights[i]);

            // Outline a text string
            context.strokeText(""+barHeight, currentX+
                            shadowX, currentY+shadowY);

            // Fill a text string
            context.fillStyle = "#F00";
            context.fillText(""+barHeight, currentX,
                            currentY);

        }
    }
}
    </script>
</head>

<body onload="drawGraph();">
    <header>
        <h1>HTML5 Canvas Line Graphs</h1>
    </header>

    <div>
        <canvas id="myCanvas" width="500" height="300">
                No support for Canvas
        </canvas>
    </div>

    <input type="button" onclick="drawGraph();return false"
            value="Update Graph Values" />
</body>
</html>
```

The JavaScript function `drawGraph()` in Listing 10.4 is invoked when the HTML5 page is loaded, and this function consists of three distinct loops. The first loop calculates the vertices for three distinct line graphs and stores the calculated values in the arrays `barHeights`, `barHeights2`, and `barHeights3`, respectively.

Next, a new array is created that references the vertices of the three line graphs using the following code:

```
multiLines[0] = barHeights;

multiLines[1] = barHeights2;

multiLines[2] = barHeights3;
```

Now that the line graph arrays have been initialized, we can proceed with rendering the three line graphs. This is accomplished by a nested loop, where the outer loop iterates through the elements of the array `multiLines`, and the inner loop renders one line graph, as shown here in high-level form:

```
for(var h=0; h<multiLines.length; h++) {

    currHeights = multiLines[h];
    // code omitted

    // draw line segments...
    for(var i=0; i<barCount; i++) {
      // code omitted

    }

    // render the dots
    for(var i=0; i<barCount; i++) {
      // code omitted

    }

}
```

Figure 10.4 renders a set of line graphs based on the code and data values in Listing 10.4.

HTML5 Canvas Line Graphs

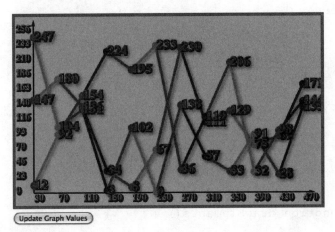

FIGURE 10.4 A set of line graphs.

RENDERING AREA GRAPHS

A bar chart consists of contiguous rectangles, but an area graph consists of a set of contiguous trapezoids that sit on the same horizontal line segment (which is often the horizontal axis for the graph). Because rectangles have two pairs of parallel sides, whereas trapezoids have only one pair of parallel sides, bar charts and area graphs are programmatically similar. We will, however, render an area graph by rendering line segments via the moveTo() method. The HTML page AreaGraph2.html contains four pages of code that is similar to code that you saw in the HTML5 page MultiLineGraphs2.html. Consequently, Listing 10.5 displays only the function drawElements() that contains a new section of code, and you can find the entire code listing on the DVD.

Listing 10.5 AreaGraph2.html

```
<!DOCTYPE html>
<html lang="en">
 <head>
  <meta charset="utf-8" />
  <title>HTML5 Canvas Area Graph</title>
```

```
<style type="text/css">
  canvas {
    border: 5px solid #888;
    background: #CCC;
  }
</style>

<script type="text/javascript">
  // code omitted for brevity

  function drawElements() {
    for(var i=0; i<barCount-1; i++) {
      currentX1 = leftBorder+i*barWidth;
      currentY1 = maxHeight-barHeights[i];
      currentX2 = leftBorder+(i+1)*barWidth;
      currentY2 = maxHeight-barHeights[i+1];

      gradient1 = context.createLinearGradient
                  (currentX1, currentY1,
                   currentX1+barWidth,
                   currentY1+barHeights[i]);

      gradient1.addColorStop(0,   '#f00');
      gradient1.addColorStop(0.3,'#000');
      gradient1.addColorStop(0.6,'#ff0');
      gradient1.addColorStop(1,   '#00f');

      context.beginPath();
    //context.fillStyle = fillColors[i%4];
      context.fillStyle = gradient1;
```

```
            context.shadowColor    = "rgba(100,100, 100,.5)";
            context.shadowOffsetX = 3;
            context.shadowOffsetY = 3;
            context.shadowBlur     = 5;

            // this code renders the current trapezoid
            context.moveTo(currentX1, currentY1);
            context.lineTo(currentX2, currentY2);
            context.lineTo(currentX2, maxHeight);
            context.lineTo(currentX1, maxHeight);

            context.fill();
        }

        drawTheDots();
        drawBarText();
    }

</head>

<body onload="drawGraph();">
  <header>
    <h1>HTML5 Canvas Area Graph</h1>
  </header>

  <div>
   <canvas id="myCanvas" width="500" height="300">
         No support for Canvas
   </canvas>
   </div>
```

```
<input type="button" onclick="drawGraph();return false"
        value="Update Graph Values" />
</body>
</html>
```

The JavaScript function `drawGraph()` in Listing 10.5 is invoked when the HTML5 page is loaded, and this function consists of three distinct loops, similar to previous examples in this chapter. The first loop calculates the vertices of the line segments that represent the top of the contiguous trapezoids. The second loop uses the values of the vertices in order to construct each trapezoid. The final loop renders a set of circles on the end points of the line segments. Figure 10.5 renders an area graph based on the code and data values in Listing 10.5.

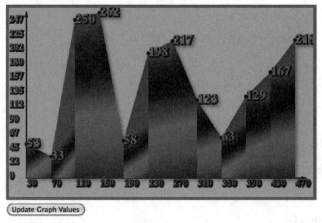

FIGURE 10.5 A simple area graph.

RENDERING PIE CHARTS

Pie charts are very popular for representing data in a graphical manner, and you often see presentations rendering a set of data in a pie chart as well as a bar chart. The HTML5 page `PieChart1.html` in Listing 10.6 contains the code that renders a pie chart.

Listing 10.6 `PieChart1.html`

```
<!DOCTYPE html>
<html lang="en">
 <head>
  <meta charset="utf-8" />
  <title>HTML5 Canvas Pie Chart</title>

  <style type="text/css">
    canvas {
        border: 5px solid #888;
        background: #CCC;
    }
  </style>

  <script type="text/javascript">
    var basePointX   = 200;
    var basePointY   = 150;
    var sumAngles    = 0;
    var endAngle     = 0;
    var startAngle   = 0;
    var fontSize     = 16;
    var shadowX      = 1;
    var shadowY      = 1;
    var currentX     = 0;
    var currentY     = 0;
    var pieAngle     = 0;
    var piePercent   = 0;
```

```
var legendWidth  = fontSize;

var legendHeight = fontSize;

var wedgeRadius  = 140;

var wedgeCount   = 6;


var maxAngle     = 360/wedgeCount;

var minAngle     = 3*maxAngle/4;

var pieAngles    = new Array(wedgeCount);

var wedgeAngles  = new Array(wedgeCount);

var fillColors   = new Array("#F00", "#FF0",
                   "#0F0", "#00F", "#F0F", "#0BB",
                   "#B44", "#44B", "#484", "#888",
                   "#0FF", "#BB0");


var elem, context, gradient1;

function drawGraph() {
   elem = document.getElementById('myCanvas');
   if (!elem || !elem.getContext) {
      return;
   }

   context = elem.getContext('2d');
   if (!context) {
      return;
   }

   drawGraph2();
}

function randomPieValues() {
   sumAngles    = 0;
   totalPieCount = 0;
```

```
      for(var i=0; i<wedgeCount; i++) {
         pieAngle = maxAngle*Math.random();

         if(pieAngle < minAngle) {
            pieAngle = minAngle;
         }

         pieAngles[i] = pieAngle;
         totalPieCount += pieAngle;
      }

      wedgeAngles[0] = 0;

      for(var i=1; i<wedgeCount; i++) {
         wedgeAngle = Math.floor(pieAngles[i]*360/
                    totalPieCount);
         wedgeAngles[i] = wedgeAngles[i-1]+wedgeAngle;
      }
   }


function drawGraph2() {
   // clear the canvas before drawing new pie chart
   context.clearRect(0, 0, elem.width, elem.height);

   randomPieValues();
   drawElements();
   drawPieText();
   drawLegend();
}
```

```
function drawElements() {
    for(var i=0; i<wedgeCount; i++) {
        startAngle = wedgeAngles[i]*Math.PI/180;


        if(i==wedgeCount-1) {
            endAngle = 360*Math.PI/180;
        } else {
            endAngle = wedgeAngles[i+1]*Math.PI/180;
        }


        context.fillStyle = fillColors[i%fillColors.
                length];
        context.shadowColor   = "rgba(64,64,64,.5)";
        context.shadowOffsetX = 3;
        context.shadowOffsetY = 3;
        context.shadowBlur    = 5;


        context.beginPath();


        context.moveTo(basePointX, basePointY);
        context.arc(basePointX, basePointY,
                wedgeRadius, startAngle, endAngle, 0);


        context.closePath();
        context.fill();
    }
}
```

```
function drawPieText() {
    // Define some drawing attributes
    context.font = "bold "+fontSize+"pt
            New Times Roman";
    context.lineWidth   = 2;
    context.strokeStyle = "#000";

    for(var i=1; i<wedgeCount; i++) {
        context.fillStyle = "#000";

        pieAngle = (wedgeAngles[i]-wedgeAngles[i-1]);

        currentX = basePointX+(wedgeRadius-20)* Math.
                cos(wedgeAngles[i] *Math.PI/180);

        currentY = basePointY+(wedgeRadius-20)* Math.
                sin(wedgeAngles[i]*Math.PI/180);

        context.moveTo(currentX, currentY);

        piePercent = Math.floor(100*pieAngle/360);

        // Outline a text string
        context.strokeText(""+piePercent, currentX+
                    shadowX, currentY+shadowY);

        // Fill a text string
        context.fillStyle = "#F00";
        context.fillText(""+piePercent, currentX,
                    currentY);
    }

}
```

```
function drawLegend() {
    // Define some drawing attributes
    context.font = "bold "+fontSize+"pt
            New Times Roman";
    context.lineWidth   = 2;
    context.strokeStyle = "#000";

    for(var i=0; i<wedgeCount; i++) {
        currentX = basePointX+11*wedgeRadius/10;
        currentY = basePointY-wedgeRadius /2+i*
                (fontSize+4);

        context.fillStyle = fillColors[i%fillColors.length];

        context.fillRect(currentX, currentY,
                    legendWidth, legendHeight);

        context.fillText("Company "+(i+1), currentX+2*
                    legendWidth, currentY+
                    legendHeight);
    }
}
</script>
</head>

<body onload="drawGraph();">
    <header>
        <h1>Canvas Pie Chart</h1>
    </header>
```

```
<div>
 <canvas id="myCanvas" width="500" height="300">
       No support for Canvas
 </canvas>
 </div>


 <input type="button" onclick="drawGraph();return false"
       value="Update Graph Values" />
 </body>
</html>
```

The JavaScript function `drawGraph()` in Listing 10.6 is executed when this HTML5 page is loaded in a browser. This function uses the `random()` function in order to initialize the array `wedgeAngles` with values for a set of angles (measured in degrees).

The second loop uses the HTML5 Canvas `arc()` method with the values in the `wedgeAngles` array in order to render the pie chart. Note that the angle span of the wedges changes in a random fashion when users reload this HTML page. The second loop uses the loop variable as an index into the array `fillColors` to select a standard color for rendering each wedge of the pie chart. In addition, each wedge is rendered with a shadow effect with the following code block:

```
context.shadowColor    = "rgba(100,100,100,.5)";
context.shadowOffsetX = 3;
context.shadowOffsetY = 3;
context.shadowBlur     = 5;
```

Figure 10.6 displays a pie chart based on the code and the data values in Listing 10.6.

Canvas Pie Chart

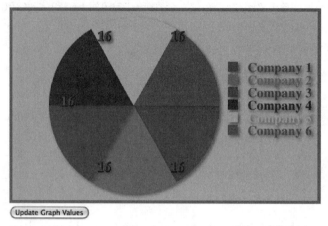

FIGURE 10.6 A pie chart in HTML5 `Canvas`.

RENDERING MULTIPLE CHARTS AND GRAPHS

Now that you have completed this chapter, you know techniques that can be used to create many types of charts and graphs, and also how to add custom modifications. The example in this section is based on the code for a bar chart, line graph, and a pie chart that you have seen in previous examples. Because the code is virtually the same it is not covered, but you can find the entire listing on the DVD. Figure 10.7 displays a bar chart, a line graph, and a pie chart based on the code in the HTML5 page `Bar-Chart2LG1Line1Pie1.html` and the CSS3 stylesheet `BarChart2L-G1Line1Pie1.css`, both of which are on the DVD.

Bar Chart, Line Graph, and Pie Chart

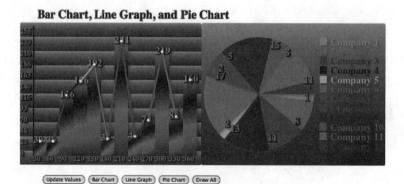

FIGURE 10.7 A bar chart, line graph, and pie chart in HTML5 `Canvas`.

SUMMARY

This chapter showed you how to create charts and graphs with linear gradients defined in HTML5 Canvas and also linear gradients defined in CSS3 selectors. You learned how to render the following:

- bar charts with gradient shading
- 3D mouse-enabled bar charts
- simple line graphs and multiline graphs
- area graphs
- pie charts

This chapter concludes the HTML5 Canvas portion of the book, and because it's also the last chapter of the book, you are ready to delve deeper into some of these topics, or perhaps venture into areas that were not covered in this book. Regardless of the direction that you choose, good luck in your journey!

INDEX